58.00

D1194053

NEGRO LEAGUES BASEBALL

NEGRO LEAGUES BASEBALL

ROGER BRUNS

LANDMARKS OF THE AMERICAN MOSAIC

 GREENWOOD

AN IMPRINT OF ABC-CLIO, LLC
Santa Barbara, California • Denver, Colorado • Oxford, England

Copyright 2012 by ABC-CLIO, LLC

All rights reserved. No part of this publication may be reproduced, stored in a
retrieval system, or transmitted, in any form or by any means, electronic, mechanical,
photocopying, recording, or otherwise, except for the inclusion of brief quotations in
a review, without prior permission in writing from the publisher.

Library of Congress Cataloging-in-Publication Data

Bruns, Roger.
  Negro Leagues baseball / Roger A. Bruns.
       p. cm. — (Landmarks of the American mosaic)
  Includes index.
  ISBN 978-0-313-38648-0 (hardback) — ISBN 978-0-313-38649-7 (ebook)
1. Baseball—United States—History.   2. Negro leagues.   3. African American
baseball players.   4. Discrimination in sports—United States.   I. Title.
  GV863.A1B784   2012
  796.357'6408996073—dc23   2011052169

ISBN: 978-0-313-38648-0
EISBN: 978-0-313-38649-7

16   15   14   13   12   1   2   3   4   5

This book is also available on the World Wide Web as an eBook.
Visit www.abc-clio.com for details.

Greenwood
An Imprint of ABC-CLIO, LLC

ABC-CLIO, LLC
130 Cremona Drive, P.O. Box 1911
Santa Barbara, California 93116-1911

This book is printed on acid-free paper ∞

Manufactured in the United States of America

Contents

Series Foreword

The Landmarks of the American Mosaic series comprises individual volumes devoted to exploring an event or development central to this country's multicultural heritage. The topics illuminate the struggles and triumphs of American Indians, African Americans, Latinos, and Asian Americans, from European contact through the turbulent last half of the 20th century. The series covers landmark court cases, laws, government programs, civil rights infringements, riots, battles, movements, and more. Written by historians especially for high school students on up and general readers, these content-rich references satisfy more thorough research needs and provide a deeper understanding of material that students might only otherwise be exposed to in a short section in a textbook or superficial explanation online.

Each book on a particular topic is a one-stop reference source. The series format includes

- Introduction
- Chronology
- Narrative chapters that trace the evolution of the event or topic chronologically
- Biographical profiles of key figures
- Selection of crucial primary documents
- Glossary

- Bibliography
- Index

This landmark series promotes respect for cultural diversity and supports the social studies curriculum by helping students understand multicultural American history.

Introduction

In March 1968, the eminent civil rights leader Dr. Martin Luther King Jr. visited his friend Don Newcombe in Los Angeles. King was planning a trip to Memphis, Tennessee, to support striking sanitation workers in their fight for fair treatment and wages. Newcombe, now over 40 years old and retired from a Hall of Fame career as a pitcher, almost entirely with the Brooklyn Dodgers, had been one of the first black players from the Negro Leagues to integrate major league baseball. Following his teammate Jackie Robinson, who broke the long-standing color barrier in 1947, Newcombe, along with other black players who first appeared on major league clubs—men such as Larry Doby of the Cleveland Indians, Willie Mays of the New York Giants, Roy Campanella of the Dodgers, and others—had endured death threats, taunts, ridicule, and humiliating treatment meted out not only by fans and opposing players but even, on occasion, by teammates. They had been pioneers and Dr. King realized it.

While eating together in a restaurant, King said to Newcombe, "Don, you'll never know how easy you and Jackie and Doby and Campy made it for me to do my job by what you did on the baseball field." It was praise Newcombe cherished. He later said, "Imagine, here is Martin getting beaten with billy-clubs, bitten by dogs and thrown in jail, and he says we made his job easier" (Vecsey 2009).

On that trip to Memphis, a month after his conversation with Newcombe, King was assassinated on April 4, 1968, at the Lorraine Motel. It was a place where, in the mid-1950s, Newcombe, Robinson, Campanella, and other black players had stayed during winter trips to play exhibition games in the South.

The story of black baseball from the time of the American Civil War to the integration of the major leagues in the late 1940s is far more than a story about sports; it is also the story about the fight for civil rights and human dignity and the battle against racism and bigotry.

Ernest Burke, who was in the Negro Leagues with the Baltimore Elite Giants, remembered some of the conditions black players encountered—the lack of accommodations, the few places to eat, the constant degrading incidents:

> When we played outside of Baltimore, ah travel conditions, like I said before, it was bad, because if we stayed, went to a small town, especially a southern town, and pulled up to a gas station or something like that, they would come out and say what do you niggers want here, what can I what, what do you want, and we'd say we want gas. And they'd tell us to pull over to the side we'll get you in a minute. And I can remember one time we stayed at a service station almost two hours, before they came out and said ". . . I'll give you five gallons of gas, and get your ass out of here . . ." I could never believe that people would be so harsh, and so, so evil against another man because of the color of his skin. (Burke, 1998)

Nevertheless, black players enthusiastically embraced the game. They organized teams and leagues, played before admiring black fans, took on with much success some of the best major league players in off-season exhibition games, gained a following from black sportswriters, and battled for recognition. For over half a century, black players, many with talent equal to any player in the major leagues, took the field in the shadow of white baseball. Yet, in the end, baseball became one of the first areas of American society to integrate—before the armed forces, before public schools, and before many of the historic civil rights battles of the 1960s. This is the story of fortitude and courage—of players, owners, and sportswriters who, in giving their all to the sport they loved, were part of a long march, against great odds, to due respect and admiration.

REFERENCES

Burke, Ernest. 1998. Excerpts of Interview, Special Collections Department, Langsdale Library, University of Baltimore.

Vecsey, Peter. 2009. "From Jim Crow to Obama, Newcombe Has Seen it All," *New York Post,* January 20. http://www.nypost.com/p/sports/more_sports/item_AjvXS 2VJKbxzfxZAX3BmtK.

Chronology of Negro Leagues Baseball

1860s	Although without professional organization, baseball is widely popular across the country. For example, a story in the Washington, DC, *Daily National Intelligencer* on September 11, 1866, calls baseball "a perfect mania."
	Several black amateur teams organize, such as the Colored Union Club, in Brooklyn, and the Pythian Club, in Philadelphia.
1867	The National Association of Base Ball Players, at its annual convention, officially bars Negroes from its teams.
1869	The all-white Cincinnati Red Stockings become the first professional baseball team with salaried players.
1871	The first professional baseball league, the National Association of Professional Base Ball Players, is established. It continues through 1875.
1873	Bud Fowler becomes the first known black to join a minor league professional baseball team, the Live Oaks, of Lynn, Massachusetts, of the International League.
1876	The National League of Professional Baseball Clubs, or the National League, is formed. It has no black players.
1882	A second major league, the American Association, is founded.

1883–1884   Moses "Fleetwood" Walker, a star catcher at Oberlin College, joins the minor league Toledo Blue Stockings. When the Blue Stockings join the major league American Association in 1884, Walker becomes the first Negro major leaguer. He is cut from the squad after the season, but continues to play in organized baseball with minor league teams. Several African American players are active on the rosters of white minor league teams during the period.

1885   New York's Cuban Giants become the first salaried professional black baseball team.

1887   The National Colored Base Ball League, the first attempt at a professional Negro league, is formed. The league includes Lord Baltimores (Baltimore), Resolutes (Boston), Browns (Cincinnati), Falls City (Louisville), Gorhams (New York), Pythians (Philadelphia), Pittsburgh Keystones, and Capital City Club (Washington).The league soon fails because of lack of attendance.

July 1887   The new International League, the most prominent of the minor league organizations, bans future contracts with black players.

1894   Bud Fowler and Grant "Home Run" Johnson form the independent "Page Fence Giants" in Adrian, Michigan, with the support of Wallace Page, president of a woven fence company. The Giants become one of the most colorful of the traveling barnstorming teams, equipped with their own railroad car.

1896   In the case of *Plessy vs. Ferguson* the U.S. Supreme Court upholds Louisiana's law requiring "separate but equal" public facilities for blacks. The decision establishes racial segregation throughout the South and much of the country.

The Page Fence Giants and the Cuban Giants play a series of games they bill as a "national championship." The Page Fence club wins 10 of 15 games.

1899   Bill Galloway, outfielder for Woodstock of the Canadian League, appears in 20 games. He is the last black man to play on a white professional team until 1946.

1901   In an attempt to bypass the color barrier, Baltimore Orioles manager John McGraw introduces a new player as Chief Charlie Tokohama, purportedly a full-blooded American

Indian. McGraw's plan backfires when scores of black fans show up to root for Grant, thus revealing his race.

1907 Star black pitcher Andrew "Rube" Foster begins his managerial career with the Leland Giants as a player-manager.

February 13, 1920 At the Paseo YMCA in Kansas City, Missouri, Rube Foster, owner and pitcher of the Chicago American Giants, organizes the first black professional baseball league, the Negro National League (NNL). It consists of eight teams: Chicago American Giants, Chicago Giants, Dayton Marcos, Detroit Stars, Indianapolis ABC's, Kansas City Monarchs, St. Louis Giants, and Cuban Stars. The NNL would operate successfully until 1931.

1920 The Negro Southern League (NSL) begins play in such cities as Atlanta, Nashville, Birmingham, Memphis, New Orleans, and Chattanooga.

1922 An antilynching bill aimed at curbing the increasing violence of whites against blacks, mainly in the South, passes the House of Representatives but dies in the Senate from a filibuster of Southern senators.

1923 The Eastern Colored League (ECL) is formed on December 16, 1923, by Edward H. Bolden, owner of the Hilldale Athletic Club of Darby, Pennsylvania, and Nat Strong, owner of the Brooklyn Royal Giants. The six-team league begins with the Brooklyn Royal Giants, Hilldale Club, Atlantic City Bacharach Giants, Lincoln Giants, Baltimore Black Sox, and Cuban Stars.

October 1924 First Negro Leagues World Series is played between the ECL champions, the Hilldale Club, and the NNL champions, the Kansas City Monarchs. Kansas City wins the series championship 5–4.

1924 In Alabama, Leroy "Satchel" Paige joins the semipro Mobile Tigers Ball Club. Later, the flamboyant and talented pitcher will move to the Pittsburgh Crawfords and the Kansas City Monarchs, where he will help them win half a dozen Negro Leagues championships from 1939–1948.

1928–1929 The ECL collapses in the spring of 1928 but the member teams reemerge in 1929 as the American Negro League (ANL).

1930   The Kansas City Monarchs, among the more successful and prestigious clubs in black baseball, withdraws from the Negro National League and returns to independent play. The NNL folds the following year.

1932   The Depression years begin a very difficult time for black baseball. The NSL is the only black professional league to survive the year.

1933   A second NNL is formed, and becomes the only black professional league operating until 1937. Organized by Pittsburgh bar owner Gus Greenlee, the league launches its inaugural season with such teams as Cole's American Giants (Chicago), Detroit Stars, Baltimore Black Sox, Pittsburgh Crawfords, Nashville Elite Giants, and Columbus Blue Birds.

September 1933   The black teams begin an all-star game competition. Known as the East-West Colored All-Star Game, it would be played each summer at Chicago's Comiskey Park. The first game, played before over 20,000 fans, is won by the West by the score of 11–7.

1937   Teams in the South and the Midwest form the Negro American League (NAL). The NAL begins its inaugural season with such teams as the Kansas City Monarchs, Chicago American Giants, Cincinnati Tigers, Memphis Red Sox, and St. Louis Stars.

                The Homestead Grays, playing home games at both Forbes Field in Pittsburgh and Griffith Stadium in Washington, begin a nine-year run as the champions of the NNL with the power-hitting duo of Josh Gibson and Buck Leonard and star pitcher "Smokey" Joe Williams.

March 18, 1942   Jackie Robinson and Nate Moreland, two black players, ask the Chicago White Sox for a tryout. Manager Jimmy Dykes grants both players a workout, but neither makes the Sox roster.

1945   Jackie Robinson, shortly after his discharge from the U.S. Army, joins the Kansas City Monarchs of the NAL and plays with such baseball stars as Satchel Paige and Cuban great Martin Dihigo.

April 16, 1945   Jackie Robinson and two other black players, Sam Jethroe and Marvin Williams, participate in a Boston Red Sox tryout at Fenway Park. The Red Sox elects to sign none of the three.

October 30, 1945 Brooklyn Dodgers' executive Branch Rickey signs Jackie Robinson to a minor league contract. Robinson will play the entire 1946 season with the Montreal Royals of the International League.

April 18, 1946 Jackie Robinson makes his minor league debut for the Montreal Royals, the International League affiliate of the Brooklyn Dodgers. Robinson becomes the first African American to play in organized baseball in the 20th century. Robinson collects a home run and three singles in his debut, on his way to the International League batting title.

April 15, 1947 Robinson plays first base for the Brooklyn Dodgers against the Boston Braves. The major league color line is broken.

1947 Larry Doby is signed by the Cleveland Indians and becomes the first black player in the American League.

1948 Satchel Paige is signed by the Cleveland Indians and becomes baseball's all-time oldest "rookie" at the estimated age of 42.

South Carolina Governor Strom Thurmond, candidate of a States' Rights Party that opposes integration and African American empowerment, carries four states in the presidential election won by Harry Truman.

1949 The NNL is absorbed in the NAL, which operates as the last black major league.

1952 By the end of the major league season more than 150 former Negro Leagues players have been integrated into organized baseball. Without its greatest stars, and struggling with low attendance, Negro Leagues baseball would slowly come to a close.

1

A National Pastime Separated by Race

In post-Civil War America, baseball swept the country as a national game. Across the United States, in sandlots from Illinois to Georgia, young boys followed their dreams of making the rosters of famous teams. And, a large percentage of those who did don the uniforms of such baseball powerhouses as the Chicago White Stockings came from poor immigrant backgrounds, many from nearly penniless families. Such superstars as Michael Kelly, an Irish kid from Boston, now went by the nickname of "King." A *New York Times* reporter wrote about the fans whose lives had been unleashed at the ballparks as they jumped "about like colts, stomped their feet, clapped their hands, threw their hats in the air, slapped their companions on the back, winked knowingly at each other, and, viewing it from a baseball standpoint, enjoyed themselves hugely" ("Many Baseball Contests" 1888, 3).

Black Americans shared in this love of baseball. Yet, in the aftermath of the war, little had changed in their social status. The images on those newly created baseball cards tucked in packages of cigarettes were not black faces. None of them! And yet, black kids had their own passions for baseball, and although largely hidden from the eyes or notice of most Americans, they took to the field.

As early as the mid-1800s, black baseball in Washington, DC, according to a local newspaper, was a mania of sorts. Throughout the city, the sight of balls and bats wielded by black kids was not unusual. Some teenagers and young men formed teams and played wherever they could scratch out a ball field. Gradually, such teams as the Mutuals and the Alerts began playing some serious games. Charles Remond Douglass, the son of the celebrated abolitionist Frederick Douglass and a former member of the Union Army during the Civil War, played on both of those teams. Frederick and Charles Douglass, themselves, formed a number of baseball clubs, hired officials, and scheduled games.

By the end of the 1860s, black teams had formed in a number of cities. Such teams as the Philadelphia Excelsiors, the Chicago Uniques, and the Camden Blue Sky began to draw crowds of curious onlookers. Shortly after the war, an activist and social leader formed a club that would dominate the early years of black baseball.

OCTAVIUS CATTO AND THE PHILADELPHIA PYTHIANS, 1866–1871

Born in 1839 to free black parents, Octavius Catto graduated from the prestigious Institute for Colored Youth in Philadelphia and became a teacher at the school for 12 years. Through the tumultuous years of the Civil War, he enthusiastically joined in both Republican Party politics and civil rights activities, becoming one of the leaders of the National Equal Rights League. During the war he worked with a recruitment committee to encourage blacks to join the Union forces. In 1866 he successfully helped lead a fight for the desegregation of the Philadelphia streetcar system.

Catto loved playing baseball. Working with fellow Institute teacher Jacob White Jr., he formed an athletic and social club in Liberty Hall, named it the Pythians of Philadelphia in honor of the ancient Greek Pythian Games, and formed a black baseball team that would gain recognition even beyond the environs of Philadelphia. An infielder, Catto also captained the team and acquired ballplayers in the Philadelphia area to challenge the Excelsiors as the dominant local team.

In its infant years, the game of baseball often featured such scores as 44–23 or 27–17 or even higher. The gloves worn by the fielders were hardly more than those worn by individuals in the winter to keep warm. Pitchers threw underhand. Catchers, without much protection, stood ten feet or more behind home plate to protect themselves from broken fingers, although most of those who played that position ended up with gnarled hands within a few years. It was not until the 1880s that pitchers began to throw sidearm and then overhand and experiment with a variety of pitches with which to baffle hitters.

Led by Catto, the Pythians, wearing their distinctive white shirts with a large gothic "P" on the chest and blue pants, nearly went undefeated in 1867, losing only to the Bachelors of Albany. It was after the 1867 season that Catto, always a racial activist as well as a ballplayer, attempted a dramatic move.

He applied for inclusion of the Pythians in the newly created Pennsylvania Amateur Baseball Association. Although a few owners of the white clubs in the association appeared ready to consider the Pythians' application, a clear majority expressed hostility and defiance to the idea that a black team be made part of the organization. Catto and his colleagues withdrew their application.

Instead of backing away from the racial challenge, Cato pressed the issue even further. He submitted an application on behalf of the Pythians to join the national governing body of professional baseball, the National Association of Base Ball Players (NABP). In December the Nomination Committee of the NABB, as did the Pennsylvania Amateur Baseball Association, decided to exclude clubs with one or more black players. The national ruling body of the game of baseball had thus formally banned black players from its organization.

The Pythians persevered. The club not only played black clubs in and near Philadelphia, it also traveled to Baltimore and Washington, where Catto played against his friend Charles Douglass.

Despite their exclusion from the NABP, the Pythians also played against white clubs, including the City Items of Philadelphia. The Pythians won the game.

In February 1870, when the U.S. Congress passed the 15th Amendment giving black men the right to vote, Octavius Catto's fire and intensity shifted from the playing fields to politics. With his usual determination, he set out to organize and encourage blacks to vote in elections scheduled for the fall of 1871. During the year, the Pythians played only a few games while Catto worked feverishly to recruit new voters.

As the October 10, 1871, election in Philadelphia approached, Catto began to receive threatening letters. Although many anticipated street violence on election day, Catto, along with students and other teachers, reported to the institute. When stories of violence reached Catto, he closed the school and headed to his Fourth Ward voting poll to vote. Assaulted in the street, Catto became one of three black men killed that day in Philadelphia. He was 32 years old. No one was ever convicted for his assassination.

On the day of his funeral on October 16, thousands of people, both black and white, lined Broad Street to pay their respects. No one in Philadelphia could recall a black person ever being given this kind of honor. The Pythians baseball team, in mourning and absent its leader, disbanded.

THE BEGINNING HORRORS OF JIM CROW

The death of Octavius Catto in 1871 not only foreshadowed increasing racial violence in postwar America, but also signaled the plight ahead for black baseball players who tried to make their way through a white society. Especially in the American South, where black teams headed in the colder months to face whatever teams willing to challenge them, life in the late 19th century became increasingly constrained and isolated. Fearful that newly freed blacks would exert unfavorable political and economic pressures, Southern state legislatures, constitutional conventions, and city governments combined to limit the power and influence of blacks, thus returning Southern life, as much as possible, to its pre-Civil War status. Southern states from the Atlantic coast to Texas established restrictive legislation for race relations that came to be called "Jim Crow" laws, a term derived from an unflattering and demeaning black character from pre-Civil War minstrel shows.

States passed laws virtually eliminating the right of blacks to vote. They required railroad stations to provide separate waiting rooms for whites and blacks and separate cars. On city streetcars, whites sat in the front; blacks in the back. Signs such as "Whites Only" and "Colored" dotted the landscape—at public water fountains, in restaurants—signs so humiliating and degrading that black Americans were reminded every day that they were second-class citizens.

Blacks were also reminded of their lowly status by reports of lynchings—mobs of whites hanging victims to their death from trees or using even more brutal methods of torture and execution. Such incidents induced a pervasive sense of dread among black communities. If slavery was no longer officially allowed by law, whites maintained control through a rigid caste system that left blacks little hope and almost no power to control their lives.

Between 1870 and 1884, 11 Southern states legally banned interracial marriages. School segregation laws also appeared in nearly every Southern state prior to 1888, beginning with Tennessee and Arkansas in 1866. Almost all the Southern states passed statutes restricting voting rights for blacks by imposing voter registration restrictions such as literacy tests and poll taxes.

In 1890, Louisiana passed a law requiring blacks to ride in separate railroad cars. To challenge the law's constitutionality, a light-skinned black named Homer Plessy boarded a train reserved for whites and was arrested. When the local judge ruled against Plessy, the case ascended to the U.S. Supreme Court, which upheld the lower court ruling. One of the most notorious cases in American history, *Plessy v. Ferguson* decreed that Plessy's rights had not been denied because separate but equal accommodations had been available to Plessy. The "separate but equal" decision and the ways in which it gave license to segregation would haunt black Americans for generations.

BLACK BASEBALL'S MOSES

He was something of a Renaissance man—highly educated, erudite, and a gifted athlete. His name was Moses Fleetwood Walker and he was born in

1857 in Mt. Pleasant, Ohio, a town with a large Quaker population and a history of antislavery leanings, a town that in times of slavery had been a stop on the Underground Railroad for slaves fleeing for freedom.

When Walker was a youngster, the family moved to Steubenville, Ohio, where his father became a doctor and then a minister. Walker first attended black schools and later an integrated high school. His father became one of the wealthiest black professionals in the state of Ohio. In 1878 it became possible for Walker to enroll in Oberlin College, a school recognized for its acceptance of both black and women students.

In 1881, Oberlin formed a baseball team, the school's first intercollegiate athletic squad. Fleet, who had played baseball during his childhood, became a star catcher, and was joined on the team by his newly enrolled brother, Weldy, who played in the outfield.

In 1882, Walker transferred to the University of Michigan where he played a complete season at Ann Arbor. He had signed up to study law but the lure of professional baseball drew him away from college.

The summer of 1883 proved to be notable not only for a young black catcher but also for the history of baseball. His catching abilities had caught the eye of a number of professional baseball scouts, and the Toledo, Ohio Bluestockings of the Northwestern League offered Walker a spot on the team. He accepted and he excelled.

With Walker handling the difficult catching duties at a time when pitchers were beginning to throw overhand and to experiment with breaking pitches, the Toledo team dominated the Northwestern League.

Walker continued to shine on the field. The racial issue, however, constantly dogged him whenever he performed and whenever his name appeared in print. He endured degrading insults in some places. Never was he just Walker, a catcher. He was Walker and he was an oddity, a spectacle—*colored* or *dusky* or *mulatto*, or worse, *coon*. A simple notice in an 1883 game said it routinely:

Game to-day at 3:30
Only one game this week
Secure your season tickets at once
See Walker, the great colored catcher. (Zang 1995, 33)

In August 1883, the Chicago White Stockings, a powerhouse team of the National League, arrived in Toledo to play an exhibition game, led by the premier player in the major leagues, Adrian "Cap" Anson. Six feet, two inches and about 220 pounds, Anson was an aggressive and proud leader of his "Heroic Legion of Baseball." While on the road the White Stockings team rode into towns like a conquering army in handsome, open carriages drawn by white horses. Anson liked to deliver speeches to crowds gathered to watch the her-alded team's arrival. Cap did not like black people and was not in the least inclined to hide the fact. On this day, he declared to the management of the Toledo team that his "Heroic Legion" would not take the field if the "nigger" was in the lineup.

To his great credit, manager Charlie Morton was in no mood to be intimi-dated by such a threat. Walker played. Anson backed down, realizing that his team would lose money by not playing. But this was not the last of the bigotry that Fleet Walker would hear from Cap Anson.

In 1884, Toledo officially became part of the American Association, which at that time was considered a major league. Thus, Fleet Walker became the first black player to have any extended career in the majors. Fleet's brother, Weldy, joined the Bluestockings and played in five games in 1884, and thus, he too competed in baseball's major leagues.

Nevertheless, the hate level directed against Fleet Walker and epitomized by Cap Anson did not lessen as the season of 1884 progressed. In September, before Toledo was to travel to Richmond, Virginia, for a three-game series, manager Morton of the Bluestockings received a letter threatening vigilante action against Walker: "We the undersigned do hereby warn you not to put up Walker, the Negro catcher, the evenings that you play in Richmond, as we could mention the names of 75 determined men who have sworn to mob Walker if he comes on the ground in a suit," the letter said. "We hope you will listen to our words of warning, so that there will be no trouble; but if you do not there certainly will be. We only write this to prevent much bloodshed, as you alone can prevent." Unknown to the authors of the letter, Walker had suf-fered a broken rib from a foul tip and was already out for the season (Peterson 1992, 23).

The Toledo Bluestockings, reeling from financial difficulties, decided not to ask either of the Walker brothers to return after the 1884 season. The team disbanded a year later. Although both Fleet and Weldy Walker made overtures to other major league teams, none would agree to sign them. The word had spread throughout organized white baseball about the difficulties encoun-tered by Toledo and its star black catcher. No other team owner wanted to incur such disruption even if it meant passing on a chance to improve his squad's talent.

Although dispirited, Walker didn't give up his baseball career, or his dream of again playing major league ball. He joined a number of integrated minor league teams. In 1887, Walker, now catching for Newark of the International League, was joined by another black player, George Stovey, a talented left-handed pitcher. According to one sportswriter, Stovey's breaking ball was wicked, so good that the pitches looked "as large as an alderman's opinion of himself," but when they reached the plate could not be hit "with a cellar door." Another writer, who had seen Stovey pitch with the Cuban Giants, called him "the brunette fellow with the sinister fin and demonic delivery." With Stovey on the mound and Walker behind the plate, the *Sporting News* declared early on, using a weak racial pun, "Verily they are dark horses and ought to be a drawing card" (Zang 1995, 53).

Stovey and Walker performed masterfully in 1887, Stovey winning an International League record 35 games and Walker handling the difficult catching duties with great skill. Despite the successes of the two, 1887 proved to be a lamentable watershed for black baseball and race relations.

On July 14, Walker's old racial nemesis Cap Anson and his Chicago White Stockings arrived in Newark to play an exhibition game. Once again, as he had done when Walker was in Toledo, Anson demanded that no black players be allowed on the field against his team. This time, he had earlier made his demand a term of agreement. Neither Walker nor Stovey took the field against the White Stockings.

Ironically, on that same day in 1887, owners of teams from the International League reached an agreement no longer to issue contracts to additional black players. The decision was a direct result of a number of protests from white players throughout the league, who increasingly voiced their abhorrence of playing against blacks such as Walker and Stovey, as well as a talented second baseman of Buffalo, Frank Grant, and left-handed pitcher Robert Higgins of Syracuse.

In marking an indelible, official, and defiant color line, the International League thus paved the way for other leagues and other teams to turn away even the most talented black players. By the turn of the century, there would be no black players in organized professional baseball.

THE CUBAN GIANTS, 1885

The story of the Cuban Giants began at an exclusive hotel on Long Island, New York, called the Argyle, a resort that catered to wealthy patrons. The hotel formed a baseball team to add to the entertainment of its guests. Organized by Frank Thompson, the recruited players came mostly from Philadelphia and Washington, DC. While not entertaining on the diamond, they worked as waiters, porters, and bellhops.

The Cubans were not Cubans; they were dark-skinned men but they were not from Cuba. If the name Cubans was meant to fool anyone about the racial composition of the team, it became something of a joke with most people, who were fully aware that the players were American blacks playing professional baseball. Nevertheless, the effort at disguise did point out the racial sensitivities alive in America's post-Civil War culture.

In its first year, the Giants played extensively in Florida, centered in St. Augustine, where rich investors were turning a swamp into a luxury hotel destination for the rich. The following year, Walter Cook, a wealthy business-man in Trenton, New Jersey, bought the team and the Giants began playing mostly in the East against a variety of minor league, college, semipro, assorted amateur teams, and even, occasionally, major league teams.

It was a successful business operation, and the talented black players earned more with the Giants than they could on other squads. Through the years, the Giants enjoyed the services of such superb players as Frank Grant, George Stovey, Grant "Home Run" Johnson, and Sol White.

White, a sure-handed second baseman, later played for a number of black teams, became a manager, and was also the first historian of black baseball. White wrote that "the 'Cuban Giants' were heralded everywhere as marvels of the base ball world. They were not looked upon by the public as freaks, but they were classed as men of talent." Nevertheless, advertisements for exhibi-tion games with major leaguers portrayed the team in the same light as Buf-falo Bill's Wild West Show and other circus performers (Newman 2007, 81).

While most black players were purists about the game and believed that it must be played with dignity at all times, those teams and players who put on a show brought larger numbers of fans to the gates. The Cubans put on a show. Third baseman Ben Holmes, for example, became well known for various kinds of horseplay, especially his cakewalk along the foul lines.

It was all part circus, part sport, but it also enabled the players to show off their athletic skills. Gradually, as the team played exhibition games against the most highly skilled white players in the country, it because increasingly clear that these players were not merely comedy performers but competitive ath-letes. And that fact, along with simple, engrained racism, made many white players openly hostile even to be on the same field with the black players. Embarrassment for the whites was a scary proposition.

The white press did not generally report games of black teams as serious athletic events but as sideshow entertainment. On October 5, 1885, the Cuban Giants played the New York Metropolitans at the Polo Grounds. The *New York Times* described the event as "a farcical game of ball. . . . A nine of the ebon sons of Africa, running in all coffee shades from black Mocha to café au lait, who call themselves the Cuban giants, gave a minstrel performance on the di-amond, and the Mets enjoyed it." The game, said the account, was interesting only for the "gibes of the grand stand and the repartee of the players" ("Cuban Giants Beaten" 1885, 2).

Nevertheless, a number of articles in the *Sporting News* during these years praised the skills of many of the Cuban Giants players. Some even suggested that they might be of major league caliber. A correspondent for the magazine wrote in 1888: "There are players among these colored men that are equal to any white players on the ballfield. If you don't think so, go and see the Cuban Giants play. This club, with its strongest players on the field could play a favorable game against such clubs as the New Yorks or Chicagos" (Malloy 2005, 7).

The Giants team took on all clubs up to its challenge and earned a reputation as the most talented black team in the country. In an exhibition game in 1887 against the major league World Series champion Detroit Tigers, it led 4–2 in the eighth inning, only to lose the game because of fielding lapses.

Yet, the issue of race was never far from the surface. In September 1887, a number of players of the St. Louis Brown Stockings of the American Associations signed a letter to Christian von der Ahe, the German American entrepreneur and owner of the Giants team, objecting to the scheduling of an exhibition game against the Cubans in New York. The letter read: "Dear Sir: We, the undersigned members of the St. Louis Baseball Club, do not agree to play against negroes tomorrow. We will cheerfully play against white people at any time, and think, by refusing to play, we are not only doing what is right, taking everything into consideration and the shape the team is in at present." The owner acceded to the wishes of the players and cancelled the game ("Color Line . . ." 1887, 1).

THE BASEBALL ODYSSEY OF BUD FOWLER

John Jackson was born near Cooperstown, New York, the son of a hop-picker and barber. When he began his baseball career, he changed his name to Bud Fowler. In 1878, he joined the Live Oaks of Lynn, Massachusetts, a team in the white, minor league International Association. His appearance in a Lynn uniform marked him as the first black player to integrate a team in organized professional baseball's minor leagues. But his career in integrated baseball was constantly battered by racial incidents. He was constantly the target not only of verbal assaults from players and fans but also of players intentionally spiking him at second base and throwing at his head while at the plate. Most of time, he was the only black on integrated teams. He later said, "If I had not been quite so black, I might have caught on as a Spaniard or something of that kind. . . . My skin is against me" (Ward and Burns 1994, 40–41).

Fowler became something of a baseball hobo, roaming from town to town, from team to team, taking itinerant work as a player wherever he could get it, enduring the humiliations but excelling on the diamond: Worchester, Massachusetts (1878); Malden, Massachusetts (1879); Guelph and Petrolia, Ontario, Canada (1881); New Orleans, Louisiana (1882); and Richmond, Virginia (1882).

Fowler was not only a skilled player but also an organizer and promoter at heart. In early 1883, he joined several interested parties, including a St. Louis tavern owner, in attempting to form a black league. It never panned out, and Fowler was back on the road. He went to Youngstown, Ohio, and joined the local Niles Grays for a short time and then joined a team in Stillwater, Minnesota.

While playing for Stillwater in 1884, Fowler endured yet another slashing spike attack. The St. Paul *Daily Globe* reported, "Fowler, the lightning colored catcher for the Stillwaters, had his foot spiked by a base runner at home plate breaking the bone of his big toe." After a surgeon had announced that "It will be several days before he can play again," the determined Fowler was soon back in the lineup, rapping out a double and stealing two bases (Hillen 2010).

Fowler came up with a solution to the spiking problem. He began to play second base and catcher with the lower parts of his legs protected by handmade wooden guards. White players slashing their cleats into Fowler suddenly found that they had hit wood rather than flesh, a rather disappointing feeling for those seeking bigoted satisfaction.

As Fowler's roaming continued—Keokuk, Iowa (1884); Pueblo, Colorado (1885); and Topeka, Kansas (1886)—he once again found himself in the middle of an effort to form the first national black league. Led by Walter Brown, former newspaperman for the *Cleveland Gazette* and now owner of a black club in Pittsburgh, a group met to form the National Colored League. The meeting, held in Pittsburgh on December 9, 1886, even made the pages of the *New York Times.* "The new rules of the national agreement were unanimously adopted," reported the *Times,* "and committees on constitution and schedule were appointed. The convention then adjourned to meet in this city in March. The promoters are enthusiastic and say the success of the new organization is assured" ("Colored Baseball . . ." 1886, 5).

The success of the new organization was in no way assured. The league managed to open in May, but within two weeks, after only 13 games, it disbanded because of financial woes. Bud Fowler was once again back on the road—Binghamton, New York (1887), and Montpelier, Vermont (1887).

In 1888, Fowler signed a contract with a team in Lafayette, Indiana, that was part of the Central Interstate League. When Fowler showed up, the startled management of the team quickly voided his contract. They had not realized that he was black. A local newspaper, the *Logansport Pharos,* reported: "John W. Fowler . . . arrived in Lafayette Saturday night, having been engaged to fill the position of pitcher . . . It was thought that Fowler was a white man, and quite a surprise was in store for the Lafayette players when they discovered that he was a genuine darkey. The manager of the club concluded that he wanted only strawberry blondes, and the contract with Fowler was annulled." (McKenna, "Bud Fowler").

Fowler was back on the road: Santa Fe, New Mexico (1888); Greenville, Michigan (1889); Galesburg, Illinois (1890); Burlington, Iowa (1890); Lincoln, Nebraska (1892); and Findlay, Ohio (1891).

After spending two years with the independent team in Findlay, Fowler decided on a grand new plan. He would form his own team. He and a fellow Findlay player, shortstop Grant "Home Run" Johnson, became partners in the venture. After a frustrating effort to locate financial backing in Ohio, the two finally took their idea to Michigan, where they met white businessman J. Wallace Page, president of the Page Woven Fence Company in Adrian, 30 miles southwest of Ann Arbor. The company manufactured barbed wire. Page loved baseball and saw the advertising possibilities in a traveling black baseball team. In 1895, the Page Fence Giants hit the road.

As the Cuban Giants had been in their heyday, the Page Fence Giants were not only ballplayers but also showmen. They clowned. They traveled in a private 60-foot railroad coach paid for by the company that served not only an advertising purpose but also as isolation for the black players from the Jim Crow white world through which the team traveled. The train not only had sleeping quarters but a private chef. Across the side of the train were the words "Page Woven Wire Fence Co. Adrian, Mich." As they left the train for the games, the players, dressed in elaborate black uniforms with "Page Fence Giants" emblazoned on the fronts, wearing firefighters hats and on bicycles provided by another sponsor, the Monarch Bicycle Company of Massachusetts, paraded from the train to whatever parks hosted the games. The players even sold tickets.

Fowler began to bring together the beginnings of a formidable team of black players, including Sol White, a squad that dominated most of its competition. Page Fence played the Cincinnati Reds in a two-game exhibition. Although the Reds won both games, Fowler, now 37 years old, managed to get one hit and fielded superbly.

Fowler also obliged *Cincinnati Enquirer* reporters who asked for an interview. He told them he was nearly 50 years old, exaggerating for effect. He talked about playing in every state in the Union, about competing for trappers' furs in the West, about taking on farmers' teams in the Midwest, about lonely pioneer settlements and mining camps where he faced any men who challenged him on whatever crude fields they might have carved out. The *Enquirer* reporters were not only dazzled by his stories but gushed with praise for the athleticism displayed on the field by this aging physical wonder.

Ironically, but not surprisingly, Bud Fowler, the man most instrumental in forming the Page Fence Giants, did not stay with the team for an entire season. Once again, his wanderlust took over. In mid-season, Fowler suddenly found himself with an offer to play again on an integrated white team. He left Page Fence and joined the Lansing Senators of the Michigan State League. When the league collapsed the following season, Fowler had played his last game with an integrated minor league team in organized baseball. He had played, in all, 10 seasons of his career in the minor leagues, far more than any other black player.

The Page Fence Giants lasted three more seasons. Fowler did not rejoin them, instead returning to play on the Findlay, Ohio, semipro team in 1896, where he stayed for three years, something of a record of longevity for the wandering Fowler. In July 1899, Fowler's teammates had tired of having a black on their squad and insisted to the management that he be removed. Management went along with the players. Bud Fowler would play on no more integrated teams.

But Fowler stuck with baseball. With the help of some moneyed interests, he organized a traveling black team called the All-American Tourists, which, in many ways, adopted the style of the Page Fence Giants. The players rode in a railroad car, and when arriving at a playing site, they appeared in white vests, opera hats, carrying silk umbrellas.

In 1901, Fowler formed the Smoky City Giants in Pittsburgh, and then, once again, moved on a year later, to Indiana. In 1904, he again tried to form a black league but failed to find backers. He told a newspaper reporter that in the near future someone with enough nerve would take the chance to form a black league and they would make a lot of money.

Fowler reestablished the Black Tourists for a few more years and then retired. It would be many years before his prophecy of a black league would become fact.

At the turn of the century, the color line had been drawn throughout all of professional baseball. A young black player for the Columbia Giants would soon find out just how rigid that line had become.

CHARLIE GRANT, AKA CHIEF TOKOHAMA OR TOKOHOMA OR . . .

Charlie Grant Jr. from Cincinnati, Ohio, joined the Page Fence Giants at age 18, replacing at second base the great Bud Fowler, who had gone on the road once again to explore the possibilities of integrated baseball. By 1901, Grant, an especially talented fielder, was a member of the Columbia Giants, a black team based in Chicago.

In the off-season Grant had taken a job as a bellhop at the Eastland Hotel in Hot Springs, Arkansas, a favorite town for players to train for the coming season. Here, vacationers sought refuge from the winter's cold of the North to luxuriate in the thermal springs, bathe in the sunshine, visit Bathhouse Row, and enjoy the nightlife, including gambling. Baseball players headed there before the season to engage in the same pursuits as the vacationers but also to train a little to prepare for the upcoming season. Owners and managers, while enjoying the amenities, met with colleagues, and especially in 1901, looked for new players to add to their rosters. This was the year that a new league had been formed—the American League—and baseball executives from a number of teams were on the prowl to find new talent. In late February, players from the Baltimore Orioles, Chicago White Sox, Pittsburgh Pirates, and Brooklyn Dodgers showed up along with several managers and owners.

Among those in Hot Springs was John McGraw. A stocky, fierce competitor—one of the best infielders in the late 19th century—McGraw was in 1901 player-manager of the Orioles, one of the teams in the newly formed American League.

Also working at the hotel was Dave Wyatt, a middle infielder and teammate of Grant with the Columbia Giants. Wyatt, who later became a sportswriter, said that it was he who introduced Grant to McGraw. On the grounds of the hotel, McGraw worked out Grant, hitting balls to him and throwing batting practice. Impressed, McGraw decided to offer Grant a contract. But there was the matter of his race. Light-skinned, with straight black hair, Grant had the general appearance of an American Indian.

Wyatt later explained the scheme. "Grant was one of our greatest baseball players," he wrote. "Some years ago he accompanied the writer to Hot Springs where we hatched a plan to better the condition of colored players. I placed the same before McGraw, whom I knew personally. . . . We manufactured [a name]—Grant-a-Muscogee. This made a hit with McGraw, but in the meantime some newspaperman got 'hep' to us and sent the news broadcast that the Indian find's name was Tokohoma. The idea that McGraw did not know Grant was a colored man is all bosh" (McKenna, "Charlie Grant . . .").

Whatever the inside details of the scheme had been, McGraw announced to the press that he had hired a new infielder of American Indian blood to join the Orioles for the beginning of the 1901 season. Press reports referred to Grant's false name with various spellings—Tokohoma, Tokahoma, Tokahana—and some even began to give him nicknames—To Ka Ho Ma, Tokie, and Toke. The name is close to Tuskahoma, Oklahoma, the name of the capital of the Choctaw Nation in Oklahoma, but Grant was being passed off as a Cherokee.

When asked about his lineage, Grant, who was eager to join the Baltimore club, told a *Milwaukee Daily News* reporter on April 1 that his mother was a Cherokee Indian and that his father was white.

Lucius Harper, a columnist of the *Chicago Defender*, telling the story in 1942 of the Grant-McGraw episode, said that two of Grant's former teammates revealed the true identity of Chief Tokohama to the press. With various papers now reporting that the chief was actually Grant, McGraw's plot soon unraveled.

In Chicago, where Grant had played for the previous few years, McGraw's Indian came to the attention of President Charles Comiskey of the Chicago

White Sox, a rival of the Orioles in the new American League. Comiskey declared: "I'm not going to stand for McGraw ringing in an Indian on the Baltimore team. If Muggsy really keeps this Indian, I will get a Chinaman of my acquaintance and put him on third. Somebody told me that the Cherokee of McGraw's is really Grant, the crack Negro second baseman from Cincinnati, fixed up with war paint and a bunch of feathers"(Peterson 1970, 56).

Harper later wrote that Ban Johnson, head of the American League, "called in McGraw, Wyatt, and Grant and after a lengthy conference decided 'that the league could not go on record as deceiving the fans by fostering a player under false identity' and instructed McGraw to forthwith release Grant. McGraw had no choice" (Harper 1942, 1).

Wyatt said that McGraw told Johnson that it was wrong for a man to be barred from baseball because of his race. Nevertheless, Johnson was adamant and McGraw was forced to tell Grant that their efforts were lost. When the 1901 season began, Tokohama/Grant was not in the starting lineup for the Orioles, but was soon on his way back to the roster of the Columbia Giants.

John McGraw would leave the Baltimore Orioles and the American League in 1902 and take over as manager of the National League New York Giants. For more than 31 years, "Little Napoleon"—as he became known unflatteringly in the press—would lead the Giants to 10 National League pennants and three world championships.

After finishing the 1901 season with the Columbia Giants, Grant went on to play for a number of black teams including the Philadelphia Giants, Cuban X Giants, New York Black Sox, and finally, the Cincinnati Stars for the last three years of his career. He remained in Cincinnati, his original hometown, for the remainder of his life, which ended tragically in 1932 when a motorist lost control of his car, hopped a curb, and fatally struck Grant.

The McGraw-Grant episode in 1901 demonstrated the fact to all in professional baseball that black players, even ones pretending to be Native Americans, faced an inflexible wall of segregation.

GREAT BLACK TEAMS AND BARNSTORMING GLORY

When the Page Fence Giants team took to the road (or, in its case, to the tracks by railroad car) to play teams across the United States, it became one of the first successful professional black barnstorming teams.

Originally, the term "barnstorming" applied to traveling theater companies bringing plays to the 19-century American frontier where they frequently performed in barns. The acting companies carried with them their stage equipment, costumes, and all other necessary accoutrements. Barnstorming baseball teams did the same thing, loading their bats, gloves, uniforms, and other accessories and hitting the road to play whatever competition they could find that would draw crowds and make money.

Barnstorming black teams had one especially towering accomplishment—they began to demonstrate the quality of many of the black players heretofore so obscure to most of the public. Especially in the off-season, in the winter months when black teams and players were paired against major leaguers in exhibition games, many black stars showed their brilliance.

In 1910 a black squad played 12 games in Havana, Cuba, against the Detroit Tigers, a dominant major league team that boasted a lineup that included the great Ty Cobb. The Tigers won the series, 7–4, with Cobb hitting .371. Cobb's average, however, was fourth best in the series, behind black stars John Henry Lloyd at .500, Grant Johnson at .412, and Bruce Petway at .390.

Five years later, fireballing pitcher Smokey Joe Williams led his Lincoln Giants to a 1–0 shutout victory over the Philadelphia Phillies, a team fresh off a World Series appearance. That same year, major league teams played eight exhibition games against black teams. They won four. It is not surprising that many white owners, managers, and players became increasingly reluctant to face black barnstormers.

In Philadelphia, one of the dominant barnstorming black teams of the early 20th century emerged—the Philadelphia Giants. Organized in 1902, the Giants, led by player-manager Sol White, boasted rosters that included such stars as Frank Grant, Charlie Grant, and "Home Run" Johnson. For a decade, the team romped over challengers. When White left at the end of 1908, the team began an organizational restructuring that ended in its demise.

In Indianapolis, Indiana, the American Brewing Company organized a black team that it appropriately titled the "ABC's." Led by one of black baseball's most resourceful managers, C. I. Taylor, the ABC's featured superstars Oscar Charleston, perhaps the best centerfielder in the game, and the second baseman Bingo DeMoss, a sparkling defensive player with great range. Although it was not unusual for Taylor to clown around in the third-base coaching box for the entertainment of the fans, his team was a dynamic collection of hard-nosed competitors.

In Homestead, Pennsylvania, on the banks of the Monongahela River near Pittsburgh, an industrial team made up of black steelworkers evolved into one of the most successful black teams in history—the Homestead Grays. Its leader was Willis "Cum" Posey. Born to enterprising parents in Homestead in 1880, Posey's father, after working as a riverboat engineer, became general manager of a coal company. His mother, the first black woman to graduate from Ohio State University, later became a teacher at the institution.

The light-skinned Posey attended the University of Pittsburgh and later Duquesne University under a fictitious name to hide his racial background.

He played both basketball and golf. But his great passion became baseball. When the Homestead Grays first organized in 1910 as a semipro team, Posey joined as a player and shed the fictitious name and also any doubts about his lineage. With his educational background and sharp mind, it soon became apparent that Posey had many skills beyond the playing field. In 1912, he took over many of the team's administrative duties, including booking games. He instituted discipline among his players, something that had been notably lacking among teams of all races in baseball's formative years. He established the team on a relatively sound financial footing. It would remain a powerhouse throughout the history of black baseball.

In Darby, Pennsylvania, a suburb of Philadelphia, a team called the Hilldale Daisies became a formidable black club. Its leader was Ed Bolden. After spending much of his early life working in the post office and becoming active in a number of fraternal and social organizations in Philadelphia, the likeable Bolden made many friends and associates.

By 1916, the Daisies had become professional, playing most of their games on a 60/40 basis, with the winner of the game getting the greater share. Bolden managed to bring to Hilldale such players as Judy Johnson, perhaps the greatest third baseman in the history of the Negro Leagues; premier catcher James "Biz" Mackey; and the lightening-fast outfielder Spottswood Poles.

In Chicago, at the turn of the century, a strapping teenage pitcher from Texas began a career that would earn him a unique place in the history of black baseball. In 1902, Andrew Foster joined Frank Leland's Chicago Union Giants and was an immediate sensation. In one memorable barnstorming duel, he defeated the legendary white pitcher Rube Waddell and thus acquired a nickname. With an unusual repertoire of pitches, including a wicked screwball, Rube Foster, like most black youngsters, moved from one team to another, seeking better paychecks. He pitched with the Cuban X Giants and the Philadelphia Giants; traveled to Cuba, where he managed a team; and returned to Chicago in 1907 to manage and play once again for Leland's Giants.

In 1910, after a split with Leland, Foster decided to organize his own team, stocking the club with players from Leland's Giants and the Philadelphia Giants. The leader of Foster's new team, the Chicago American Giants, was one of most celebrated black stars in the early 1900s—John Henry "Pop" Lloyd. He was such a commanding presence at shortstop that some black writers began to call him the "Black Honus Wagner"; others went even further, saying that Wagner should be called the "White Pop Lloyd."

In 1911, the American League's Chicago White Sox moved into the newly built Comiskey Park on Chicago's south side. Foster seized an opportunity. Entering into a partnership with John M. Schorling, Comiskey's son-in-law, Foster was now able to use the former White Sox home at South Side Park for American Giants games. Foster molded the American Giants to fit a scrappy style of play. Loaded with good pitching, superior fielders, and great speed, the Giants played with intelligence and resourcefulness and were admired throughout black baseball.

Thus, after the turn of the century, several dominant black teams flourished. Some, such as the Hilldale Daisies, the Chicago American Giants, the Indianapolis ABC's, and the Homestead Grays, would survive into the 1920s and even beyond. Others would rise and fade or morph into other clubs. But for one very interested observer, an ex-player, much bitterness and anger remained over the rigid, demeaning racial segregation of the sport.

THE LAMENT OF FLEET WALKER

Moses "Fleet" Walker retired from baseball in 1889. His days of flailing at the segregation and humiliations of the sport had ended. For the well-educated and introspective Walker, life after baseball oscillated between a swirl of accomplishment and despair. In Syracuse, New York, in April 1891, Walker was belittled and attacked by a group of white men. One of the men struck Walker in the head with a rock, and in the ensuing struggle, Walker stabbed to death one of his assailants. He was acquitted on a charge of second-degree murder. He began drinking to excess and to carry a gun. He took various jobs, one as a railway postal clerk that led to a charge of mail theft. He was convicted and jailed. He returned to Steubenville and reunited with his brother, Weldy. They opened a hotel and later managed several movie theaters. With his sharp intelligence, Walker became so knowledgeable about motion picture technology that he patented a number of inventions.

But his mind remained filled with the race issue that he had so forcefully engaged his entire life. He and Weldy began to publish a small newspaper called the *Equator* that tackled head on various so-called race studies that claimed the biological inferiority of blacks and other issues related to the future of black citizens in America. In 1908, he printed a 47-page book on America and race, concluding that the best avenue for blacks was to leave the country, that the United States was irremediable in its racism and bigotry. In *Our Home Colony,* Walker wrote: "it is contrary to everything in the nature of man, and almost criminal to attempt to harmonize these two diverse peoples while living under the same government" (Walker, 1908, preface).

Moses Walker was a pioneer and the pressure, in certain ways, broke his spirit. A new generation of black players was now taking the field.

REFERENCES

"A Colored Baseball League," 1886. *New York Times,* December 10, 5.
"A Color Line in Baseball," 1887. *New York Times,* September 12, 1.
"The Cuban Giants Beaten," 1885. *New York Times,* October 6, 2.

Harper, Lucius. 1942. "'Dustin' off the News," *Chicago Defender,* August 8, 1.

Hillen, Blair. 2010. "Who's Who in the Integration of Baseball," Pennsylvania Center for the Book, Fall. http://pabook.libraries.psu.edu/palitmap/Fowler.html.

Malloy, Jerry. 2005. "The Birth of the Cuban Giants," in Bill Kirwin, ed. *Out of the Shadows.* Lincoln: University of Nebraska Press, 1–14.

"Many Baseball Contests." 1888. *New York Times,* May 31, 3.

McKenna, Brian. "Bud Fowler," The Baseball Biography Project, Society for American Baseball Research (SABR). http://bioproj.sabr.org/bioproj.cfm?a=v&v=l&bid=3116&pid=19716.

McKenna, Brian. "Charlie Grant," The Baseball Biography Project, Society for American Baseball Research (SABR). http://bioproj.sabr.org/bioproj.cfm?a=v&v=l&bid=3056&pid=19711.

Newman, Roberta. 2007. "Pitching behind the Color Line: Baseball, Advertising, and Race," *Baseball Research Journal,* 81.

Peterson, Robert. 1970. *Only the Ball Was White.* New York: Gramercy Books.

Peterson, Robert. 1992. *Only the Ball Was White.* New York: Oxford University Press,

Walker, M. F. 1908. *Our Home Colony: A Treatise on the Past, Present, and Future of the Negro Race in America.* Steubenville, OH: Herald, preface.

Ward, Geoffrey, and Ken Burns. 1994. *Baseball: An Illustrated History.* New York: Alfred A. Knopf.

Zang, David. 1995. *Fleet Walker's Divided Heart.* Lincoln: University of Nebraska Press.

2

Black Baseball
Post-World War I

THE GREAT MIGRATION

Although virulent racism existed in parts of Northern cities and although blacks were limited in where they could live and work, at least in places such as Chicago there seemed to be better opportunities. Here, they could attend better schools, have greater access to public services, could vote, and have a chance to join workforces in expanding steel mills, packing houses, and service jobs.

Although some blacks had decided to move to the North in the later years of the 19th century, it was not until the onset of World War I that the exodus began in earnest. As warring nations in Europe sought American industrial products and as President Woodrow Wilson's administration began to prepare for possible U.S. involvement in World War I, Northern factories began to accelerate production. In order to satisfy demand, those factories needed a far greater workforce than was available. For the first time, industrialists needed black workers from the South. In steel mills, railroad yards, and defense-related industrial plants, blacks from Alabama, Georgia, Mississippi, and other Southern states suddenly found job openings.

The impetus to leave behind the degradation of Jim Crow was now, for many, like a fever. It was aided by the editors and writers of the *Chicago Defender,* the most widely read black newspaper in the South.

How did the *Chicago Defender,* a paper that often styled itself as the spokesperson for "the Race," get into the hands of an increasing number of black readers in states in the deep South? It got there, in many cases, by stealth. Although circulation of the newspaper was restricted in various Southern towns and cities, copies arrived in the hands of Pullman porters on the Illinois Central Railroad, entertainers, and black baseball players on barnstorming circuits. Copies of the paper circulated in barber shops and bars, and from family to family. Readers learned in its pages about those new jobs in the steel mills and garment shops, about growing black nightlife in Chicago, about schools, and were reminded that the Jim Crow laws under which they suffered in the South did not exist in Chicago or Detroit or New York. They read notices of individuals and families arriving from various Southern destinations. In May 1917, the paper even called for "a Great Northern Drive"—a migration of blacks away from their near-slavery to cities of opportunity.

Between 1916 and 1919, nearly half a million blacks from the South moved North. Some of those arriving in Chicago and other cities had draped banners on the sides of the trains hailing their "Second Emancipation" and "Bound for the Promised Land."

The migrants would soon realize that life for most would still remain a tough slough. Just as such immigrant groups as the Irish and the Polish had done, blacks began to congregate together in the various cities. In Chicago, it was on the city's south side. They would still find parts of the cities off limits for housing and recreation. They would find few political opportunities. They would also find, in many cases, virulent racism, as white groups began to see this growing black population as a distinct threat, especially as their numbers increased, their neighborhoods grew in size, and they filled jobs formerly off limits to them.

The migration produced more than resentment and anger; it produced race riots. A number of cities erupted in violence. In Chicago, in 1919, an incident at a beach involving white gangs known as athletic clubs left 38 people dead and more than 500 injured. Businesses burned; neighborhoods burned. National Guardsmen helped quell the violence. But, through it all, more and more blacks shed the subservience that had burdened them for so long and fought back.

Although most blacks filled only semiskilled or service jobs and usually received wages lower than whites, they were now far more in control of their own lives than they had been in the South. This was not nirvana, but it was better here than from where they had come.

By 1918, the *Chicago Defender* could claim much success in its campaign. "The black workmen left the South with trembling and fear," said a *Defender* editorial. "They were going—they didn't know where—among strange people, with strange customs. The people who claimed to know best how to treat them painted a frightful picture of what would befall the migrators if they left the land of cotton and sugar cane. But they left in droves, are still leaving, and only a few have returned." The necessity of labor economics, said the *Defender,* brought together white and black workers in the North. "There is a long fight still ahead of us—a fight with brains, not brawn. Our entrance into the economic world sounds the death knell of discrimination and oppression" ("Migration . . ." 16).

Although that death knell would be generations coming, the migration had, indeed, opened up new opportunities, not only for black workers, but for black entrepreneurship.

RUBE FOSTER MAKES HIS DREAM HAPPEN—A NEGRO LEAGUE

He had been a superb pitcher and an innovative manager. But Rube Foster would be remembered most of all as the man who created the first truly national Negro major league. Foster had harbored for years a dream of organizing black teams into a league like those of major league baseball. With the growth of black populations in large cities, Foster believed the time was now right to strengthen black baseball from its chaotic movement of players and teams and disorganized, ad hoc schedules into a full-fledged, professionally run league with more stable management. Black baseball, Foster was convinced, could be one the greatest entertainment attractions for urban black populations.

The big Texan, who carried around a revolver to match his oversized personality, was a convincing character—confident, persuasive, the perfectly audacious leader needed to bring together a group of baseball owners with their own formidable egos. After approaching a number of owners over the course of a year, Foster, on February 13, 1920, called them to a meeting, along with media representatives, at the Kansas City YMCA to outline how this new league would be run. Sportswriter Ira Lewis called it "perhaps the most singular and noteworthy meeting ever held in the interest of our sport life" (Hogan 2006, 161).

Foster presented a constitution at the meeting, which laid down rules of conduct during games and prohibited team-jumping and raiding other teams for players, among other restrictions. Foster said his goal in forming the league was "to create a profession that would equal the earning capacity of any other profession . . . keep Colored baseball from the control of whites [and] do something concrete for the loyalty of the Race." The owners accepted the agreement and named Foster the league's first commissioner. Within the year, the Negro National League (NNL) played its first contest ("Rube Foster . . ." 2012).

He wanted the league to rival the white major leagues and eventually play them in a World Series true to its name. He said of the NNL, "We are the ship; all else the sea." His words became the league's motto (Ward and Burns 1994, 157).

The NNL comprised the following teams: Foster's own team, the Chicago American Giants; the Kansas City Monarchs, the only team in the league to have a white owner, J. L. Wilkinson; the Chicago Giants, a club without a home field that played against all the other teams at their home sites; the Dayton Marcos, an outstanding barnstorming attraction for a decade; the Detroit Stars, a team founded in 1919 that would become one of the most stable and powerful clubs in the league; the Indianapolis ABC's, featuring one of the greatest black players in the game, Oscar Charleston; the St. Louis Giants, an independent club that had regularly played the Chicago American Giants and the Indianapolis ABC's; and the Cuban Stars, a team comprised almost entirely of Cuban players, organized in Cincinnati, Ohio.

Cary Lewis, a sportswriter for the *Chicago Defender,* announced Foster's plan with much anticipation. A new league had been Foster's dream for years, he wrote, "to see men of his Race have a circuit of their own . . . Mr. Foster is planning night and day for the coming season. Every businessman in Chicago is back of him. He has the confidence and respect of the press and fans. No man in baseball has more influence than 'Rube' Foster" (Lewis 1919, 11).

The new league immediately became a sensation in the various cities. As opening day approached, black newspapers and sportswriters issued a mighty call for fans. In Cincinnati, where the Cuban Stars would often play their games at the city's League Park, the *Union* published this advertisement:

Coming!

Famous Colored Teams

The Base Ball Fans here are in a frenzy of enthusiasm over the Opening Games of the Colored Base Ball Teams at League Park, beginning Saturday, April 30th. The Famous "A.B.C.'s" of Indianapolis will cross bats with the renowned "Cuban Stars." Both teams are "Way Out In the Front" in the Base Ball World. Col. C.I. Taylor of Indianapolis will be here in person, and all who know "C.I." realizes that he always stands for the best there is in America's Great National game. During the absence of the Reds this season Colored Teams have games scheduled. Best of Order. Best of Accommodations. Popular Prices! DON'T FORGET— The coming games take place Saturday, April 30th, Sunday, Monday, Tuesday, and Wednesday, May 1st to 4th. (*Union* 1921, 1)

And the fans did come. Opening games in the various cities in early May 1920 drew huge crowds that surrounded the parks. In Detroit, fans jostled to get inside for a game between the Detroit Stars and the Cuban Stars. A reporter wrote of the pandemonium: "Never in the baseball history of Detroit was there enacted a scene such as was staged here last Sunday when countless thousands of excited and enthusiastic devotees of baseball lined up on Mack Avenue for blocks, surrounded entrances to the park and nearly stampeded the officials and guards of the enclosure in their eagerness to gain admittance." The scene demonstrated one salient fact: the Detroit park and others in the cities of the new league "are not sufficient in either seating or standing capacity to accommodate the eager throngs that want to witness the games between the various teams that swing around the new baseball circuit" (Wyatt 1920, 9).

Charles Starke, the sports editor of the *Kansas City Call,* wrote of the sense of racial pride and confidence that erupted with the creation of the new league. "Baseball is a great thing for the race in a big way," he said. "We have tasted in a national way the meaning of league baseball, and we have approved of it and declared it all right for adult and child—we the people" (Hogan 2006, 159).

Foster took great satisfaction in what he and his fellow black team owners were able to accomplish with their scant resources, particularly when compared with their counterparts in the major leagues. Where big league owners had "wealth counted in millions," Foster said, he and his fraternity had "only the faith in the weather man. . . . We are willing and know what can be done, but have nothing to do it with" (Carroll 2006, 34).

While exuding infectious confidence, Foster still knew well that the entire venture was fraught with challenges. Could the godfather of the NNL, for example, successfully negotiate with white stadium owners to play in large venues necessary to hold thousands of fans? Could he, working with the black press, generate the kind of publicity and enthusiasm necessary to keep the league afloat?

Smoking a large pipe and calling everyone "Darlin'," Foster settled in to his role not only with gusto but with a keen sense of what would be necessary to bind the entire operation together. One of his first moves involved Oscar Charleston, who had recently moved from the Indianapolis team to sign with Foster's Chicago American Giants. Foster asked Charleston to return to Indianapolis to help balance the league's talent. He followed with other negotiated moves to keep certain teams competitive. He helped bankroll both the Dayton and Detroit clubs. While pulling strings as commissioner, he also continued his managerial role for the Giants.

Foster controlled the NNL as a king did his subjects. He hired the umpires, handled bookings, and settled disputes among players and owners, sometimes to the considerable irritation of the various parties involved.

Foster managed to establish the NNL on such a sound footing that salaries for players jumped from $100 per month to $250 a month. Crowds on Sundays and holidays in the various venues often topped 8,000.

Not only was Foster's ambitious enterprise of starting the NNL a success, so was his team. Playing at Schorling Park on the south side of Chicago, Foster's American Giants dominated the new league. Led by Cristobal Torriente, a stocky, pull-hitting, strong-armed outfielder from Cuba, and Dave Brown, an ace left-handed pitcher, the American Giants won championships in the first three years of the league.

Sportswriter W. Rollo Wilson marveled at Foster's command of his enterprise: "A loud-voiced man with a smelly pipe who kids his opponents and makes them like it . . . The Master of the Show who moves the figures of his checkerboard at will. The smooth-toned counselor of infinite wisdom and sober thought. The King who, to suit his purpose, assumes the role of the Jester. Always the center of any crowd, the magnet, attracting both the brains and the froth of humanity. . . . Known to everybody, knows everybody. That's Rube" (Wilson 1924, 6).

BARNSTORMING, JUDGE LANDIS, AND BABE RUTH

In the fall of 1919, scandal rocked major league baseball. Several members of the Chicago White Sox, succumbing to the lure of professional gamblers, accepted money to throw the World Series to the Cincinnati Reds. Devastated by the besmirching of the game, baseball owners appointed federal judge Kennesaw Mountain Landis as the first commissioner of baseball. Given almost dictatorial powers to enforce baseball law and order, Landis took office on January 12, 1921.

A man of huge ego, Landis played the part of the grand dispenser of judicial wisdom in both appearance and demeanor. Severe looking, with long white hair and a wispy thin body, he seemed like a man always in the throes of grand decision making that would make ordinary judges tremble with apprehension. "His career," wrote colorful newspaper columnist Heywood Broun, "typifies the heights to which dramatic talent may carry a man in America if only he has the foresight not to go on the stage" (Fimrite 1993, 76).

As a federal judge, many of his courtroom decisions were overturned by appellate rulings. One of his prominent actions was a decision in 1913 that black heavyweight champion fighter Jack Johnson be banned from boxing for allegedly transporting a white woman over state lines for prostitution.

In August 1921, Landis banished from baseball eight of the White Sox players—they would thereafter be known as the Black Sox. In handing down the ruling, he virtually discarded the fact that the players had just been exonerated through a technicality in a criminal court. Although a few of the players had certainly taken money to throw Series games, it remains uncertain whether all of those banned from the game by Landis had done so, especially "Shoeless Joe" Jackson, who actually hit for a high average in the games. Nevertheless, true to his harsh reputation, Landis proclaimed that none of the players would ever again compete in the major leagues. None of them ever did.

And now, in late 1921, the imperious Landis was on another mission. He decided to enforce a long-ignored rule in baseball prohibiting members of a World Series team from barnstorming in the off-season. In attempting to enforce the rule he was taking on the game's greatest star and its most eager barnstormer—Babe Ruth.

In 1921, Babe Ruth was in the early years of what would be an unprecedented baseball career, one that would mark him as an American icon. Ruth grew up in the rough dock section of Baltimore. He was the son of a bartender and at age seven entered St. Mary's Industrial School, an institution for underprivileged boys. At St. Mary's he learned to be a tailor; mostly, however, he learned to play baseball. From those early days, the round-faced, burley kid displayed a prodigious talent for the game. When he left St. Mary's, he began to play semiprofessional ball in Pennsylvania as a pitcher and was then signed by the Baltimore Orioles of the International League in 1914. It was his hometown team and he excelled. Soon, he was on the train to Boston, signed to a contract to play for the American League's Boston Red Sox. For five years, the left-hander compiled a successful record, winning twice as many games as he lost. But Ruth's fame would not come from the pitching mound. As his hitting prowess became increasingly evident, Ruth became an outfielder.

In 1920, in one of baseball history's most historic mistakes, the Red Sox decided to sell its new prodigy to the New York Yankees. It was there, in Yankee Stadium, that Ruth, with his unprecedented display of home-run power and his jovial personality, would become the Babe of legend—of towering blasts in parks across the country, of pennants and World Series victories, of a personality both ribald and warm that thrilled fans wherever he played. So dominant became Ruth in the American social fabric that one company would even produce a candy bar named Baby Ruth.

For all of his talent and the attention lavished on him by fans and writers, Ruth lacked what many of the ballplayers of his day displayed often—racial prejudice. He loved competing in barnstorming games with black players in the off-seasons. He knew firsthand their skills and their love of the game. There was some talk among the black community that Ruth himself had a black ancestor. Throughout his career, he made friendships with many black barnstormers. One said: "He was quite a guy, always a lot of fun. All the guys really liked him" (Jenkinson 1998, 291).

Following the 1920 season, after he had walloped an astounding 54 home runs, Ruth played a number of exhibition games against black players. He also traveled to Cuba, joining players from John McGraw's National League New York Giants to play a series of very competitive games against a team of black and Latino players.

In October 1921, the Yankees played the Giants in the World Series. As he had done in the past, Ruth once again, after the series ended, began a robust barnstorming schedule.

For baseball executives not involved with barnstorming, the practice seemed fraught with problems. First, there was the possibility that the players might injure themselves, thus jeopardizing their careers and their contracts with the major league teams. Second, the major league teams and their owners did not make money on barnstorming; the profits went directly into the hands of the players. And third, many of the barnstorming contests increasingly demonstrated the abilities of black players, an embarrassing problem for the whites-only policies of professional baseball.

Yankees co-owner Col. Tillinghast Huston, who had seen enough reports of barnstorming major leaguers losing to black teams, said: "I agree with the gentlemen who think this barnstorming business is getting past a joke. First, I was all for the boys. I couldn't see why they should be deprived of earning the extra money in the fall, but, gee whillikens, some of the happenings in these barnstorming trips have made me sit up and take notice. Think of several teams of major leaguers losing farcical contests to colored teams. Either they ought to quit playing or at least draw the color line" (Barthel 2007, 105).

Commissioner Landis, more than willing to reinforce the color line, soon came to the rescue of those baseball executives who were tired of hearing about black players demonstrating their skills against major league players. The commissioner learned of a largely ignored rule on the books since 1911 that prohibited players from teams involved in World Series games to play barnstorming games. Major league baseball had feared that the players of the two teams in the World Series could theoretically take the show on the barnstorming road and feature additional so-called World Series games in towns around the country. The rule makers intended to prevent such a spectacle that would demean the World Series itself.

As he had done in the Black Sox scandal, Landis once again saw an opportunity to exert his power, and not incidentally, grab much personal media hype. In early December 1921, Landis fined Ruth his World Series earnings of over $3,000 and suspended the slugger until May 20 of the 1922 season, a term amounting to nearly 40 games. Outfielder Bob Meusel and pitcher Bill Perry suffered similar sanctions. In his written decision, Landis declared: "This situation involves not merely rule violation, but rather a mutinous defiance by the players to present the question: Which is the bigger—baseball or any individual in baseball" ("Ruth is Suspended . . ." 1921, 25).

Told of Landis's decision, Ruth said simply that the commissioner should "go jump in a lake." Quick to respond to the slugger's challenge to his authority, Landis declared, "it seems I'll have to show somebody who's running this game" (Fimrite 1993, 76).

Many in the country were apprehensive. A petition signed by 10,000 New York fans arrived on Landis's desk. Even President Harding spoke out on the ban, voicing hope that the matter would be resolved so that the country would not be deprived of watching baseball's magnificent hitter in action.

Landis ignored the pleadings. The 1922 season began for the Yankees with Ruth out of the lineup. Without Ruth as a draw, empty seats in Yankee Stadium as well as other venues in which the Yankees played on the road immediately increased in number, driving down baseball's profits. Finally, on May 20, 1922, the slugger returned to the lineup. The rule banning barnstorming by World Series players was soon rescinded.

In October, Ruth resumed postseason barnstorming. He played against the Kansas City Monarchs on October 22 and began a long tour that started in rural Kansas and Oklahoma. He played against Negro Leagues teams after every season in the 1920s.

After the legendary 1927 season in which Ruth drilled 60 home runs, he visited the Guardian Angel Home for Negroes in Kansas City. Photographers snapped pictures as Babe held a black child in his arms.

ED BOLDEN AND THE EASTERN COLORED LEAGUE

Ed Bolden, somewhat shy and physically small, seemed an unlikely rival to the nearly iconic figure of Rube Foster. And yet, it was Bolden who, with the help of his creative and energetic friends, established a league to challenge Foster's Negro National League.

As the Hilldale Daisies became one the powerful black teams in the eastern United States, Bolden decided on a strategy to form a league of teams to rival the NNL, whose teams were based in the Midwest. Bolden wrote: "The fans have loyally supported the club and there is little doubt they will continue doing so, but I think they are entitled to better competition among our clubs, and the best way to secure it is through an organized circuit" (Metcalf 2000, 59).

Allied with white businessman, promoter, and booking agent Nat Strong of New York, Bolden called a meeting in December 1922 to form the Mutual Association of Eastern Colored Baseball Clubs, or Eastern Colored League (ECL). Like Foster's NNL, the organizing meeting of the new league took place at a YMCA, this one in Philadelphia.

Beginning with the 1923 season, the ECL launched its inaugural schedule with six teams: Bolden's Hilldale club; the Brooklyn Royal Giants, a team founded early in the century that was purchased and now run by Nat Strong; the Lincoln Giants of New York, led by player-manager Cyclone Joe Williams, an aging but still effective right-handed hurler; the Atlantic City Bacharach Giants, an excellent club led by outfielder Charlie Mason; the Baltimore Black

Sox, led by four players that would come to be known as the "Million Dollar Infield"; and the Cuban Stars, a team owned by Alejandro "Alex" Pompez, a New York executive whose immigrant family members were cigar manufacturers who had moved to the United States from Cuba. Thus, both leagues had one team each filled with players from Cuba and other Latin American countries.

Bolden's Hilldale club won pennants in each of the first three years of the ECL, just as Foster's American Giants had won the first three pennants of the NNL. But Bolden's league soon incurred Foster's wrath as teams from the East began offering higher salaries than the teams from the Midwest league had been paying their players. A number of NNL stars, such as "Biz" Mackey of the Indianapolis ABC's, began heading for more lucrative playing pastures. The exodus from the Indianapolis club to the ECL during the first two years of the new league became so critical that the team's caliber of play plummeted.

The bidding war escalated, along with a war of words between the league executives and owners. Negro Leagues baseball had, sooner than expected, become a big business enterprise and the competition between the two leagues had become fierce.

FIRST NEGRO LEAGUES WORLD SERIES, 1924

In 1924, negotiations between Foster and Bolden and other officials of the two leagues resulted in another logical step in the evolution of professional Negro Leagues baseball—a World Series. The officials who gathered in a meeting in New York in September 1924 not only agreed to a series between the winners of the two respective leagues—the Kansas City Monarchs of the NNL, managed by long-time star pitcher Jose Mendez, and the Hilldale Daisies of the ECL, managed by infielder Frank Warfield—but they also created a novel approach to the series, very unlike that of the major leagues. Instead of the venues being limited to the cities of the two winning teams, this series would be played in two additional cities that did not field league winners—Baltimore and Chicago—thus giving fans in those cities the chance to be part of the first Negro fall classic.

The series would be the best of nine games. The first two games were scheduled for Hilldale, followed by two in Baltimore, three games in Kansas City, and the final two games, if necessary, in Chicago.

The series looked to be a match between the Monarchs' offensive juggernaut and Hilldale's pitching strength. Both teams boasted established stars. Kansas City featured pitcher and slugger Bullet Rogan and Hilldale countered with infielder Judy Johnson.

In an age in which pitchers tended to use exaggerated windup motions, Bullet Rogan used none. Starting his motion at the belt, he threw sidearm, augmenting a respectable fastball with an assortment of changeups—forkball, palmball, and the occasional spitball. According to press reports, Rogan once struck out Bob Meusel of the New York Yankees four times in a barnstorming game. Rogan was also a feared hitter.

Judy Johnson was considered by most black sportswriters in the 1920s as the best third baseman in the Negro Leagues. A skilled fielder with quick hands and great range and a heady, line-drive hitter, Johnson became a Hilldale club member in his early days of professional ball and a mainstay for the club for several years. W. Rollo Wilson, a writer for the *Pittsburgh Courier,* spoke for many fans who considered Johnson the best player in the Negro Leagues: "We nominate as the outstanding baseball player of the year—Julius Ceasar Johnson, which is slang for Judy, pride of Hilldale . . . we have elaborated on this bird so much that to try to say more would be painting the lily" (Smith, 1924, 7).

Johnson himself later remembered his early days in the ECL: "After the Eastern Colored League was formed in 1923, we had our own park in Darby, and our crowds were so large they had to enlarge the park. Not just for Negroes, for white fans too. The Athletics and Phillies were down then, and people were getting season tickets to see us. You couldn't buy a box seat" (Holway 1989, C12).

And now as the first Negro Leagues World Series was set to open, Hilldale's slick-fielding shortstop, Jake Stephens, was out with an injury and manager Warfield had to shuffle the club's lineup. The versatile third baseman Johnson moved to short and the equally versatile catcher Biz Mackey moved from behind the plate to third base. Reserve catcher Louis Santop took over as catcher. With the injury to Stephens and considering the Monarchs' superior hitting, much of the black press leaned toward the Monarchs as a slight favorite.

Nevertheless, Hilldale had its own dominant pitcher capable of throwing many strong innings. His name was Nip Winters, and he was considered by many the best pitcher in the ECL. If Winters, the left-hander with a wicked curve, who had amassed a sensational won-lost record with Hilldale in the league's first years, could hold up, many felt, Hilldale had a decent shot at the championship.

On October 3, 1924, at the Baker Bowl in Philadelphia, home of the Philadelphia Phillies, over 5,000 fans saw Bullet Rogan frustrate the Hilldale lineup; Kansas City took game one by a 6–2 score. Rogan held the Daisies scoreless until two outs in the ninth inning.

With a win in Philadelphia secured, a confident Monarchs team took the field in game two. The players left the field after the last out in the ninth with much less confidence. Hilldale, behind Nip Winters, shut out Kansas City 11–0.

On October 5, the scene shifted to Baltimore. All afternoon and into increasing darkness, the teams battled. When the teams reached the end of the 13th inning with the score tied 6–6, the umpires called the game.

After Hilldale took game four in Baltimore, the teams headed to Kansas City with the Monarchs down one game. When the home team's train reached Union Station in downtown Kansas City, more than 5,000 fans crowded the platform along with a 50-piece band. The team then watched a parade in its honor. In the black community of Kansas City, the World Series was no small event.

On October 11, Bullet Rogan of the Monarchs and Nip Winters of the Daisies treated fans at Muehlebach Park to a memorable duel of pitching superiority. Despite giving up two runs in the first inning, Winters settled in and began mowing down Monarchs hitters inning after inning. Through eight innings, Rogan had given up only one run. The ninth inning proved crucial. Helped by defensive lapses by the Monarchs, Hilldale managed to get two men on base with the dangerous Judy Johnson coming to the plate. Before a stunned stadium crowd, Johnson drilled a three-run inside-the-park home run to put the game away for Hilldale. Nip Winters retired 25 of the last 26 Monarchs hitters he faced.

With Hilldale holding a 3 to 1 edge in the series, Kansas City rallied in the next two home games. In the last game in Kansas City, which went 12 innings, manager Jose Mendez took the mound briefly in relief and set Hilldale hitters down to get the win.

The series was now tied, and the destination was Shorling Park in the south side of Chicago, the home of Rube Foster's Chicago American Giants. It was here that the World Series would be decided. Foster's great regret over the series, of course, was the fact that his own Giants were not representing the NNL. Nevertheless, he played the gracious host.

The first game in Chicago was pivotal in the series. The loser would have to win two games in a row to win the best of nine. The game was in the firm grasp of Hilldale—for eight innings (baseball is a game of nine innings.). Pitcher Rube Currie, pitching with exemplary efficiency, took a 2–0 lead into the bottom of the ninth inning. Suddenly, his defense failed the hurler. Three costly errors led to three runs and a 4–3 Monarchs' victory.

The blown lead so infuriated both Currie and manager Warfield that their shouts and epithets resounded through the locker room—Warfield screaming at Santop for dropping a foul pop-up, Currie screaming generally at the world. A *Kansas City Call* reporter described Currie: "The wrath of Mr. Currie was being expressed in the clubhouse in language which beggers description. . . . It was cold outside, but it was plenty hot in the Hilldale quarters" (Hogan 2006, 177).

A day later, on October 19, Hilldale bounced back from the devastating ninth inning of the previous game, beating the Monarchs 5–3 with a two-run rally of own in the ninth. Thus, with the series tied at four games each, the stage was set for a one-game showdown for the championship.

October 20 was a raw day in Chicago—low temperatures, a biting wind sweeping across the field. Many of the most ardent fans decided that even this game was not worth the physical torture of the moment. And so a sparse, shivering crowd awaited the most significant game in the brief history of the professional Negro Leagues.

Manager Mendez of the Monarchs had a tough decision. All of his starting pitchers were nursing sore arms or nearly worn out from the grinding series of games, some of which had gone into extra innings, one of which went into extra innings and was then called off.

When Jose Mendez was a kid in Cuba, he worked in the sugarcane fields. The hard labor, he said later, accounted for his powerful arms and strong fingers that belied his five-foot, eight-inch, 150-pound frame. When he took up the game of baseball, his friends knew where he belonged on the field—on the pitcher's mound. He threw pitches that seemed to explode and dart. When players from the Cincinnati Reds visited Cuba in 1908 on a barnstorming tour, Mendez, then 21 years old and playing with a Cuban team, blew pitches past the major leaguers as no Cuban pitcher had ever done. He pitched a one-hit shutout.

Later, he faced players from the Detroit Tigers and the New York Giants, prompting manger John McGraw of the Giants to compare Mendez to his own ace pitcher, Christy Mathewson. If Mendez had been white, McGraw reportedly remarked, he would have offered $50,000 for his release from the Cuban team to play for the Giants. In Cuba, he became "El Diamante Negro," or "The Black Diamond," and was the country's first baseball legend. Often, when he would walk into a restaurant in Cuba, patrons would stand and applaud.

Mendez came to the United States and played on a number of black teams. In 1912, he barnstormed with J. L. Wilkinson's All-Nations team. After injuring his pitching arm, he played shortstop for a time. In 1920, he signed with Wilkinson's Kansas City Monarchs.

And now as the player-manager of the Kansas City squad, with the game of his life at hand, Mendez made a gutsy move—he decided to pitch the game himself. He had already thrown a few effective innings in relief. But starting this crucial game was another matter entirely.

The decision startled his fellow players, the Hilldale team, the press, and everyone else close to the game. Mendez had been told by a doctor who had operated on his pitching arm earlier in the year that pitching a full game might injure him permanently. The veteran ignored the advice and inserted his name in the starting lineup.

Mendez was far from the young El Diamante Negro who had burned fastballs past helpless hitters. Although his title was player-manager, he had been more manager than player in recent years. His damaged pitching arm ached from years on the mound. His skills were diminished. But Mendez had other attributes that day. During the long series with Hilldale, he had studiously watched the tendencies of the Hilldale hitters and believed that he could baffle them with slow stuff, keep them off-balance. With the small crowd donning fur coats and bracing themselves against the wind and cold, most believed that Mendez would surely be adversely affected, as all sore-armed pitchers are on cold days. Nevertheless, the Cuban walked to the mound to face Hilldale.

His pitching opponent for Hilldale was Holsey "Scrip" Lee, a submarine right-hander who could buckle the legs of even the most disciplined right-handed hitters. Lee had been with a National Guard unit that had fought against Pancho Villa's forces at the Mexican border in 1916. He had been with the 372nd Infantry serving in France during World War I and had earned two Battle Stars and a Purple Heart. He was certainly not intimidated by the final game of the World Series.

From the beginning, it was a monumental pitching duel. Mixing speeds with an assortment of pitches, Mendez put down Hilldale hitters in rapid succession, most of them on meek pop-ups or fly balls. For seven innings, Lee was just as tough. When Mendez put down Hilldale again in the top of the eighth inning, it seemed as if the game would go on endlessly. However, in the bottom half of the inning, the dike broke for Lee; Kansas City broke through for five runs. Mendez closed out the game in the ninth with another scoreless inning.

The Kansas City Monarchs were the first World Series champions of the Negro Leagues. Jose Mendez's performance—complete game, no runs, three hits—became the stuff of legend—an aging hurler, going against the advice of his physician, pitched a shutout in the most important game Negro Leagues fans had ever witnessed.

The stars of both teams played like stars. Judy Johnson led both teams in hitting, rapping five doubles, a triple, and a home run and hitting .341 for the series. For Bullet Rogan, the series became a stage on which he exhibited not only his pitching mastery but also his versatility and stamina. He won two games out of three games that he started, relieved in another, and compiled an impressive 2.57 ERA. In addition, when not on the mound, he played the outfield in six games, hitting .325. Nip Winters had also proved to be nearly unhittable in the series. He threw four complete games, winning three of them and allowing slightly more than one run a game.

After the series, sportswriter Frank Young of the *Chicago Defender* said that the games had been such a success that they had drawn the interest of even the sports departments of daily white newspapers in both Kansas City and Philadelphia. The Kansas City *Journal Post*, Young wrote with much delight, had even run pictures of Nip Winters and Bullet Rogan. It was the only time, Young said, that the paper had featured the pictures of black individuals—except for criminals and boxer Harry "The Black Panther" Wills.

Of the final game, Young raved: "To say that the game was one of the best ever played in Chicago by any two teams would not be exaggerating, and to say it was one of the best seen in recent years would be only telling the truth" (Young 1924, 1).

SATCHEL AT RICKWOOD FIELD

Walking today into the green ballpark on the west side of Birmingham, Alabama, is like walking back into a rich history of baseball—both white and black. Built in 1910, two years before Boston's Fenway Park, Rickwood is the oldest surviving professional baseball park in the United States. Named after A. H. "Rick" Woodward, chairman of Woodward Iron Company and owner of the Birmingham Barons, the park, in its life of over a century, has on its grass and dirt seen players such as Babe Ruth, Satchel Paige, Ty Cobb, Josh Gibson, Rogers Hornsby, Hank Aaron, and a host of others. In 1947, a young high school kid who had not yet graduated from nearby Fairfield Industrial High School played at Rickwood after briefly joining the Negro Leagues Birmingham Black Barons—his name was Willie Mays.

But in the spring of 1926, a tall, lanky, right-handed pitcher took the mound at Rickwood for the Chattanooga Giants against the Black Barons. This was no ordinary young colt taking an awkward shot at pro ball; this was a kid who threw darts. Some hitters claimed that they had difficulty even seeing LeRoy "Satchel" Paige's fast stuff.

He grew up in the poorest section of south side Mobile, Alabama, the son of a usually out-of-work landscaper. His mother earned 50 cents a day traveling across town to clean the houses of wealthy whites. Buck O'Neil, a Negro Leagues player who later became something of a spokesman for black baseball when history had forgotten it, said of Paige: "Satchel came from nothing, even less than most black people did back then, and he had a burning desire to prove himself" (O'Neil 1997, 111).

When he was about seven years old, the boy worked briefly at a railroad station carrying luggage. He later said that when he began loading several pieces on a pole, a young redcap said that he looked like a "satchel tree." Hence, the nickname was born, at least in that particular retelling of Paige's early days. Like so many other facets of his life and career, no one, it seems, knows for certain.

One thing is irrefutable. The young man from his earliest days could throw a baseball with much velocity and precision. When he was about 12 years old, he landed in the Industrial School for Negro Children at Mount Miegs, Alabama, after swiping a piece of costume jewelry. It was at the school, under the tutelage of baseball coach Edward Byrd, that the boy first played the game that would shape his own life and the life of the sport.

In December 1923, still in his late teens, the gangling youngster, well over six feet, left the industrial school for life on a baseball road. After playing for a team called the Mobile Tigers, he was picked up in 1926 by the Chattanooga Black Lookouts of the Negro Southern League. With a high leg kick and an assortment of delivery motions, Paige baffled hitter after hitter, all the while chatting away at them from the pitcher's mound. Years later, when Ralph Kiner, a Hall of Fame white outfielder, had faced Paige in a barnstorming game, he remembered Paige calling out his pitches—a "bee at yo' knee, a taste at yo' waist, and better at yo' letters" (Gay 2010, 39).

Paige would become not only perhaps the game's greatest pitcher of all time but also one of its consummate showmen. On a number of occasions, Paige directed his outfielders to head to the bench; he did not need them. Almost every time he pulled this showboat antic, he prevailed, striking out eager hitters who saw an empty outfield. On other occasions, he would intentionally load the bases with walks just to frustrate the next three hitters as he blazed balls past them.

Pepper Martin, the feisty and talented infielder of the St. Louis Cardinals who faced Paige in off-season barnstorming games, once said of the lanky hurler: "You can't see nuthin' but dat foot. It hides the ballpark and Satch, too. Sometimes you don't know the ball's been pitched till it plunks behind you" (Gay 2010, 66).

Paige would travel not only the United States but also to South America, from team to team, entertaining the fans and the press with memorable quips, showing off a wicked repertoire of pitches, and making news even in the mainline newspapers and periodicals. He often entertained fans by showing off his pinpoint control. During his warm-up pitches, he stuck the foil wrapper from a stick of gum on home plate and then threw one pitch after another directly over it.

But, now in the spring of 1926, with his legend in its infancy, Satchel toed the pitching rubber in the park that would also become legendary. Behind Satchel, the Chattanooga squad prevailed that day against the Black Barons. So impressed was the management of the Birmingham team that it immediately offered Paige a salary of $275 a month to switch teams. Since Satchel was only making $50 a month for Chattanooga, the decision was not difficult.

The Black Barons would soon be invited into Rube Foster's Negro National League. Paige would continue to dominate whatever hitters stood 60 feet, 6 inches from his "bee ball" or whatever fast pitch or breaking ball he chose to throw.

And Rickwood Field would continue to host games, both of black teams and white. Although the games were not integrated, most of the games had seats filled with both races. Piper Davis, a superb Negro Leagues player who organized the Black Barons, talked later about how baseball, given the chance, could bring together people, not separate them. "My dad and I would go to games," he said, "and, while standing in line for tickets, actually talk to white men about baseball—pennant races, famous players. I don't just mean Black Barons games, but the white Barons, too. Until I was grown and in college, I don't remember talking to a white man, really having a conversation with him, about anything except baseball" (Barra 2010, 72).

AN ERA PASSES; NEW STARS EMERGE

On December 9, 1930, at the age of 49, Rube Foster died of a heart attack. On a day in 1925, he had fallen unconscious in his room from a gas leak and was pulled from the room suffering near asphyxiation. He never recovered, displaying increasing symptoms of erratic behavior, and eventually, dementia. In 1926, in the fog and darkness of mental erosion, Foster was placed in an asylum in Kankakee, Illinois. He stayed there for the rest of his life. In Chicago, mourners, numbering more than 3,000, remembering the giant contributions that Foster had made to black baseball and to the black community, stood in frigid wind and rain to pay respect.

When Foster entered the asylum, Dave "Gentleman Dave" Malarcher took over as player-manager of the American Giants. A highly skilled third baseman, Malarcher joined the American Giants in 1920 and became an important component of the baseball machine constructed by Foster. Now, taking over Foster's reins, the new manager continued to preach to his players what his mentor had taught them—discipline and defense. And although Foster could now never fully appreciate their accomplishments, the team he built went on to achieve the heights of Negro Leagues baseball. After winning NNL pennants in both 1926 and 1927, the American Giants defeated the champions of the ECL, the Bacharach Giants of Atlantic City, in the two Negro Leagues World Series.

In July 2010, the United States Postal Service honored Negro Leagues baseball by unveiling two stamps. One depicted an artist's rendering of an action play at home plate; the other was a portrait of Rube Foster.

Ultimately, with the loss of Foster and the financial pressures of the Great Depression beginning to grip the country, professional black baseball declined in the late 1920s. With the increasing strains on family budgets within black communities, attendance eroded. Strained by financial pressures and plagued often by administrative mismanagement, various teams struggled to stay afloat. In 1928, the ECL folded. Although the NNL limped along until 1931, it, too, dissolved.

Many individual teams survived, scratching out an independent existence for a time, as they had done before the advent of the Negro Leagues structure. Players moved from team to team seeking the best offers; others played in the Caribbean venues. Nevertheless, there would be other black executives who, like Rube Foster, would lead black baseball to a revival of league play in the 1930s.

In April 1930, the owner of the Kansas City Monarchs, J. L. Wilkinson, attempting to inject new excitement into the world of black baseball, invested much of his life savings into a new invention. He introduced a traveling lighting system to black baseball.

The system was powered by giant gas engines and generators. There were four trucks. Each of the trucks carried a set of six floodlights, elevated on two poles, and each mounted in the truck beds. One truck of lights was placed down the left field line, one down the right field line, another one behind right field and the fourth behind left field. Additional lights were mounted on the top of the grandstands.

On a night in Enid, Oklahoma, as the Monarchs played a game against Phillips University, the teams took the field under Wilkinson's new lights. "What talkies are to movies, lights will be to baseball," Wilkinson proudly proclaimed (Clark and Holway "1930 Negro National League").

For two months, Wilkinson and the Monarchs took their lighting system on the road—to small towns and large cities. In St. Louis, 4,000 fans turned out to see that city's first game under the lights. In Chicago, the black press of the Windy City gushed with exuberance, the *Chicago Defender* calling the occasion "The most spectacular event in all baseball history" ("City Fans . . ." 1930, 8).

All of this came five years before the first night game in major league history. In May 1935, the Cincinnati Reds hosted the Philadelphia Phillies under lights at Crosley Field.

For black baseball, the Monarch's traveling light exhibitions seemed to herald the beginning of a new era. Under the lights at Pittsburgh's Forbes Field, the catcher for the Homestead Grays suffered a broken finger when he had difficulty picking up a pitch. His replacement was a teenager who had generated much buzz on the local sandlots for his towering home runs. His name was Josh Gibson.

In the early 1930s the names of a new generation would showcase the Negro Leagues—men such as Satchel Paige, Josh Gibson, James "Cool Papa" Bell, Buck Leonard, Martin Dihigo, Ted "Double Duty" Radcliffe, and many others, who were just now, in the early 1930s, gaining star status. The new decade would also give rise to the dominance of such power-laden teams as the Pittsburgh Crawfords and the Homestead Grays. These would be the men and teams highlighted in the sports sections of the black newspapers, cheered on by black fans crowding major stadiums, and talked about among keen observers of the sport and by white stars who in exhibition games played against them. Later, their skills would be known through stories and lore and formal recognition by the larger American public. But for now their feats still remained, for most of the country, despite J. L. Wilkinson's lights, mostly in the shadows.

REFERENCES

Barra, Allan. 2010. *Rickwood Field: A Century in America's Oldest Ballpark*. New York: W. W. Norton & Company.

Barthel, Thomas. 2007. *Baseball Barnstorming and Exhibition Games, 1901–1962*. Jefferson, NC: McFarland and Company.

Carroll, Brian. 2006. "Early Twentieth-Century Heroes: Coverage of Negro League Baseball in the Pittsburgh Courier and the Chicago Defender," *Journalism History*, 34.

"City Fans to See Night Baseball," 1930. *Chicago Defender*, June 21, 8.

Clark, Dick, and John B. Holway. "1930 Negro National League," SABR Research Journals Archives. http://research.sabr.org/journals/1930-negro-national-league.

Fimrite, Ron. 1993. "His Own Biggest Fan," *Sports Illustrated*, July 19, 76.

Gay, Timothy. 2010. *Satch, Dizzy, and Rapid Robert*. New York: Simon & Schuster.

Hogan, Lawrence. 2006. *Shades of Glory*. Washington, D.C: National Geographic.

Holway, John. 1989. "Judy Johnson a Master of Playing the Angles," *Washington Post*, June 25, C12.

Jenkinson, Bill. 1998. "Babe Ruth and the Issue of Race," *American Business Law Journal*, Winter, 291.

Lewis, Cary. 1919. "Baseball Circuit for Next Season," *The Chicago Defender*, October 4, 11.

Metcalf, Henry. 2000. *A Game for all Races*. New York: Metro Books.

"Migration and Its Effect," 1918. *Chicago Defender*, April 20, 16.

O'Neil, Buck. 1997. *I Was Right on Time*. New York: Simon & Shuster.

"Rube Foster—The Negro National League," 2012. http://sports.jrank.org/pages/1529/Foster-Rube-Negro-National-League.html

"Ruth Is Suspended: Fined Series Money," 1921. *New York Times*, December 6, 25.

Smith, Rollo. 1924. "Eastern Snapshots," *Pittsburgh Courier*, October 25, 7.

Union (Cincinnati), April 30, 1921, 1.

Ward, Geoffrey, and Ken Burns. 1994. *Baseball: An Illustrated History*. New York: Alfred A. Knopf.

Wilson, W. Rollo. 1924. "Rube Foster Dominating Figure in World Series," *Pittsburgh Courier*, October 11, 6.

Wyatt, Dave. 1920. "Big Crowd See Stars Battle," *Chicago Defender*, May 22, 9.

Young, Frank. 1924. "Kansas City Wins Championship," *Chicago Defender*, October 25, 1.

3

Great Teams, Great Players

BLACK CLUBS IN YANKEE STADIUM

It had been seven years since Yankee Stadium had first opened its gates. Under the leadership of Yankee president Jake Ruppert and the presence in the lineup of young slugger Babe Ruth, the Yankees, in the spring of 1923, were in their early days of baseball dominance. But seven years later, on July 5, 1930, about 20,000 fans filed into the "house that Ruth built" to see a double-header in which neither Ruth nor any other white player participated. Ruppert opened the doors of his magnificent stadium to two black teams—the New York Lincoln Giants and the Baltimore Black Sox.

This was a charitable event on behalf of the Brotherhood of Sleeping Car Porters, a union founded in 1925 under the direction of labor leader and magazine publisher A. Philip Randolph. For over two decades there had been efforts to bring together porters into a labor union to fight for fair pay and other basic rights. Now, in the midst of the Great Depression, the porters and other workers continued to battle for recognition and collective bargaining rights from the Pullman Company. Their motto: "Fight or Be Slaves."

Led by Secretary-Treasurer of the Brotherhood Roy Lancaster, the union managed to convince Ruppert and other Yankee officials to help sponsor the fundraising effort. When the Yankees agreed, an ebullient Lancaster declared that the "great Yankee Stadium" had been "given to the porters free, to aid them in their fight for a higher standard of living. Truly, we have friends in both races" (Hogan 2006, 257).

The game itself became something of a showcase of power hitting by Herbert "Rap" Dixon of the Black Sox and Chino Smith of the Giants. The teams split the two games of the doubleheader while Dixon hit three homers and Smith two. Player-manager of the Giants, John Henry "Pop" Lloyd, in the last years of his halcyon playing days, also liked the confines of Yankee Stadium. Pop banged out four hits in the doubleheader.

Between games, the tap dancer Bill Robinson, known as Bojangles, ran a race backwards (with a head start, naturally) against YMCA track stars. In addition, a band from the 369th Infantry Regiment, known as the Harlem Hell Fighters, also performed. The Brotherhood of Sleeping Car Porters became $3,500 richer because of the affair.

Pittsburgh Courier reporter William Nunn called the event "One of Outstanding Athletic Achievements in Race History." He described the excitement in Harlem as so great that it was like a holiday. He talked about the Broadway celebrities and city officials who turned out to fill the box seats. In describing the five home runs belted by Dixon and Smith, Nunn said, "Four of the home run swats sailed into the right field bleachers, the place where the battering 'Babe' socks most of his. And the ferocity of those liners which jumped into the bleachers from the bats of these two attested to their hitting strength." Blacks in the "days of our old age," he said, will "look back upon Yankee Stadium, July 5, 1930, as one of the red-letter days of our lives" (Nunn 1930, A4).

When Yankee Stadium opened its gates to black teams that day in 1930, wise black baseball men knew the ultimate importance. Journalist St. Clair Bourne Sr. said later, "When these guys came along and started playing this kind of ball and people saw them here at Yankee Stadium, people would come out." They would see for themselves the quality of play. And, sooner or later, "owners were going to get smart enough to realize that the real part of baseball was green, not black or white" (Hogan 2006, 260).

Cumberland "Cum" Posey, owner and manager of the Homestead Grays of Pittsburgh, was another of those wise men. Posey later said that the 1930 promotion at Yankee Stadium "had a great bearing on colored baseball of the future" (Hogan 2011).

In 1977 Pop Lloyd was elected to the Baseball Hall of Fame. His plaque recognized that, among other things, he was "instrumental in helping open Yankee Stadium to Negro baseball in 1930."

THE MIGHTY HOMESTEAD GRAYS

In the 1920s, much of black baseball had centered around two determined executives—Rube Foster, the owner of the Chicago American Giants and the father of the Negro National League, and Ed Bolden, owner of the Hilldale

Daisies and father of the Eastern Colored League (ECL). By the early 1930s, with the country wracked by severe economic depression, especially in black communities, neither league had survived. But two leading, off-the-field figures emerged to lead black baseball into a storied era of magnificent players and legendary teams—Cum Posey of the Homestead Grays and William "Gus" Greenlee, owner of the Pittsburgh Crawfords and organizer of a second Negro National League.

When the Eastern Colored League organized in 1923, Posey's Grays remained independent. He also began to draw the wrath of ECL owners when he continually lured league players to the Grays with offers of higher salaries. The team gradually became a cohesive collection of hitters and pitchers that outclassed almost any opponents up to their challenge, including collections of barnstorming major and minor leaguers.

In 1929, Posey enlisted the Grays in what proved to be a one-year venture—the American Negro League. When the league quickly disbanded, wrecked by Depression-era financial woes, the Grays, under Posey's guidance, retained their footing as an independent club and picked up even more stars as other clubs folded or floundered.

By 1931 Posey had assembled a magnificent group of players. They included five who were eventually voted into the major league Baseball Hall of Fame:

First Base: Oscar Charleston—Son of a Sioux father and a black mother from Indianapolis, Indiana, Charleston, after a stint in the army while a teenager, joined his hometown Indianapolis ABCs. Extraordinarily fast, he began his career as a center fielder. When he joined the Grays, he was already an established star, both in the field and at the plate. Now in his mid-30s in 1931, he played mostly at first base. When asked how to pitch to Charleston, St. Louis Cardinals pitcher Dizzy Dean, one of the most celebrated hurlers in the game's history who faced Charleston while barnstorming, said that the only thing he could suggest was to throw and duck. After watching Charleston's exploits on the field, famed major league manager John McGraw offered this opinion: "If Oscar Charleston isn't the greatest baseball player in the world, then I'm no judge of baseball talent" (Schulian 2005, Z2).

Third Base: Jud "Boojum" Wilson—A fierce competitor who often scrapped with opposing players and jawed with umpires, Wilson purportedly got his nickname from the sound of line drives he drilled into the walls of the various parks in which he played. In 1931, Wilson was also an established star who could effectively play any of the infield positions. Satchel Paige once said that Wilson was one of the toughest hitters he personally faced in his long career.

Pitcher: Smokey Joe Williams—A towering and imposing sight on the pitching rubber, the six-foot, four-inch Williams earned a number of nicknames in his storied career—"Strikeout," "Cyclone," and the one that was used most often, "Smokey Joe." Now in the twilight years of a legendary career, Williams had matched pitches with major leaguers such as Walter Johnson and Grover Cleveland Alexander and had so impressed Ty Cobb that the Georgian, not known for his praise of black players, admitted that in the major leagues Williams could have probably won 30 games a year. In August 1930, now 44 years old, he pitched the Grays to a one-hit, 12-inning shutout of the Kansas City Monarchs. Williams became a powerful influence on some of the younger players on Homestead's formidable team.

Pitcher: Willie Foster—Rube Foster's half brother, Willie Foster was in the prime years of a pitching career that left lasting marks in the history of the Negro Leagues, mostly on behalf of Rube Foster's Chicago American Giants. The left-hander mixed an assortment of off-speed pitches with a decent fastball and razor-point control. In the Negro Leagues World Series in 1926, he compiled an earned run average of 1.27. He would only be on the Grays for 1931, but his presence helped solidify the team as one of the greatest of all time.

Catcher Josh Gibson—Born in Georgia, Gibson moved to Pittsburgh in 1923. He entered a vocational school to become an electrician but, at age 16, began playing organized baseball for a team sponsored by Gimbels department store, where he started working as an elevator operator. It was then that the kid's phenomenal slugging prowess was soon the talk among many knowledgeable black baseball followers in the city. The youngster was powerful and muscled—six foot, two inches, with speed and a powerful throwing arm. One Negro Leagues player who saw him homer in a sandlot game said later, "The boy is a marvel. He hit the ball out of existence. They didn't even go after it. It went over a mountain" (Hogan 2006, 279).

At the plate he had a simple, short swing that generated extraordinary bat speed. When he caught the sweet spot on a pitch, the ball rocketed, sometimes to distances never before seen by onlookers. By 1928 he was playing for the semiprofessional Pittsburgh Crawfords. In late July 1930, Cum Posey persuaded the youngster to join the Grays. Although Gibson's presence on the team cemented the team's preeminence of all black squads by 1931, Gibson's personal life, as it would do throughout his career, plunged into torment. His wife, Helen, died giving birth prematurely to twins. The children would be raised by Helen's parents.

In addition to these five stars who became Hall of Famers, the Grays in 1931 also boasted versatile pitcher/catcher Ted "Double Duty" Radcliffe, who acquired his nickname from noted sportswriter Damon Runyon, who watched him pitch one game of a doubleheader and then catch the second game. Like many Negro Leagues players, Radcliffe moved from team to team. In his long career, Radcliffe played for over 40 different teams. In 1931, however, he played for the Grays, and this was a team very difficult to defeat.

The Grays played all challengers—other independent teams, semipro teams, Negro Leagues teams, major league barnstormers. None could match this imposing lineup and pitching staff. When historians of baseball scoured archives, newspapers, and any other evidence of game results they could find of the 1931 Grays, they all came away astonished at what they found. The team played around 150 games in 1931 and won approximately 95 percent of them.

"Remarking about the Grays," Radcliffe said, with more than a hint of exaggeration, "it didn't matter if we got behind by four or five runs because Josh would hit in 12 runs all by himself. Josh was some kind of hitter" (Hill 2007).

For many years Radcliffe told a story about a game in which an old lady sat on her front porch far from the field. "Wasn't no fence in this particular park," Radcliffe recalled. "Someplace in Pennsylvania, I think it was. She's way out there in centerfield rockin' away when Josh hits one. And Josh made that old lady jump" (Schulian 2000, 90).

Gibson later said that the 1931 Grays were the best team on which he had ever played. Posey agreed, saying that the 1931 team was "the strongest club the Grays ever assembled and the strongest club of modern Negro baseball as far back as we can remember" (Snyder 2003, 40).

GUS GREENLEE AND THE PITTSBURGH CRAWFORDS

King of the Hill District

The Hill District is Pittsburgh's oldest black neighborhood. Beginning in the late 1920s, part of the Hill District became a place of nightspots and good times, a place to congregate where much was happening. It became such a haven largely because of William A. "Gus" Greenlee.

If Cum Posey learned much in an academic setting, Gus Greenlee learned it on the streets. If Posey was a man averse to the spotlight; Greenlee was a man who craved attention and a following.

Born in North Carolina., Greenlee moved to Pittsburgh in 1916 with no money but filled with ambition and energy. Working at lowly jobs, he saved enough to buy a taxicab. When the United States entered World War I, Greenlee left the cab and the streets of Pittsburgh and served in the army in France. When he returned, the country had begun its grand experiment of Prohibition, attempting to rid the country of the evils of liquor. A large number of U.S. citizens, however, had no intention of obeying such a government edict. Thus, suddenly, there was a great demand for a product with no legal supply. Greenlee gave up the taxicab business but kept the taxi. He used it to provide a bootleg liquor supply to citizens of Pittsburgh's Hill District. Some began to call him "Gasoline Gus."

The son of a white man and a black woman, Greenlee was round-faced and barrel-chested, with reddish-orange hair. His friends called him Big Red. In the mid-1920s, Greenlee expanded his illegal operations beyond that of boot-legging. He purchased an underground lottery business. The numbers game, popular among a wide section of urban black communities, not only helped make Greenlee a rich man but also enabled him to achieve political influence. He became close associates with county commissioners and Pittsburgh City Hall figures, many of whom, for payoffs, enabled Big Red to become a man of very big stature in the black communities of the city.

By the early 1930s, Greenlee not only owned two hotels with speakeasies, a pool hall, and a café but also the Crawford Grill on Wylie Avenue, where, on the third floor, some of the hottest musicians of the era, a kind of Hall of Fame of jazz, performed at various times. Performers included Dizzy Gillespie, Ella Fitzgerald, Count Basie, Duke Ellington, Cab Calloway, Lena Horne, and Louis Armstrong. Like the Cotton Club in Harlem, the Crawford attracted both black and white entertainers along with racially mixed audiences. Art Rooney, owner of the Pittsburgh Steelers football team and friend of Greenlee, often visited the Crawford Grill.

With the political power and economic impact wielded by Greenlee in Pitts-burgh came obligations. To consolidate the support of the community, he built a reputation of generosity and social consciousness and became a benefac-tor on whom the black residents of the Hill could appeal in tough times. He helped provide money for young people to go to college; helped folks in the community buy homes, pay rent, and acquire medical care; and even operated a soup kitchen during the dark days of the Depression. Since most members of the black community had difficulty securing loans from mainline banking institutions, Greenlee became, for many, their best hope of finding financial support to start business

The Crawfords

In 1925, young black players formed a baseball team that that was spon-sored by the Crawford Bath House and Recreation Center, a public facility that was open to immigrants and blacks. They called the team the Crawfords and became a well-known juggernaut in the city's recreation sandlot league. As the team's reputation grew, so did donations to the center, much of them from Greenlee, who, for example, bought team uniforms for the players.

In 1931 Greenlee, whose interests and fascinations often took breathtaking turns, decided he wanted a baseball team that could challenge that other team in Pittsburgh, the Homestead Grays, and that other black leader in the city who was getting so much local press, Cum Posey. Greenlee set out to change the neighborhood recreation powerhouse, the Crawfords, into a professional team that could reduce Posey and the Grays to second best in Pittsburgh.

In 1932, Greenlee took on Posey in the most direct way that a baseball owner can take on another—he raided the Grays, offering outstanding players much greater salaries than Posey was able to offer. The Greenlee-Posey rivalry and feud was thus joined.

The Crawfords signed Judy Johnson, Oscar Charleston, and Josh Gibson in a bitter bidding war. Greenlee's success was Posey's defeat—at least in the short run. The Grays were no longer the behemoths of black baseball; it was now the other club from Pittsburgh, the Crawfords, who fielded the fearsome lineup. Satchel Paige, Cool Papa Bell, Josh Gibson, Judy Johnson, and Oscar Charleston were all now members of the Crawfords. Many baseball enthusiasts claim that the 1935 Pittsburgh Crawfords were perhaps the greatest team in Negro Leagues history. If that is true, it is primarily because the Crawfords in 1935 had many of the same players that other baseball enthusiasts regarded as the best team in Negro Leagues history—the 1931 Homestead Grays.

The source of Greenlee's money and power, especially the numbers racket, was not a secret. The players themselves often commented openly. Judy Johnson, for a time Greenlee's stalwart infielder, remembered Greenlee carrying "$100 bills all over his pockets. Gus made a lot of money. He didn't know how much money he had." Dick Seay, another of Greenlee's players, recalled: "Greenlee . . . dressed neat, big expensive hats, always a big crowd around him" (Santa Maria 1991, 20).

Walter "Buck" Leonard, one of the early baseball players who knew Greenlee, said, "Everybody knew what was going on—the chief of police . . . everybody. When the county was going to come in for a raid, Greenlee would get a notice and everybody would close down. There would be no business that day or night. The police would come in and search . . . and then they'd go away. . . . Of course, you know for that kind of protection, you were payin' something" (Santa Maria 1991, 20).

Greenlee Field, 1932

As Greenlee invested his money into this new venture, he characteristically did it his own way—with much bravado and fanfare. He purchased a plot of land from a brick company and set out to do what no other black professional baseball man had ever done—build his own stadium. At an estimated cost of $100,000, the red-brick stadium, situated in the middle of the Hill District, near his Crawford Grill, seated 7,500 fans. Greenlee estimated that a huge percentage of the fans who attended the games would not have to take public transportation to see the games—they could walk.

Soon, Greenlee, following the lead of the Kansas City Monarchs, who had been traveling around the country with their own lighting system, added a permanent lighting structure for the new stadium. It also sported an overhead tarp that covered fans from the weather. Not surprisingly, he called the new venue Greenlee Park. It opened in late April 1932.

Sportswriter Chester Washington was impressed: "All the color, glamour, picturesqueness that usually attends the opening of a big league ball park was in evidence as Goodsen's New York Black Yankees helped the popular Pittsburgh Crawfords dedicate new Greenlee Park . . . the band played . . . an impressive dedicatory speech was made . . . spectators stood to pay homage to Gus Greenlee, builder of the park. . . . electrified radio amplifiers announced the batteries . . . and the game was on" (Washington 1932, A5).

THE NEW NEGRO LEAGUES

Greenlee now had his team and his park. He was not content. He had learned about Rube Foster's estimable efforts in creating the first of the Negro Leagues a decade earlier. He knew of the league's demise. He knew of several aborted attempts by other entrepreneurs to create other league structures. But despite the economic pressures of the Great Depression that seemed to argue against yet another attempt, Greenlee, as in his other ventures, zealously moved ahead. He would resurrect the Negro Leagues on his own terms and in his own domain. Pittsburgh, home of both the Grays and the Crawfords, would be the center of the next league of black players.

Thus, the National Negro Association, later called the second Negro National League (NNL), was formed before the 1933 season. Greenlee served as the league's president. The league had formidable teams representing cities from Chicago to Pittsburgh. It did not include Kansas City. The Monarchs, in the midst of the Depression, decided to continue to play exhibition games in small towns across the country—a kind of in-season barnstorming schedule. Led by stalwart Wilbur "Bullet" Rogan on the mound, the Monarchs remained one of the most intimidating black teams in all of baseball and managed to garner enough gate receipts in their wanderings to survive.

The NNL, under Greenlee's stewardship, brought some order to the chaos that had been black baseball. The league consisted of teams in such cities as Chicago, Detroit, Baltimore, Pittsburgh, Nashville, and Columbus. The owners contracted with more than 100 players, with the average salary being about $250 per month for a four-month season. The league limited the size of team rosters and imposed a salary cap on each of the teams to reduce the raiding of players within the league by owners.

As did Rube Foster in the 1920s, Greenlee endured much criticism from fellow owners and from the press for various actions or inactions they saw in his leadership. But black sportswriter W. Rollo Wilson strongly defended Greenlee's efforts to shore up Negro Leagues baseball. "They knocked him," wrote Wilson, "they said he wanted to be a czar but they neglected to say, also, that it was his money that was paying salaries for other owners, that he was assuming bills for clubs other than the Crawfords. . . . All that he has received for his efforts has been ill-advised criticism from those unacquainted with the facts and even from the very men who accepted his money to pay their personal bills" (Lester 2001, 12).

In 1937 Kansas City Monarchs owner Wilkinson decided to abandon the year-round barnstorming of his squad and launched a second black professional league. Called the Negro American League (NAL), it brought together the strongest squads from the Midwest and upper South, led by the Monarchs. They included teams in Chicago, Cincinnati, Memphis, Detroit, Birmingham, Indianapolis, and St. Louis.

Chronic personnel turnover and financial woes would plague both the NNL as well as the NAL. Nevertheless, large numbers of people attended Negro-league games; the teams and players earned wider recognition, even in the mainline press, as the number of big league parks hosting their games increased; and, more than ever before, the leagues gained a degree of organizational acumen that had been woefully lacking in the early years of black baseball.

Within a few years of their founding, Gus Greenlee could say that the leagues "by hard work, effort, and large sums of money spent in organizing, developing and training its personnel, management and players since 1933, has made organized negro baseball a substantial business . . . employing hundreds of persons and enjoying the good will and respect of organized baseball and the public which it serves." Greenlee went on to say that since black players were unable, because of segregation, to play in white professional baseball, the Negro Leagues have "given opportunity and employment to hundreds of Negro baseball players, has given American Negro youth a chance to display and develop his talents in the National sport and has provided entertainment for millions of Negro baseball fans" (W. A. Greenlee resolution).

THE EAST-WEST GAME

Gus Greenlee, the king of Pittsburgh's Hill District—the driving force behind the Pittsburgh Crawfords and the leader of the new Negro National League—was also the principal creator of what became among black communities one of the premier athletic events in all of sports—the East-West All-Star Game.

The idea for the game came not from Greenlee himself but from two black sportswriters—Roy Sparrow of the *Pittsburgh Sun-Telegraph* and Bill Nunn of the *Pittsburgh Courier*. The two men approached Greenlee at the Crawford Grill, and their discussions led to a meeting in Chicago with Robert Cole, owner of the Chicago American Giants. Greenlee wanted the game to be played in Comiskey Park, home of the major league's Chicago White Sox. What better place could there be than Comiskey to bring national attention to the game? Cole had the necessary connections to lease the stadium, and the first game was scheduled for September 14, 1933. Greenlee became the major financial backer, along with Cole and Tom Wilson, owner of the Baltimore Elite Giants.

The players for the East-West Negro Leagues All-Star Game were selected by fans who cast votes with either of the two major black newspapers in the United States—the *Pittsburgh Courier* and the *Chicago Defender*. The competing teams were comprised of players representing distinct geographic areas. In the first game, for example, the East team was filled almost entirely with players from Pennsylvania—the bulk from the Pittsburgh Crawfords and others from the Homestead Grays and Philadelphia Stars. The West included players mostly from the Chicago American Giants and the Nashville Elite Giants.

The East-West game was an immediate fan favorite. The first contest went to the West in a slugfest, including a double and a mammoth home run in the upper tier of the left field stands by 230-pound Mule Suttles of the American Giants, one the great long-ball hitters in the history of the Negro Leagues, a fearsome sight at the plate wielding a 50-ounce bat. Despite inclement weather, nearly 20,000 watched from the seats of Comiskey. It was a grand day for black baseball, and Greenlee and Cole celebrated at Jim Knight's Tavern on 47th Street.

The East-West game soon became the most popular event in black baseball. Players were honored to be chosen by the fans. They eagerly checked into Chicago's Grand Hotel, which served as their headquarters. They hit the nightspots that featured Ella Fitzgerald, Count Basie, Fletcher Henderson, and other entertainers who arranged their schedules to be in Chicago when the East-West game was to take place.

Red, white, and blue banners draped the park. A jazz band played between innings. So many people purchased tickets to the game from various parts of the country that the Union Pacific Railroad added extra cars to some of its lines to Chicago from places as far away as Texas and Mississippi.

Fans dressed in their finest clothes, hats, and spit-shined shoes and joined the players at night in some of the hot spots around town. On several occasions, the East-West game at Comiskey outdrew the attendance of major league all-star games.

As Greenlee and the other promoters had hoped, the East-West games brought widespread attention to black baseball, even drawing a surprising number of white newspaper reporters from major dailies. The black community was already familiar with the likes of Paige and Gibson and other greats. Now, because of the East-West game, their names and others became more widely known—men whose talents were now on display on a national stage— not only Paige and Gibson but also a number of stars who would eventually be named to baseball's Hall of Fame, men such as Cool Papa Bell, Walter "Buck" Leonard, Martin Dihigo, and Monte Irvin.

Born to Mississippi sharecroppers in 1903, James Bell left the South in 1920 to live in St. Louis, Missouri, with relatives. His professional baseball odyssey began in 1922, when he first pitched for the local St. Louis Stars, a team on which he starred for over a decade. It was the beginning of a career that would last nearly 30 years as a player and a coach. At first he was a left-handed pitcher, and a good one. The story of his nickname derives from his first year with the Stars, when Bell fanned a hitter at the end of a tight game and one of his teammates gave him the moniker Cool Papa.

Soon, however, Bell's extraordinary athletic skills, particularly his speed, propelled his career in a new direction: he would be a center fielder, perhaps the greatest center fielder in all of black baseball in the 1930s and 1940s. Like most black stars, he moved from team to team—Detroit Wolves, Kansas City Monarchs, Homestead Grays, Pittsburgh Crawfords, Memphis Red Sox, Chicago American Giants, Detroit Senators, and Kansas City Stars as well as several years in Cuba, Mexico, and the Dominican Republic. His speed astonished all who watched. A sports editor of the *Denver Post* once quipped that he had at last found someone who could steal first base. Satchel Paige claimed later that, in his opinion, Bell was likely a faster runner than the legendary Olympic star Jesse Owens. In 1933, Bell played in the first East-West All-Star Game as a member of the Crawfords. He would appear in eight all-star games.

Buck Leonard, left-handed, power-hitting first baseman for the Homestead Grays, anchored an awesome lineup that many years included catcher Josh Gibson and that led the Grays to nine consecutive Negro National League championships between 1937 and 1945. Leonard had begun his baseball career as a semipro star in his hometown in Rocky Mount, North Carolina, but in 1933 he was forced by the Depression to leave home to pursue a professional career. Smokey Joe Williams saw him playing and connected him with the Grays. Beginning in 1935, Leonard became a regular fan favorite at the all-star classic.

At Latin American Stadium in Havana, Cuba, there is a statue that reads "The Immortal." All Cuban baseball fans know the identity of the bust as that of Martin Dihigo, a player of a vast array of baseball skills—pitcher, infielder, outfielder, exemplary both at the plate and in the field. He displayed his athletic gifts not only in Cuba but in the Negro Leagues, the Venezuelan League,

Santo Domingo, and the Mexican League. Often he played baseball 12 months a year. Like Buck Leonard, he first showcased his skills in the East-West game in 1935.

Willie Wells played in eight East-West games. The slick fielding shortstop was generally considered the best at his position in the Negro Leagues during the 1930s and early 1940s. Cool Papa Bell said of Willie Wells. "I haven't seen no ballplayers who could beat Wells. They used to send scouts out to scout the colored ballplayers to pick the All-Stars and they had some scouts looking at Wells and one of the scouts wrote back that, 'They got a shortstop out there that you could put six big-league shortstops out there and they couldn't catch the balls that he catch, if you put them all out there at one time. But we used to say little things like that, but he was the greatest fielder I've seen" (Interview with James "Cool Papa" Bell).

Monte Irvin, born in Alabama, raised in New Jersey, was one of the few Negro Leagues players that had the opportunity to attend a college. After his student days at Lincoln College in Oxford, Pennsylvania, Irvin joined the Newark Eagles, owned and run by Abe and Effa Manley. Unlike Josh Gibson, Cool Papa Bell, and so many other Negro Leagues greats, Irvin began his career at a time when the Negro Leagues had become a more established institution, when owners of major league teams were under increasing pressure to consider breaking down the segregation barriers of the sport. After a stellar decade with the Eagles, Monte Irvin would later join the New York Giants and achieve in the major leagues an equally stellar career.

Irvin remembered the East-West games fondly, especially one in which Satchel Paige starred.

> He was a big drawing card, you know. He proved that day why everybody wanted to see him. Our first baseman, the Newark Eagles' first baseman, was the first batter up. His name was Len Pearson. So I told him I felt sorry for him, and he said, "Why?" I said, "Well, since you're the first batter, you know Satchel's gonna want to strike you out. But you go on up and do your best." And then he said, "Well, don't remind me, would you?" So he went up and took three strikes and sat down. I said, "How'd he look?" and he said, "I don't know. I didn't see it, he was throwing so hard." ("Interview with Monte Irvin" 2000)

The 1935 East-West spectacle exceeded all expectations for skill and drama and cemented the interest in succeeding games. First, there was Josh Gibson, rapping four hits around Comiskey as if he were a hitting machine. Then, with the game tied at four runs each, the teams went into extra innings. In the top half of the 10th inning, the East struck for four runs; the game appeared to be over. Yet, in the bottom of the 10th, the West staged an unlikely rally to tie the score once again. It was now 8–8 going into the 11th inning. The East team failed to score in the top half of the inning, and Martin Dihigo, of the New York Cubans, went to the mound to try to extend the game. With two men on and two outs, he faced fearsome Mule Suttles, who had already drawn four walks in the game because pitchers worked him carefully. With two men on base, Dihigo took on Big Mule. Suttles settled the game, rocketing a shot over the farthest part of Comiskey some 450 feet from the plate. The fans stood and gave the teams a long ovation.

Sportswriter Ed Harris of the *Philadelphia Tribune* recounted the glories of the game in a rather hapless attempt at poetry. Part of it read:

Mule Suttles was up, Oh Faithful moved
And Dihigo burned one down the groove
The bat met ball, the ball passed fence
And with it went the East team's chance. (Harris 1935, 77)

SATCHEL, DIZZY, -AND BARNSTORMING

Like Satchel Paige, Dizzy Dean was an American original. Just as Paige's antics and quips were fodder for the black reporters covering Negro Leagues games, Dean's observations, uttered in a Southern drawl, ungrammatical but often insightful, enlivened the pages of newspapers across the country.

Dean was born Jay Hanna Dean on January 16, 1910, in Lucas, Arkansas, to sharecroppers Alma and Albert Dean. In 1918, Dean's mother died of tuberculosis, leaving Albert with three sons to raise—Jay, Paul, and Elmer. He took them to Oklahoma, and the father and his three barefoot boys—shoes were too expensive for the family to afford—worked the cotton fields along with other poor families trying to scratch out a living.

When he was 16 years old, Dean convinced the U.S. Army that he was 18 and enlisted, looking for better living conditions and food. It was there that the youngster, who should have been barely a junior in high school, began firing fastballs past army hitters during recreation hours. It did not go unnoticed. Word spread quickly that a new star was in the making.

It was the St. Louis Cardinals who eagerly waved a contract before Dean when he left the army. He enthusiastically signed on and spent a short time in the team's farm system beginning in 1930. As a rookie with the Cardinals in 1932, Dean led the league in strikeouts and innings pitched and won 18 games. In 1933 he became a 20-game winner and in 1934 led the National League in wins (30), complete games (24), shutouts (7), and strikeouts (195); was named the National League most valuable player (MVP); and led the Cardinals to a World Series victory, in which he was named series MVP. He was now recognized as perhaps the best pitcher in major league baseball.

For Dean, who had made his way out of poverty, barnstorming became yet another gift, a chance to earn greater income by playing the game he loved. Like migrant workers following the crop seasons, barnstormers tended to play in the East and Midwest immediately after the World Series; in the West around harvest time; and in California, Mexico, and the Caribbean in the winter. Both Dean and Satchel Paige followed the sun and the games and, often, each other.

The first recorded meeting of a Dizzy Dean barnstorming team facing a Negro Leagues squad was on October 4, 1933, in the middle of Nebraska farm land in a town near the Kansas border called Oxford. The town itself was little over 200 people, but news of barnstorming baseball games could travel many miles. The Kansas City Monarchs had played before crowds on many occasions, but this day was something special for the Monarchs and for baseball fans of rural Nebraska. Dizzy was bringing fellow major leaguers Pepper Martin, Paul Waner, Larry French, and others. The local paper, the *Oxford Standard,* gushed over the event and the fact that nearly 7,000 onlookers had swarmed the small park. "The admission charge of 60 cents was thought by many local fans to be excessive," said the paper, "but the expression was heard many times before the game, that had the charge been a dollar the same crowd would have been there, for they came from a long distance" (Gay 2010, 51).

Dizzy pitched into the third inning against the Monarchs but was hit on the elbow while at bat. Nursing his wounded arm, Diz moved himself to left field and continued in the game. His team won a tight contest, 5–4. Dean had thus begun a long career separate from his celebrated seasons as a major league Hall of Fame hurler for the St. Louis Cardinals. He had begun a barnstorming career marked by frequent games against black baseball's elite players.

Like Babe Ruth, Dean appreciated the skills of the Negro Leagues players, loved the competition, and always put on a show. As a boy he had picked cotton with his brothers alongside workers both white and black. In those sweltering fields, struggling with others to make the barest of livings, somehow the stereotypes of racial superiority were lost on Dizzy. And now, pitching against hitters as dangerous at the plate as any he had faced in the majors, seemed a natural thing, not an aberration. These guys could hit, and Diz had to throw his best stuff to get them out.

The barnstorming duels between Paige and Dean, always the occasion for good-natured taunts and quips, always entertaining fare for fans who often had to drive several hours to see the games, became annual road trips. On some occasions, Dean was able to find a number of major leaguers to accompany him on the jaunts; on other occasions, he had to fill some of his squads with the best local semipro talent available. But when major leaguers faced Paige at the plate, Satch's concentration and intensity ratcheted up. Wally Berger, a member of the Boston Braves who distinguished his career with a lifetime

.300 batting average, later remembered getting two hits off Paige—the only two hits the Dean team mustered in the game. After the second hit, Satch walked over to Berger and asked him how he managed to accomplish the feat. Paige then returned to the mound and struck out the next three hitters.

Satch talked to everyone during games—to the hitters, umpires, fans, even to base runners. When Dizzy tripled off Satch in a game in Dayton, Ohio, a blooping hit that managed to land near the right field line, Dean stood proudly on third with no outs. Dean later recalled the aftermath: "The fans were yellin' their heads off for me when ol' Satch walks over and says to me, 'I hope all your friends brought plenty to eat, Diz, because if they wait for you to score, they're gonna be here past dark. You ain't goin' no further.' Then he fanned the next three." Dean also told a story about a time in Oklahoma when he joked to a radio show announcer before a game that Satchel had no idea how to throw a curve. When Dizzy first came to the plate that afternoon, Satch yelled at him. "Hear say you're goin' around tellin' people I ain't got a curve. . . . Well, then, you tell me what this is." He threw three curves. Dizzy swung three times with no luck. "How's that," Satchel laughed, "for a guy who ain't got a curve ball?" (Tye 2010).

Dean later said that he was once in a barber shop where a group of men were arguing about who was the best pitcher in all of baseball history. The names of Lefty Grove, Walter Johnson, and Lefty Gomez were suggested, along with the famous pitcher in the barber shop that day. Dean set them straight. The best pitcher he ever saw, he instructed them, was Satchel Paige. He also said that it was too bad that the black players were not in the majors. Dean later expanded on his claim, saying that if he and Satch were on the same team they would win 60 games, clinch the pennant by the Fourth of July, and go fishing until the World Series.

Each year, when the barnstorming major leaguers returned to their teams and spring training, the black players, of course, did not join them. Some played in the Negro Leagues. Others played in Mexico or the Caribbean. Some kept on barnstorming with independent teams. For black players, the traveling life remained plagued by racial hatred.

Although barnstorming through the South was dangerous and difficult, black players also faced humiliation in many areas of the North. Ted "Double Duty" Radcliffe, veteran of many barnstorming excursions, later said:

Traveling was tough back then! When we were playing in Southern Illinois and Indiana it was just like Mississippi. You had to go to the back of a grocery store to get a bologna sandwich. Segregation is pretty bad when you got to go to the back of a grocery store for a sandwich! The black ballplayers caught hell but we kept playing. We had to play because you couldn't make no money working. We had to do the best we could.

We couldn't get no hotel, couldn't take no bath. I've gone four or five days at a time without taking a bath. Back in those days they used to have barber shops where you could take a bath for a quarter. Some of the white people would let me take a bath because they'd feel sorry for me. Two or three of us would go in there. They used to have a sign in Illinois down by East St. Louis along the railroad said, "No niggers allowed." You know the dictionary says that anyone can be a nigger if they're low grade but the white man put it on us to degrade us. It didn't bother me but they did it. (McNary 1994, 25)

As much as Satchel Paige and other black stars enjoyed the competition with Dizzy Dean and other major league players, as much as they respected those white players who saw past skin color and recognized talent, it was impossible not to feel bitterness. In an interview, Paige once reflected on how people would say that Satch and Diz were so similar, "like two tadpoles." But Paige reminded everyone that Dean went back to the limelight of the majors; he and the other blacks went back to the chitlin' circuit. Or, in 1937, courtesy of a dictator from the Dominican Republic, some black players headed for the Dominican Republic.

DOMINICAN REPUBLIC—BASEBALL FEVER

In the late 19th century, the sport of baseball, as it had earlier in Cuba, found life in the Dominican Republic. Baseball diamonds appeared in major cities and even in rural areas; professional teams took form. Baseball had become such a dominant force in the country's athletic landscape by the 1930s that teams from the Dominican Republic were playing games with teams from other Caribbean nations and, occasionally, with teams from North America.

In 1930, Rafael Trujillo became president of the Dominican Republic. He was a military man, trained as an officer in the Constabulary Guard, rising to the rank of general and then commander-in-chief. He came to the presidency as the result of a political revolt. When elections were called after a temporary provisional government, Trujillo decided to run for the presidency. From his earliest days as an active political figure, Trujillo built a reputation for violence, intimidation, and even murder in his ascent to power.

With boundless vanity and ego, Trujillo, in time, persuaded the city council of the country's largest city, Santo Domingo, to change the name to Ciudad Trujillo. He renamed many of the provinces after himself and members of his family. Streets and monuments throughout the country began to bear his name. He created a number of national honors and decorations that, not surprisingly, were bestowed on him.

As his reelection approached in 1937 (the result a foregone conclusion), he nevertheless engaged an unusual tactic in the reelection campaign—he used the baseball championship series as the spotlight. Who could assemble the championship team—Trujillo or the pretenders to his office? He called his team the Dragones de Ciudad Trujillo. He even labeled the baseball playoffs the National Baseball Championship for the Reelection of President Trujillo.

With the political campaign underway, Trujillo searched for a way to ensure that the Dragones de Ciudad Trujillo became invincible. His own interest in and knowledge of baseball and the exploits of barnstorming black players in Cuba and other Latin American sites led him to a devious plot. Since the Negro Leagues in the United States were certainly more vulnerable to the raiding of players than would be the major leagues, he would do what Gus Greenlee had done to Cum Posey—he would offer substantial money to certain Negro Leagues players to come to the Dominican Republic, help his team win the championship, and elevate his already formidable political power and, he believed, the adoration of the people.

Not surprisingly, Trujillo's main target was the Negro Leagues's most celebrated star—Satchel Paige. As the Crawfords assembled in New Orleans to begin their spring training, Trujillo sent agents to offer Paige the kind of money he could not begin to make for a season playing in the Negro Leagues—several thousand dollars up front with perhaps more to come if he convinced others to head to the island. Always willing to be lured by the greater paycheck, Paige not only agreed but persuaded other Crawfords to join him, including mainstay Cool Papa Bell.

The secret machinations began in early May 1937, when a Pan American plane, hired by Trujillo, whisked away several members of the Pittsburgh Crawfords to join the Ciudiad Trujillo team. Paige said later that the players were treated like heroes when their plane landed in the Dominican. Nevertheless, they realized early on that they were under intense pressure to win. During a party at one of Trujillo's plantations, Paige was told by a local journalist that the leader does not ever like to lose and that there might be consequences if his baseball team was not successful.

Following lectures by team spokesmen, the players were for the first time shown to their rooms, told to stay there and to go to sleep early. Armed Dominican soldiers were stationed in front of the hotel's doors to prevent the players from exploring the nightlife of the city. The pressure was, indeed, on.

By May 1937, the Negro Leagues had been raided of 17 top players, 10 of them members from the Pittsburgh Crawfords—an irony certainly not lost on Gus Greenlee. When the owners of Trujillo's principal baseball adversaries realized that black players were joining the Ciudad Trujillo, they countered his moves by attempting to do the same thing. Compared to Trujillo, they were only mildly successful. Nevertheless, the powerful Santiago team managed to import such Negro Leaguers as pitcher Chet Brewer from the Kansas City Monarchs and infielder George Scales from the New York Black Yankees. They also recruited Cuban superstar Martin Dihigo. San Pedro, another of Trujillo's baseball rivals, also managed to entice several less celebrated players.

Meanwhile, back in Pittsburgh's Hill District, Greenlee was still a king, a man whose business interests were not to be brazenly attacked. Foremost, he was a fighter. In reacting to the Dominican Republic fiasco, he first tried to get court orders barring the players from remaining with Trujillo's team. When that effort proved fruitless, he tried another avenue. He would attempt to make the entire episode an international diplomatic affair.

Led by Greenlee, the owners of a number of Negro Leagues clubs met in Philadelphia on May 27, 1937, drew up a resolution condemning the actions of the Dominican Republic, and agreed to approach a number of members of Congress and the Department of State for redress of grievances. Several members of the State Department and congressional representatives were forthright in explaining that the actions of the Dominican Republican government did not appear to violate either the general principles of international law or the treaty rights between the United States and the Dominican Republic. Nevertheless, league owners traveled to Washington to meet with U.S. government officials. Lawyers for the Negro Leagues also approached the Dominican Consulate and were told that the question was one of a private nature and of no concern to the Dominican authorities. Gus Greenlee's ire intensified.

On the baseball field in the Dominican Republic, president Trujillo's Dragones faced off against the team from Santiago, and the seven-game series became a tense struggle—not only an athletic event, in Trujillo's mind, but also a political one. With the championship tied at three games apiece, Paige took the mound for the Dragones in the deciding showdown.

Satchel was as nervous on the mound as never before. From the stands he heard shouts yelled in English that he had better win or else. "By the seventh inning, we were a run behind and you could see Trujillo lining up his army," Paige said later. "They began to look like a firing squad. In the last of the seventh we scored two runs and went ahead 6–5. You never saw Ol' Satch throw harder after that. I shut them down the last two innings and we won. I hustled back to our hotel and the next morning we blew out of there in a hurry. We never did see Trujillo again and I ain't sorry" (Ward and Burns 1994, 223).

When Paige and his fellow Crawfords returned, an enraged Greenlee, whose team would never be the same again, banned the players from his league. Undaunted, Paige put together an all-star team and played much of the following year in Mexico. Eventually, most of the players who had defected to Trujillo's team would find their way back into the Negro Leagues. But 1937 in the Dominican Republic had been a wild ride.

Years later, Bell was even more emphatic in claiming that the lives of the players had been threatened. "People told us if we didn't win the title we would be executed," he recounted still nervously. "But we won" (Rogers).

SATCHEL AND DIZZY—GETTING TOGETHER ONE MORE TIME

In late May 1942, Satchel Paige's barnstorming team and Dizzy Dean's all stars met in Washington's Griffith Stadium before an estimated crowd of 22,000, the largest non–major league crowd in the ballpark's history. So eager were the fans to watch the black barnstormers and Dean's team collide that auxiliary police had to be summoned to control patrons storming the ticket booths.

Paige had joined the black press and others who were pressuring major league baseball executives to allow integration. If they continued to refuse, Paige had another suggestion. "If the Jim Crow law in baseball says no colored boys playing on white teams," he said, "I think there ought to be a full colored team in each big league. Don't think they wouldn't show those boys some baseball too. We could get up one great team. I know for sure" ("On the Line" 1941, 18).

Paige still brimmed with confidence and swagger, and, armed with a baffling array of pitches and motions, he confused hitters, kept them off balance, often reducing their hitting strokes to feeble waves. As they found their seats, fans buzzed over the promise that Paige had made in the press about the game. The collection of major leaguers, Paige promised, would get no runs.

This was not the Dizzy Dean that fans had seen prior to an injury to his arm in 1937. Although he continued to field a team of barnstormers in the off-season, Dizzy was no longer a competitive pitcher. He was now beginning a career as a baseball radio broadcaster, a career that would later take off with the advent of television broadcasting. Dizzy's homespun stories would keep Dean in the eye of baseball fans for years to come.

By this time, some of the nation's daily newspapers had begun to run stories about black players. Especially in Washington, where the Homestead Grays regularly showed off their excellence, the *Washington Post* had, on occasion, carried articles about Negro Leagues play. It was clear to any knowledgeable baseball purist who had watched the hometown Senators in Washington and also saw the potent Grays in action which team was the most skilled.

About this game in 1942 the *Post* carried a lengthy piece about the barnstorming showdown and Paige's guarantee of no runs. Although Paige did not deliver his shutout, he was nearly unhittable. The black barnstormers carried the day. "Swaggering and taunting the batters to connect with his blinding speed," the *Post* reported, "the 34-year old Kansas City Monarch ace permitted five hits but offset them with seven timely strikeouts." The all stars managed to ruin Paige's promise with a single unearned run in the fourth inning, the result of two errors and one hit. But the veteran hurler, unfazed, turned up the pressure: "Winding and uncoiling his long right arm like a giant spring, the six-foot, four-inch veteran of 17 seasons of pitching fairly blew down two of the Stars' leading hitters . . . who left the plate with somewhat awed expressions, after taking three swings apiece at balls that sped plate-ward looking as small as peas" ("Paige, Grays Beat Stars" 1942, 17).

REFERENCES

Gay, Timothy. 2010. *Satch, Dizzy & Rapid Robert*. New York: Simon & Schuster.

Harris, Ed. 1935. "At It Again: Lament on the East-West Game." *Philadelphia Tribune* (August 29). Reprinted in Lester, Larry. *Black Baseball's National Showcase: The East-West Game, 1933–1953*. Lincoln: University of Nebraska Press, 2001.

Hill, Justice B. 2007. "1931 Homestead Grays Best Ever: Team with Galaxy of Negro League Stars Dominated." MLB.com (February 26), http://mlb.mlb.com/news/article.jsp?ymd=20070226&content_id=1816465&fext=.jsp&c_id=mlb.

Hogan, Lawrence. 2006. *Shades of Glory: The Negro Leagues and the Story of African-American Baseball*. Washington, DC: National Geographic.

Hogan, Lawrence. 2011. "The Negro Leagues Discovered an Oasis at Yankee Stadium." *New York Times* (February 12), http://www.nytimes.com/2011/02/13/sports/baseball/13stadium.html.

"Interview with James 'Cool Papa' Bell." 1970 (transcripts made available). Oral History T-015. Interviewed by Arthur Shaffer and Charles Korr, Black Community Leaders Project, Western Historical Manuscript Collection, University of Missouri–St. Louis.

"Interview with Monte Irvin: The Negro League Great, Now 79, Discusses Satchel Paige, the East-West Game, and Why It's So Hard for Ex-Negro Leaguers to Make the Hall of Fame." 2000. Interviewed by Eric Enders (March 4), http://www.ericenders.com/monte.htm.

Lester, Larry. 2001. *Black Baseball's National Showcase: The East-West All Star Game. 1933–1953*. Lincoln: University of Nebraska Press.

McNary, Kyle. 1994. *Ted "Double Duty" Radcliffe*. St. Louis: McNary Publishing.

Nunn, William G. 1930. "Diamond Stars Rise to Miracle Heights in Big Game at Yankee Bowl." *Pittsburgh Courier* (July 12): A4.

"On the Line with Considine." 1941. *Washington Post* (July 22): 18.

"Paige, Grays Beat Stars, 8–1, Before 22,000." 1942. *Washington Post* (June 1): 17.

Rogers, William "Brother." "Cool Papa Bell." *Mississippi History Now*, http://mshistory.k12.ms.us/articles/277/cool-papa-bell.

Santa Maria, Michael. 1991. "King of the Hill: Looking Back at Gus Greenlee's Pittsburgh." *American Visions* (June): 20.

Schulian, John. 2000. "Laughing on the Outside: The Greatest Slugger Never to Play in the Major Leagues, Josh Gibson, Was a Jovial Teammate but, in the End, a Tragic Mystery to Almost All Who Knew Him." *Sports Illustrated* (June 26): 90.

Schulian, John. 2005. "A One-Way Ticket to Obscurity: That's What Being Black in the First Half of the 20th Century Meant for Oscar Charleston, the Greatest Baseball Player You've Never Heard Of." *Sports Illustrated* (September 5): Z2.

Snyder, Brad. 2003. *Beyond the Shadow of the Senators.* New York: McGraw-Hill.

Tye, Larry. 2010. "Barnstorming Aces Satchel Paige and Dizzy Dean." *American History* (April 1), http://www.historynet.com/barnstorming-aces-satchel-paige-and-dizzy-dean.htm.

W. A. Greenlee resolution adopted at meeting in Philadelphia, May 27, 1937, National Archives and Records Administration, RG 59, Records of the Department of State, Decimal File, 839.40634.

Ward, Geoffrey C., and Ken Burns. 1994. *Baseball: An Illustrated History.* New York: Alfred A. Knopf.

Washington, Chester. 1932. "Sportively Speaking." *Pittsburgh Courier* (May 7): A5.

4

The Drive to Integrate

THE BLACK PRESS AND ITS ALLIES
LAUNCH A CAMPAIGN

At the 10th annual New York Baseball Writers' Association dinner at the grand ballroom of the Hotel Commodore on the night of February 5, 1933, one journalist came prepared to address a subject of serious inquiry. He declared that he could see no reason why a black baseball player should not be able to participate in the major leagues. Heywood Broun was responding to an editorial that had appeared a few days earlier in the *New York Daily News* that made the same point.

Harvard graduate, leading journalist and drama critic as well as sportswriter, Broun had throughout his career written blistering columns on injustice, discrimination, and human rights. Now working for Scripps-Howard, Broun pointed out that the United States had a black athlete, sprinter Eddie Tolan, represented on its team at the 1932 Olympic Games and that actor and singer Paul Robeson, who had starred in football at Rutgers during his college years, had been named as a first-team all-American player. Why, then, was there a segregation policy in professional baseball?

Although Broun's remarks were only a minor interruption in the night's festivities, one of the sportswriters in attendance followed up with his own informal investigation into whether baseball insiders would welcome black players into the majors. Jimmy Powers, one of the writers at the *Daily News* who had triggered the paper's editorial, decided to interview a number of owners and players. He spoke with John Heydler, president of the National League; Jake Ruppert, owner of the New York Yankees; and players such as Frankie Frisch and Lou Gehrig. Powers soon wrote a column concluding that there was widespread willingness inside baseball to allow black players into the highest levels. But despite the concerns of a few white reporters such as Broun and Powers, the drive to integrate baseball would not come from the mainstream U.S. press. It would come from major black newspapers and the leading paper of American Communists.

THE *PITTSBURGH COURIER* AND THE *CHICAGO DEFENDER* ON THE ATTACK

Established in 1907, the *Pittsburgh Courier* had, by the early 1930s, achieved national prominence. This was not simply a paper that was read by black Americans in Pittsburgh; it gained a national readership and a crusading reputation. It led campaigns for improvements in housing, education, and health care and encouraged its readers to join such organizations as the National Association for the Advancement of Colored People (NAACP) and the National Urban League to fight for their rights. In the 1932 presidential election, it encouraged its readers to abandon a Republican Party that no longer could be seen in the eyes of African Americans as the party of Abraham Lincoln but as the party of entrenched capitalist titans with no regard for the interests of minorities.

And now, in 1933, the *Courier* pressed the issue of baseball integration. Sports editor Chester Washington, praising Broun and Powers for raising the issue of integration, announced that the *Courier* would conduct a symposium on baseball focusing on whether black players should be allowed to play in the major leagues. Washington and his colleagues would solicit the views of managers, owners, baseball executives, players, and sportswriters to measure opinion on the issue.

Through a four-month series of reports, some of the responses to the central question were revealing. National League president Heydler incredulously insisted that he knew of no instance in the history of the game in which a black player had been denied entrance in the majors. Had Heydler never heard of Cap Anson and his role in throwing Fleet Walker out of the majors, and was he ignorant of the lamentable stories about George Stovey and other blacks prohibited from playing just a few decades earlier? Had he never heard of the aborted attempt of Baltimore manager John McGraw early in the century to play Charlie Grant, a black man, on his team, disguising him as Chief Tokahama, a Cherokee Indian?

Although Commissioner Landis refused personally to respond to the *Courier*'s symposium, the secretary-treasurer of organized baseball, Leslie O'Connor, also approached the issue as if it did not exist. There was no law prohibiting blacks in the majors, he said, and the matter of the players on the various rosters was entirely in the hands of the owners. No mention was made of there being an unwritten law or gentleman's agreement.

Some owners rebutted the commissioner's office and said that they were, indeed, prohibited from signing blacks by rule from organized baseball. Other owners responded with lukewarm sentiments for allowing black players the opportunity to compete.

Although the *Courier*'s exploration of the issue of baseball integration was ignored by the white establishment press, the interviews and responses across a wide spectrum of the baseball world served not only to inform black readers of the issue, but it sparked increasing demands that something be done to correct this injustice. It also laid a written foundation on which emerging activists on the issue could build.

Founded in 1905, the *Chicago Defender* was by World War I the nation's most influential black weekly. Like the *Pittsburgh Courier*, its readership base spanned the country. Within a few years, the *Defender*'s slashing editorials and graphic images took on the most egregious assaults on the rights of black people—from disenfranchisement to lynching. This was a fighting paper, and its circulation in black sections of major northern cities soared. So inflammatory did some cities in the South regard the *Defender* that it was banned from newsstands. Only through smuggling by Pullman porters and others did the paper make it into the hands of blacks in the South.

On September 16, 1933, the *Defender* published a lead editorial castigating baseball's management for its persistence in preserving segregation against blacks. Some of the top white players, the editorial pointed out, had praised the skills of black athletes against whom they had played in barnstorming matchups. All manner of nationalities were represented on the playing field—"Indians, Cubans, Filipinos, Jews, Italians, Greeks." The lone exception was the American black man. "There was no Hitler movement created in America when John McGraw of the New York Giants put Andy Cohen, a Jew, on second base. It was up to Cohen to make good or go" ("What's the Matter with Baseball?" 1933).

The paper argued that the white public was not opposed to cheering for blacks. They had cheered blacks on the football field, in the Olympic Games, and in boxing. "Professional baseball has been and is losing thousands of dollars yearly by its narrow and asinine prejudiced attitude in the operation of the national game. It has been admitted that the sport needs new life. It does need new life, but in order for it to obtain new life such men as Kenesaw Mountain Landis must show an avowed courage in renouncing un-American principles in the operation of the this national sport. We ask again: What is the matter, with baseball? The answer is plain prejudice—that's all" ("What's the Matter with Baseball?" 1933).

Meanwhile, in Detroit, a young black teenager named Wendell Smith, who was the only African American student at Southeastern High School and whose father worked in Henry Ford's household as a chef, pitched his American Legion team, which featured future Chicago White Sox catcher Mike Tresh, to a playoff victory. Following the game, a professional scout signed Tresh and the opposing team's pitcher to a contract. Smith later remembered the scout's words to him: "I wish I could sign you, too, but I can't." Smith knew very well the reason (Lamb 2002, 189).

Instead, Smith decided to continue his education, enrolling at West Virginia State College near Charleston. There, at the historically black 1890 land-grant institution, he played baseball and became the sports editor for the school newspaper. He graduated in 1937 and then joined the staff of the *Pittsburgh Courier*, first as a sportswriter and then as its sports editor the following year. It was from this position that Wendell Smith would join the fight.

LESTER RODNEY AND THE *DAILY WORKER*

The American Communist Party in the United States in the 1930s was small and dedicated but widely distrusted by the overwhelming majority of Americans. Nevertheless, during the terrible economic times of the Great Depression, its message of workers' rights and justice rang true to many intellectuals. Its journalistic organ was the *Daily Worker*, published in New York, a surprisingly lively paper with commentary on not only U.S. politics and economics but on cultural matters. It also had a sportswriter—Lester Rodney.

A grandson of European Jewish immigrants, Rodney grew up in the Bensonhurst section of Brooklyn, became an avid fan of the Dodgers, and wrote sports columns for his local high school newspaper. His father was the owner of a silk factory who lost his business in the stock market crash of 1929. Rodney attended Syracuse University briefly, but, given the family's financial pressures, he never completed his degree. After taking numerous short-term jobs, he gravitated back to his most developed skill in high school—sportswriting.

He took a job with the *Daily Worker*, whose editors sought to gain the widest readership possible. Adding a sports section, they reasoned, would help. In the young Rodney, they found a crusading, tireless advocate whose instincts for the oppressed and those who had been denied justice and a fair shake matched the message of the paper.

Early on, one of Rodney's special causes became the segregation of blacks from organized baseball. On August 13, 1936, the *Daily Worker* announced its own campaign against baseball segregation, emblazoning this advertisement:

Outlawed by Baseball! The Crime of the Big Leagues!

The newspapers have carefully hushed it up!
One of the most sordid stories in American sports!
Though they win laurels for America in the Olympics—though they proved themselves to be outstanding baseball stars—Negroes have been placed beyond the pale of the American and National Leagues.

The series, said the *Daily Worker* ad, would rip the veil from the "Crime of the Big Leagues" (Silber 2003, xvii).

Rodney published interviews with both whites and blacks in baseball about the racial barrier. He highlighted the accomplishments and abilities of black stars such as Satchel Paige and Josh Gibson, attempting to inform the mostly white readership of the paper of the fact that a whole different world of baseball existed, shrouded from their view, sometimes just down the street, sometimes in the same ballparks where they had seen their favorite major league heroes. He highlighted a quote made in 1937 by New York Yankee great Joe DiMaggio that Paige was the toughest pitcher he ever faced. Most Americans had no knowledge of Paige or Gibson or even knew about the segregation issue. In one issue of the paper, Paige issued a challenge to the New York Yankees to play against a collection of Negro Leagues players. If the Yankees won, Paige declared, he and his teammates would not take a dime of the earnings. The Yankees, of course, declined to comment.

With great organizational skill, Rodney got readers of the paper involved in the protest. He led the *Daily Worker* in petition drives that ultimately led to more than a million signatures urging Commissioner Landis to take action. Rodney organized pickets outside Yankee Stadium in favor of integration. He accused Landis of willful deception in claiming that there was no agreement in organized baseball to keep blacks out of the majors.

He wrote an open letter to Landis declaring, "You, the self-proclaimed 'Czar' of baseball, are the man responsible for keeping Jim Crow in our National Pastime. You are the one refusing to say the word which would do more to justify baseball's existence . . . than any other single thing" (Goldstein 2009, B9).

In 1937, the *Daily Worker* sent Ted Benson to speak with National League President Ford Frick. His answer to the question regarding segregation in the majors was clear: there was no rule barring blacks. A player, Frick said, "must have unique ability and good character and habits . . . I do not recall one instance where baseball has allowed race, creed or color to enter into its selection of players" ("Conscience of the Trade" 2003). Thus, Ford Frick, like National League president John Heydler, pleaded ignorance of the issue.

SAM LACY MEETS WITH CLARK GRIFFITH, DECEMBER 1937

As a child, Sam Lacy saw many Senators games at Washington's Griffith Stadium, mostly as a peanut vender in the colored section of the ballpark. As a teenager, he played semipro baseball in Washington, sometimes in games against such Negro Leagues stars as Oscar Charleston and Martin Dihigo. Lacy, thus, had a firsthand grasp on the talents of players, both black and white. The inevitable question bothered him from the beginning: why were black players not allowed in the majors? He remarked,

> I was in a position to make some comparisons and it seemed to me that those black players were good enough to play in the big leagues. There was, of course, no talk then of that ever happening. When I was growing up, there was no real opportunity for blacks in any sport. It never crossed our minds as kids to aspire to the big leagues. Even the best players considered it a lost cause. But the idea stuck with me. I felt that not only were blacks being deprived of the opportunity to make some money but that whites were being deprived of the opportunity to see these fellows perform. (Fimrite 1990)

Watching the dismal hometown Senators and, in contrast, seeing the Homestead Grays before almost entirely black fans, Lacy saw early on something that Clark Griffith, president of the Senators, surely knew himself—that the best team in the city of Washington was not wearing Senators uniforms. "I had seen the teams come into play," Lacy said later. "Having seen these guys, I got to thinking that some of these ballplayers, watching them play, are no better than the guys that play in the Negro Leagues" (Gordon 2008).

While attending Howard University in Washington, DC, Lacy began a journalism career as a part-time writer at the *Washington Tribune*. After graduation he joined the paper as a full-time writer in the sports department. He soon produced columns expressing outrage against the policy of excluding blacks from professional baseball. It would become, for him, a crusade. He attempted to meet with baseball commissioner Landis. The judge ignored him. In December 1937, he managed to arrange a meeting with Clark Griffith, owner of the Senators and of Griffith Stadium.

Nicknamed the Old Fox, Griffith had been in baseball for nearly all of his 69 years. The game flowed through his veins. Pitching in the minor leagues in 1891, the short and slightly built youngster developed such doctored pitches as the spitball, the scuff ball, and others that made his rise to the major leagues an easier proposition. In his pitching career, he won 20 or more games seven times, mostly with the Chicago White Sox.

But it would not be as a player that Griffith would take his lofty spot in base-ball lore. In 1912, he became manager of the Washington Senators, a team that would, in its long history, have on its roster only a handful of great play-ers—led by fireballing star pitcher Walter Johnson. With Johnson leading the way, Griffith made the Senators, for a time, respectable. In 1919, Griffith be-came part owner of the Senators, ensured that National Park be renamed for him as Griffith Stadium, and, after the 1920 season, gave up his managerial duties. He would now be the executive face of the Washington Senators for the next 35 years. In 1924, the Senators, led by the aging Johnson, won their first and only World Series.

A tight-fisted owner with a sharp negotiating sense, Griffith kept the team on a fiscally sound foundation, if not competitive on the field against the likes of the New York Yankees or other more lucrative franchises. As the years wore on, the Senators managed to gain the embarrassing designation of "First in War, First in Peace, and Last in the American League."

In Griffith's years of guiding the team, he had not particularly endeared himself to the increasing black population of the nation's capital. During the 1920s, he put in place strict segregated seating for major league games, with blacks occupying only a certain area of the bleachers. Nevertheless, Griffith's smart business sense and strong desire to see the Senators remain in exis-tence led him to agree to rent Griffith Stadium to black teams, most notably to the Homestead Grays in the late 1930s.

Not openly racist, Griffith, indeed, often watched and enjoyed games be-tween Negro Leagues teams and often remarked on the skills of the players. For Sam Lacy, then, Griffith seemed to represent a possible breakthrough convert, an owner who might seriously consider cracking the long winter of segregation in major league baseball. And so Lacy approached Griffith's office seeking an audience. Would the owner grant the young writer an interview? When the Old Fox acquiesced, it was already a triumph of sorts for Lacy. He would become the first black sportswriter to gain a serious meeting with a baseball official of Griffith's rank.

In the meeting, the young black reporter appealed not only to Griffith's love of baseball but also to his business acumen. Placing a few black stars on the Senators, Lacy said, would produce a team worthy of Washington, DC, a joy to see, and a distinct challenge to the dominance of the New York Yankees. The seats of Griffith Stadium would rock to the cheers for a powerhouse team. Lacy floated the names of Gibson and Paige and Buck Leonard and others.

Griffith admitted that there were "some mighty good players in Negro baseball," and he even admitted that there were "very few big-league owners who are not aware of the fact that the time is not far off" for baseball to inte-grate (Lanctot 2004, 220).

Nevertheless, he would not be the one to take the revolutionary step. It was not yet the right time. He warned Lacy about the "cruel and filthy epithets" that black players would first have to endure when breaking the color barrier. Lacy, of course, knew what kinds of pressure the first black players would face. He had faced many of those cruel and filthy epithets in his own daily life.

Griffith suggested that a strong, separate black league, eventually recognized by organized baseball, might be the ultimate route. Such a league would not be a disruptive force to the Negro Leagues themselves and would build on an economic structure already in place, not threaten it. If the Senators began stocking black players, he said, the move would kill the Negro Leagues. Although he did not say it to Lacy, it also would have killed his financial interest in renting out Griffith Stadium to Negro Leagues teams.

Lacy later said of the meeting, "I approached Clark Griffith of the Washington team, and he told me it wouldn't be workable. There were too many southerners in the league and there would be too many fights. I told him that was something baseball should police if they were serious. He said baseball wasn't ready" (Mayo 2002).

Although Lacy was not able to enlist Griffith in the drive to integrate, he left the meeting with a sense that the forces of change were, indeed, in the air. If Griffith recognized the talent of black players and if he also recognized that there would, indeed, be movement of some kind toward reform, this was at least a start.

THE JAKE POWELL INCIDENT, 1938

On July 29, 1938, Alvin "Jake" Powell, an outfielder for the New York Yankees, interviewed before a game with the White Sox on a major Chicago radio station, casually used the usual racial epithet of the time in speaking about African Americans. Asked what he did in the off-season, Powell talked about working for the police department of his hometown in Dayton, Ohio, "cracking niggers over the head" ("Powell Suspended" 1938).

Although major newspapers mentioned the incident in passing, the black press, the following day, leaped on the remark like lions on prey. So quickly did the castigation of the Yankee infielder reverberate around black communities in major cities that Powell was told to stay home by Yankee management for the next game at Comiskey Park in Chicago, in a predominately black part of the city.

The following day, a delegation led by executives of such black organizations as the Urban League and including the sports editor of the *Chicago Defender*, Fay Young, demanded that the White Sox not allow Powell on the field. Before the game, the umpires met another delegation from Chicago's black community, who presented a resolution demanding that Powell not only apologize but be kicked out of baseball for life. The Associated Press reported that a formal petition would be presented to Commissioner Landis.

New York sportswriter Dan Daniel thought the whole controversy was overblown and would have little impact. Blaming the radio medium for the uproar more than the player messenger, Daniel said, "Powell could have been more careful. But he is a hustling player, aggressive, and always getting into a jam" (Lamb 1999, 21–34).

But Dan Daniel underestimated the frayed racial undercurrent that increasingly tugged at professional baseball as the various voices calling for integration of the sport gained louder volume. Not surprisingly, the *Chicago Defender* demanded that the Yankees immediately rid its team of its openly racist player. How could Yankee owner Jake Ruppert, the *Defender* questioned, ignore the outrage of thousands of black fans that regularly patronized Yankee stadium? Within a few days, talk of a boycott by blacks of games in the venerable stadium gained currency.

Indeed, Wendell Smith of the *Pittsburgh Courier,* in a scathing editorial two months before Powell's unfortunate interview, had written in favor of a boycott, chiding blacks for their continuing willingness to suffer the indignities of segregated baseball: "Why we continue to flock to major league ball parks, spending our hard earned dough, screaming and hollering, stamping our feet, and clapping our hands, begging and pleading for some white batter to knock some white pitcher's ears off, almost having fits if the home team loses and crying for joy when they win, is a question that probably never will be answered satisfactorily. What in the world are we thinking about anyhow?" Patronizing major league baseball, Smith said, was an affront to the black stars of the Negro Leagues who had toiled in relative obscurity in the white world. "Oh, we're an optimistic, faithful, prideless lot—we pitiful black folk," Smith continued. "Yes, sir—we black folk are a strange tribe" ("Smitty's Sport Spurts" 1918, 17).

Ruppert and the Yankees heard the protests and decided that something had to be done to quell a looming storm. Yankee management not only met with black journalists asking what could be done to improve relations with the black community, but also pointed out that every year the team distributed complimentary tickets to black fans, donated to the Harlem YMCA, and even hired black security guards at Yankee Stadium.

The Yankees sent Powell on something of a mission of penance. He made his way to the offices of the *Chicago Defender* to apologize. He went to bars in the black areas of Chicago and, later, in Harlem, buying drinks for the customers, assuring them that he had meant no disrespect.

During a meeting with Commissioner Landis, Powell denied any prejudicial intent. "I don't remember saying anything like that at all," Powell said, "and I certainly would never mean to say anything offensive to the Negroes of Dayton, Chicago or anywhere else. I have some very good friends among the Negroes in Dayton" ("Powell Suspended" 1938, 63).

His own views against including blacks in professional sports notwithstanding, Landis suspended Powell for 10 days, the first time a major league player had been officially sanctioned for a racist remark.

The Powell affair and Landis's decision became a sounding board for a number of political columnists. Even Westbrook Pegler, certainly not noted for views sympathetic to racial causes, charged that Powell was merely reflecting the views of the leaders in charge of major league baseball, a "business which trades under the name of the national game but has always treated the Negroes as Adolf Hitler treats the Jews." Powell, according to Pegler, was only giving crude voice to official policy (Pegler 1938, 9).

Thus, the affair did not go quietly. On August 16, when Powell returned to the Yankee lineup in Washington, DC, after his suspension, he was met with a cascade of boos from the segregated seating in the outfield. He was also met with some flying pop bottles as he patrolled left field. At one point the game was delayed for more than 10 minutes while the ground crew roamed the area around Powell removing the bottles from the field. At another point, a pop bottle vendor's carrying cart came hurtling to the stadium floor quite close to its target. Powell escaped the barrage uninjured.

In the midst of the controversy, the *Chicago Defender* turned the Powell incident into a plea for integration, editorializing, as it had many times before, that the hour had come "to open the door of opportunity to professional baseball players of all colors." A number of individual owners, by this time, had privately said that they would be willing to field black players. Many major leaguers had praised the skills of barnstormers they had faced in competition. "In cold, honest fact," the *Defender* asserted, "if black players had been in baseball, the Jake Powell incident would never have occurred, for as in Congress, legislatures, and city councils where we have elected officials, the presence of our men reminds—and demands respect. The same fact holds true in the industrial and commercial fields. Be wise, open the door, and 'Go to town.' We would like to see Mr. Comiskey and Mr. Wrigley break the ice" ("Baseball Is Next" 1938, 16).

It would not be Charles Comiskey, owner of the Chicago White Sox, or P. K. Wrigley, owner of the Chicago Cubs, that would open the door. Nevertheless, the Jake Powell affair had shaken baseball's racial condition as no other incident had ever done. In galvanizing the black press and making news throughout the baseball world, it created increasing momentum for those who wanted to see black players on major league diamonds.

Chicago Defender staff writer Al Monroe noted that repercussions from the Jake Powell affair had been palpable. Through the years, he said, baseball managers, executives, and players had tried to evade every subject relating to segregation of the sport. When writers had asked for interviews on the subject, they were invariably rebuffed. They simply had not been interested. The Powell incident, however, had shown that black protests and threats of boycotts had shaken baseball's foundation, at least for a moment.

Monroe mentioned the fact that years earlier when Ty Cobb was charged with kicking a black maid in a hotel, the incident did not gain national news. "In those days," he wrote, "there were no Race papers to fight the battles of their people. Thus when the daily scribes decided to end the discussion the Cobb episode died of its own lack of noise" (Monroe 1938, 8).

By 1938, things had changed dramatically. The forces of the black press, along with the *Daily Worker* and a few white sportswriters, were making a difference.

BLACK BALL PLAYERS—THE EQUAL OF ANY

Sportswriter Shirley Povich of the *Washington Post,* whose major responsibility had been to cover the hapless Washington Senators, knew very well the talent level of many of the Negro Leagues players. At an exhibition game in Orlando, Florida, he had sat next to Walter "the Big Train," Johnson, a Hall of Fame hurler from the days when the Senators had not been hapless. As Homestead Grays take on the Newark Eagles, Johnson sat next to Povich in the box seats, watching with much interest the high quality of baseball on display. Johnson was especially impressed with Josh Gibson. "There is a catcher," he told Povich, "that any big league club would like to buy for $200,000. I've heard of him before. His name is Gibson . . . he can do everything. He hits the ball a mile. And he catches so easy he might just as well be in a rocking chair. Throws like a rifle. Bill Dickey isn't as good a catcher. Too bad this Gibson is a colored fellow" (Povich 1939, 21).

Povich wrote in his column about the gentleman's agreement among owners: "Just how a colored player would be detrimental to the game has never been fully explained, but that seems to be the light in which they are regarded by the baseball brass hats. Perhaps it is because there is such an overwhelming majority of Southern boys in big league baseball who would not take kindly to the presence of colored athletes and would flash a menacing spike, or so. Perhaps it's because baseball has done well enough without colored players. It's a smug, conservative business not given to very great enterprise and the introduction of new and novel features" (Povich 1939, 21).

From his desk in Washington, Povich knew very well the lamentable attendance that the Senators were drawing in Griffith Stadium. At a game in early August 1938, the Senators drew fewer than 1,000 fans. A few days earlier, a doubleheader between four teams from the Negro Leagues drew more than 10,000. The quality of play in the Negro Leagues compared to that of the major leagues was certainly not lost on those who witnessed both. It had been going on for years.

In Oakland, California, in February 1936, Satchel Paige and a collection of relatively unknown black players took on a team of barnstorming major leaguers led by Joe DiMaggio, Ernie Lombardi, and Harry Lavagetto. One of the 4,000 onlookers who jammed the small ballpark was white baseball writer Eddie Murphy from New York. After watching Paige give up only two runs while striking out a dozen in a 10-inning loss, Murphy wrote: "The greatest baseball pitching attraction in the world is being passed up by scouts, club owners, and managers only because the doors of organized ball are closed to him. It is surprising some move is not planned to lift the bars and allow this fellow and other diamond greats of his race to prove their supremacy" (Murphy 1936, 13).

Now, major newsstand magazines were lauding the prowess of Paige. *Life* magazine, featuring pictures of Paige in his exaggerated windup and delivery, as well as personal photos, declared, "Barred from organized professional baseball because he is a Negro, Paige has played against many of the major-league stars in exhibition games." According to players who faced him, Paige had more than proven his big-league caliber status, the article continued ("Satchel Paige" 1941, 91).

Even baseball owners who had personally watched Negro Leagues baseball acknowledged the superior athletic ability of many of the black players. When Chester Washington, sportswriter for the *Pittsburgh Courier,* met briefly with William Benswanger, owner of the Pittsburgh Pirates, in 1938, Benswanger said: "I've seen lots of colored clubs play—in fact, I watched almost every game involving colored teams at Forbes Field for many years—and I've seen several players but not all of them—who appear to be just as good as many of our men in organized baseball" (Washington 1938, 17).

Benswanger had seen Paige; he had seen Gibson. Nevertheless, just as Clark Griffith, he was not ready to begin the revolution. The word *someday* always seemed to arise at the end of such discussions with big league owners. But the evidence was clear to men such as Benswanger and to those who watched the games. And with the increasing scrutiny and pressure from the black press, from the *Daily Worker,* and from a few white reporters, the evidence was gaining circulation.

In the early 1940s, service in the U.S. Armed Forces involved both black and white baseball players. More than 50 professional ballplayers would never return home from the war, most of them killed in combat. Hundreds more returned with serious injuries that either hurt or ended their careers. Black Americans were aware that their own baseball heroes were also answering the call to service. In the 1945 Negro Baseball Yearbook, the cover depicts two images of Homestead Grays' pitcher Ernest "Spoon" Carter. In one he is wearing his baseball uniform; in the other he is in military uniform hurling a grenade.

But despite the loss of the services of many of their star players during the war, baseball executives of the major leagues still refused to sign black players to their rosters. Instead, they signed youngsters too young for wartime service, over-the-hill players too old for the war, and any reasonably skilled player they could find—as long as his skin was not black.

PAUL ROBESON CONFRONTS COMMISSIONER LANDIS, DECEMBER 3, 1943

By 1943, Paul Robeson was a man of unique standing and accomplishment, a man whose talents and character had a profound effect on U.S. culture. Born in 1898 to the son of a former slave, Robeson rose to unimagined heights— star football player at Rutgers who was inducted into the National College Football Hall of Fame, world-renowned concert singer, and an actor on stage and screen. His musical recordings were known in most parts of the world. He was the first black actor to star in roles that dignified his race. In 1925, the music critic of the *New York Times* hailed his rendering of Negro spirituals as a master humanistic accomplishment. In 1933, Robeson donated the proceeds from his performances of *All God's Chillun* to Jewish refugees fleeing Hitler's Nazis. In 1939, he premiered *Ballad for Americans*, a cantata celebrating the multiethnic, multiracial character of the United States. In 1943, a critic called his interpretation of his title role in Shakespeare's *Othello* as the most notable and defining of the 20th century.

Throughout his career, Robeson, vigorously fought for the dignity and rights of black Americans and battled racism through various left-wing labor and political affiliations. His uncompromising battles over social issues and the resulting attacks from right-wing extremists and congressional investigations aimed at ferreting out communists would lead the government eventually to revoke his passport for eight years. But now, in 1943, Paul Robeson would lend his prestige and name to the battle against segregation in professional baseball.

On December 3, 1943, Robeson headed a delegation of blacks who met with baseball commissioner Landis and major league owners at the Roosevelt Hotel in New York City. The meeting was arranged mainly by journalist Sam Lacy, who secured the cooperation of several black organizations, including the Negro Newspaper Publishers Association, the Urban League, the NAACP, and others. That Landis agreed to allow the delegation to address the owners was a testament to Lacy's dogged efforts to have the issue publicly aired and Landis's own realization that continuing to ignore a growing momentum behind the drive toward integration would appear defensive.

Before all 16 major league team owners and both league presidents, Robeson declared:

> This is an excellent time to bring about an entry of Negro players into organized baseball. The time has come when you must change your attitude toward Negroes and keep it consistent with the rest of the country. To me, the most indicative thing that has happened in the fight against racial discrimination is the reception that I have been given in *Othello*. I was told before the play was produced that America was not ready to accept me or such a delicate theme, but I've never appeared before friendlier audiences. (Robeson and Foner 1978, 150–51)

Robeson said that he understood the fear of owners that integration would bring some opposition and even troublesome confrontations. But he looked back to his own football experience at Rutgers, which demonstrated that a black athlete, by his achievements on the field, can not only bring fans to his side but also have the beneficial effect of bringing together those of both races united to a common interest.

"I come here as an American and former athlete," he said. "I urge you to decide favorably on this request and that action be taken this very season. I believe you can be assured they will reflect the highest credit upon the game and the American people will commend you for this action which reflects the best in the American spirit" (Robeson and Foner 1978, 150–51).

Other black delegates bolstered the case. John Sengstacke of the *Chicago Defender* spoke about the evils and dangers of segregation itself: "If any American organization establishes . . . barriers . . . against any class of citizens, the security of all classes is placed in constant and potential jeopardy" (Lanctot 2004, 245).

Ira Lewis, president of the *Pittsburgh Courier*, was even more challenging in his remarks. He appealed to the owners' business sense. He pointed out that the largest baseball crowd in Chicago during the past year was the Negro Leagues East-West game. He said that a championship high school football game between Negro schools in Chicago had attracted over thousands of people. He then hammered away at the "tacit understanding" or "gentleman's agreement" against black players participating in the major leagues. "In the name of the America we all love; in the name of democracy that we associate with the word America, that you undo this wrong; that you do away with this mean precedent, this gentleman's understanding and agreement, and let our national pastime be a game for all the boys in America" (Smith 1943, 1).

Although some of the owners at the meeting acknowledged the growing demand for change, most remained either resentful of the pressure now being applied by the black press and other advocates for change or fearful that such a move would spark outrage and violence among the ballplayers, especially those with backgrounds from the South.

For Landis himself, the answer was the still the same. The commissioner denied there was any law, unwritten or otherwise, that prohibited blacks from being signed to major league contracts. There was no gentleman's agreement, he insisted, and no threats or intimidation against the owners. For the 21 years he had served as commissioner, Landis said with much solemnity, there had been no prohibition against Negro players in organized baseball. If there were winks and nods among those in attendance, none were reported by the press.

In November 1944, Judge Landis died. Hired in 1920 to clean up the sport of baseball amid the betting scandal involving the Chicago Black Sox, Landis as baseball commissioner over the years banned numerous players for various offenses. He banned more players from the game than all of his successors combined. But for blacks, Landis's actions were less about kicking players out of the game and more about not letting certain players into it. Major league baseball would now look for a new commissioner. Black players, writers, and others involved with the Negro Leagues would anxiously await the new commissioner's position on the critical issue of integration.

IZZY MUCHNICK AND THE INFAMOUS
RED SOX TRYOUT, APRIL 16, 1945

You will not find the name of Isadore Harry Yaver Muchnick in any lists of baseball players, managers, owners, sportswriters, executives, announcers, analysts, or other assorted men and women who participated in the sport throughout its history. Yet, Izzy Muchnick became an unlikely ally to those who in the early 1940s sought an end to segregation in the major leagues.

Born in Boston in 1908 to Russian Jewish immigrants, Muchnick was a precocious kid, excelling at the celebrated Boston Latin School and at Harvard Law. Like his parents, he seemed to be a born activist, finding numerous liberal causes at which to throw his considerable energies.

Despite his Jewish background, Muchnick, with much political savvy and obvious intellectual gifts, managed to win election to the Boston city council in 1941. On the council, he found himself in opposition to the majority on a number of issues, including equal pay for women and a redistricting of public schools to provide for some integration of blacks. This was 1941, not the 1960s, when the civil rights movement was in full force. Muchnick was, in many ways, ahead of his time on a number of issues.

One of those issues was the integration of baseball. As he did in proposing redistricting of public school districts, Muchnick saw the baseball issue in terms of fairness and equality. Although a lifelong Red Sox fan, he was always bothered by the inherent contradictions in baseball. It was the country's leading sport. It was supposed to set a standard for youngsters. And yet it steadfastly refused to allow obviously accomplished ball players to compete in the majors simply because they were black. Although only a lone voice on the Boston City Council, he was now in a political position to try to push for change. He leaped into a political fray on behalf of black Americans even though his district was approximately 99 percent white.

During the 1940s, the Red Sox were required to secure a permit to play baseball on Sundays. The vote required a unanimous vote from the city council. This was an opportunity that Izzy Muchnick could not pass up.

In late 1944, Eddie Collins, Red Sox vice president and general manager, received a letter he had not expected. "I cannot understand," Muchnick wrote to Collins, "how baseball, which claims to be the national sport and which . . . receives special favors and dispensation from the Federal Government because of alleged moral value can continue a pre-Civil War attitude toward American citizens because of the color of their skins" (Bryant 2003, 28).

The reply from Collins angered Muchnick, who regarded it as disingenuous and misleading. "As I wrote to one of your fellow councilors last April," Collins wrote, "I have been connected with the Red Sox for twelve years and during that time we have never had a single request for a tryout by a colored applicant. It is beyond my understanding how anyone could insinuate or believe that all ball players, regardless of race, color or creed have not been treated in the American way so far as having an equal opportunity to play for the Red Sox" (Bryant 2003, 28–29).

Muchnick began to make it clear that he would refuse to grant the Sunday waiver to the Red Sox unless the team agreed to sponsor a tryout for black players who could conceivably help the Red Sox in their pennant quest and at the same time establish the team as a responsible and enlightened force for needed change. When Mabray "Doc" Kountze, the leading black reporter in Boston, heard of Muchnick's efforts, he referred to him as something of a "white modern abolitionist."

Eddie Collins, by many accounts a no-nonsense racist who disliked not only blacks but who was also anti-Catholic and anti-Semitic, did not want to have a tryout for black players. Owner Tom Yawkey did not want to have such a tryout. Indeed, not only did the Boston Red Sox have no interest in signing a black player, the team did not have a single black individual working at Fenway Park in any capacity whatsoever, even as janitors. Nevertheless, with an insistent city councilman unwilling to back off his demands, the Red Sox complied. There would be a tryout.

With Wendell Smith of the *Pittsburgh Courier* lending assistance in the selection of the players to be invited, three emerged from the discussions. They included infielder Jackie Robinson, a former standout football player at the

University of Southern California who had recently joined the Kansas City Monarchs; Sam Jethroe, a speedy and hard-hitting outfielder of the Cleveland Buckeyes; and Marvin Williams, a power-hitting infielder from the Philadelphia Stars. The *Courier* paid for the expenses of the players' trip to Boston.

Robinson said to Smith, "I don't know if the Red Sox are going to give us a chance or not. But if we do get a chance, it will mark another chapter in the long fight for Negro players in organized baseball. And, if I can do just one little thing to make that fight become a reality, I'll be satisfied. Maybe I won't make it, but maybe it'll pave the way for some kid in the future" (Smith 1945b, 16).

On April 16, 1945, four days after the death of President Franklin D. Roosevelt, the 3 players gathered at Fenway Park, along with 10 white players, mostly young high school kids, to demonstrate their skills before Cronin and others of Red Sox management. It was not held in secret. Indeed, several reporters, including Wendell Smith, scribbled notes as the players worked out. Izzy Muchnick watched with much interest, fascinated especially by Robinson. The young player said later that he was satisfied with his own performance, even suggesting that the workout could not have gone much better.

Clif Keane, a reporter for the *Boston Globe,* witnessed the tryout. When the three players had finished their workouts and were leaving the field, Keane wrote, they heard a person from the stands, possibly a Red Sox employee, yelling a racial epithet. It would not be the first time the three men had been subjected to such treatment, and it would certainly not be the last.

After the tryout, Wendell Smith spoke with Cronin and Duffy, both of whom said the players had performed well. In reporting the tryout, Smith closed with this hopeful message to his readers: "They came here. . . . They were granted a tryout Monday morning . . . and they made an indelible impression. Will they be signed by the Boston Red Sox and become the first Negroes to ever play in the major leagues? That is one question I cannot answer. But I'm pulling for them as I never pulled for anyone in my life" (Smith 1945a, 1).

Nevertheless, Robinson told a friend that he was quite skeptical, convinced that the whole thing had probably been worthless. "Not for one minute did we believe the tryout was sincere," he said later. Sam Jethroe said that the team told him afterward that the players "had potential but it wasn't the right time" (Lanctot 2004, 257).

The evening after the tryout, Robinson accepted an invitation to have dinner in Dorchester at the home of Izzy and Ann. Robinson and the Muchnick family remained friends for the rest of their lives. When Robinson traveled to Boston, the Muchnick home was always welcome for him.

The tryout did generate some publicity outside black news organizations. The *New York Times* ran a column. "Two of three Negro aspirants for major league baseball berths—Jackie Robinson of Pasadena, Calif., and Marvin Williams of Philadelphia—impressed Manager Joe Cronin and Coach Hugh Duffy today while working out for the Boston Red Sox." Sam Jethroe apparently had not impressed the Red Sox ("Red Sox Test 3 Negroes" 1945, 31).

When he rejoined the Cleveland Buckeyes after the tryout, Jethroe called the whole affair a joke, a farce. When he looked at Cronin in the stands a number of times during the workout, Jethroe told some teammates, the manager almost always had his back turned. Nevertheless, a few years later, the fleet outfielder Jethroe would later join the major leagues.

Joe Cronin, 34 years later, recalled: "I remember the tryout very well. But after it, we told them our only farm club available was in Louisville, Kentucky, and we didn't think they'd be interested in going there because of the racial feelings at the time. Besides, this was after the season had started and we didn't sign players off tryouts in those days to play in the big leagues. I was in no position to offer them a job. The general manager did the hiring and there was an unwritten rule at that time against hiring black players. I was just the manager" (Bryant 2003, 32).

Although the tryout at Fenway did not represent a major breakthrough in the drive for baseball integration, it was, nevertheless, yet another rapping on the door, another indication that change was coming. For all of Red Sox management, the affair was a sham, with all sorts of dodging and weaving to avoid responsibility for ignoring the entire event. Owner Tom Yawkey was so resistant to the activities that day in Boston that he remained isolated, turning the entire matter over to Collins, who, as he said himself, "was just the manager." Tom Yawkey would be the last owner in the major leagues to sign a black player.

HAPPY CHANDLER BECOMES NEW
BASEBALL COMMISSIONER

On April 24, 1945, major league owners meeting in Cleveland voted to offer the job of commissioner of baseball to United States senator and former Kentucky governor A. B. "Happy" Chandler. He accepted.

Born in Kentucky, Chandler attended Harvard University, served in the U.S. Army from 1918 to 1919, graduated from Transylvania College in Lexington, Kentucky, in 1921, and received a law degree from the University of Kentucky in 1924. After practicing law, he entered the political arena, becoming governor of Kentucky in 1935 and then a U.S. senator in 1939 to fill a vacancy. He was subsequently reelected in 1942.

Chandler was an avid sports enthusiast. In his younger years, he had played semipro baseball and served as an assistant football coach. During World War II, he became a staunch supporter of keeping major league baseball alive through the war years, even when a very large number of its regular players were overseas. Baseball, he said, was a morale builder that the country needed in its most challenging times.

At a Chicago news conference on May 3, 1945, in response to a question about the possible integration of baseball, Chandler said that black players "should have a chance like everybody else." But he quickly backed away from such an assertive position, saying he had no knowledge that discrimination did, indeed, exist. He then said, "I'm sure there is room for colored players in the big leagues . . . they may want to play in their own leagues and then meet the major league champion in a playoff game" (Hill 2010).

Later that spring, when discussing the race issue with Ric Roberts of the *Pittsburgh Courier*, Chandler, perhaps to ingratiate himself with the black press, was much more encouraging. "If it's discrimination you're afraid of," he said, "you have nothing to fear from me." The heroism of black players during the war should prove to anyone that they were worthy of a chance to play in the majors, he said. "If a black boy can make it on Okinawa and Guadalcanal, hell, he can make it in baseball" (Hill 2010).

Yet, after measuring the various, sometimes conflicting statements made by Chandler in the first few months after being named commissioner, the *Pittsburgh Courier*, on September 1, 1945, could only say "'Czar' Chandler Evasive on Major League Bias."

LEON DAY AND WILLARD BROWN AT NUREMBURG, GERMANY, AUGUST 30, 1945

For German leader Adolf Hitler, the medieval city of Nuremberg symbolized the links between the gothic past of Germany and its supposed glorious future under Nazi rule. It was here in Nuremburg's magnificent stadium in 1934 that the movie director Leni Riefenstahl filmed many of the scenes of the enormous Nazi rallies, with the massive numbers of Nazi troops in perfect alignment. Her film, *Triumph of the Will*, became a propaganda masterpiece.

But now, in September 1945, five months after the death of Hitler, the Nuremberg stadium became a venue of something quite different from the rallies of goose-stepping German soldiers. It was the scene of a baseball game.

Two of the star players in the game were Leon Day and Willard "Home Run" Brown. Day, who grew up in Baltimore, left high school after two years to pitch in semipro baseball. Soon he was in the Negro Leagues, starring with the Newark Eagles. In the 1942 East-West All-Star Game in Chicago's Comiskey Park, Day, pitching for the East, bested opposing pitcher Satchel Paige and held the West team scoreless. Monte Irvin, who played shortstop with the Newark Eagles, once said of Day, "People don't know what a great pitcher he was! In my opinion, he was as good or better than Bob Gibson. He was a better fielder, a better hitter, could run like a deer. And just as good a pitcher. When he pitched against Satchel, Satchel didn't have any edge. You thought Don Newcombe could pitch. You should have seen Day! One of the most complete athletes I've ever seen. He was fantastic, that man" (Holway "One Day at a Time").

In September 1943, the 26-year-old Day was drafted by the army and joined the 818th Amphibian Battalion, driving an army "Duck" or amphibian landing truck. He drove onto Normandy's Utah Beach six days after D-Day.

Willard Brown, born in Louisiana, joined the Kansas City Monarchs in 1934 and, unlike most Negro Leagues players, stayed with the same team for his entire career. First a shortstop, he later played the outfield. A feared power hitter, he led the league in home runs in 1942 and 1943. The next year, like Leon Day, he was with the army in France, a member of the Quartermaster Corps who crossed the English Channel during the Normandy invasion.

Throughout World War II, the various armed services, in a quest to grant some sense of normalcy to troops under their command, created baseball teams that competed when there was time for recreation. The managers of the teams and the players treated the games with fierce pride. As in professional baseball, the teams were almost always segregated. A number of teams were quite talented, especially the 71st Infantry Division Red Circlers of the Third Army. Its lineup included such major league stars as center fielder Harry "the Hat" Walker of the St. Louis Cardinals; infielder Benny Zientara of the Cincinnati Reds; and a formidable pitching staff of side-arming, right-hander Ewell Blackwell of the Cincinnati Reds; left-hander Al Brazale of the St. Louis Cardinals; and left-hander Ken Heintzelman of the Pittsburgh Pirates.

"Subway" Sam Nahem, a pitcher for the Philadelphia Phillies, had also organized a team, this one to represent the Overseas Invasion Service Expedition (OISE) representing Com-Z (Communications Zone) in the European theater of operations (ETO). Composed largely of minor league players, Nahem's team did not boast the kind of talent of the Third Army team. To become competitive with the best teams in the European theater, Nahem took an unusual step. He invited Willard Brown and Leon Day to join up. There was no baseball commissioner in the armed forces to force Nahem to give up the idea, no gentleman's agreement among owners such as that which existed in white professional baseball to prevent a move to add blacks to the team.

With Day bolstering the pitching staff and Brown adding formidable power to the lineup, Nahem's team became so strong in the summer of 1945 that it challenged the Red Circlers for the ETO World Series. The five-game series, with two of the games to be played in Rheims, France, began on August 30, 1945, in the vast stadium in Nuremberg, with a massive crowd of GIs estimated by some at over 100,000.

The Red Circlers took the first game 9–2. *The Stars and Stripes,* an independent newspaper on the U.S. military, reported that Brown was "the only man who had much luck hitting Blackwell" ("Willard Brown" 2010).

The next game at Nuremburg was a triumph for Leon Day, who held the Red Circlers to a single run in a 2–1 victory. Brown drove in the go-ahead run in the sixth inning with a single.

Behind outstanding performances by both Negro Leaguers, Nahem's OISE went on to win the series three games to two. And so, in Europe, Negro Leagues stars celebrated a championship. There was one major difference from their experiences in the states. They had played on an integrated team.

REFERENCES

"Baseball Is Next." 1938. *Chicago Defender* (August 27): 16.

Bryant, Howard. 2003. *Shut Out: A Story of Race and Baseball in Boston.* Boston: Beacon Press.

"The Conscience of the Trade." 2003. *Mudville: The Voice of Baseball,* http://www.mud villemagazine.com/archives/12_2003/index.html.

Fimrite, Ron. 1990. "Sam Lacy: Black Crusader." *Sports Illustrated* (October 29), http:// sportsillustrated.cnn.com/vault/article/magazine/MAG1136283/3/index.htm.

Goldstein, Richard. 2009. "Lester Rodney, Early Voice in the Fight against Racism in Sports, Dies at 98." *New York Times* (December 23): B9.

Gordon, Patrick. 2008. "A Media Pioneer: Sam Lacy Helped Jackie Robinson Break the Color Line." *Bleacher Report* (July 15), http://bleacherreport.com/articles/37964-a-media-pioneer-sam-lacy-helped-jackie-robinson-break-the-color-line.

Hill, John Paul. 2010. "Commissioner A. B. "Happy" Chandler and the Integration of Major League Baseball: A Reassessment." *NINE: A Journal of Baseball History and Culture* (Fall), http://muse.jhu.edu/journals/nine/summary/v019/19.1.hill.html.

Holway, John B. "One Day at a Time." SABR Research Journal Archives, http://re search.sabr.org/journals/newhouser-and-trout.

Lamb, Chris. 1999. "L'affaire Jake Powell: The Minority Press Goes to Bat against Segregated Baseball." *Journalism and Mass Communication Quarterly,* 76 (1) (Spring): 21–34.

Lamb, Chris. 2002. "'What's Wrong with Baseball': The *Pittsburgh Courier* and the Beginning of Its Campaign to Integrate the National Pastime." *Western Journal of Black Studies* 26: 189.

Lanctot, Neil. 2004. *Negro League Baseball: The Rise and Ruin of a Black Institution.* Philadelphia: University of Pennsylvania Press.

Mayo, Jonathan. 2002. "Ink-tegration: Writers Lacy, Smith Played Big Role in Baseball Integration" (February), http://mlb.mlb.com/mlb/history/mlb_negro_leagues_ story.jsp?story=lacysmith.

Monroe, Al. 1938. "It's News to Me." *Chicago Defender* (September 17): 8.

Murphy, Eddie. 1936. "Daily Scribe Tells Majors of Value of Satchel Paige." *Chicago Defender* (February 8): 13.

Pegler, Westbrook. 1938. "Fair Enough." *Washington Post* (August 5): 9.

"Powell Suspended for Radio Remarks." 1938. *New York Times* (July 31): 63.

Povich, Shirley. 1939. "This Morning with Shirley Povich." *Washington Post* (April 7): 21.

"Red Sox Test 3 Negroes." 1945. *New York Times* (April 17): 31.

Robeson, Paul, and Philip Foner. 1978. *Paul Robeson Speaks: Writings, Speeches, Interviews, 1918–1974*. New York: Brunner-Routledge.

"Satchel Paige, Negro Ballplayer, Is One of the Best Pitchers in Game." 1941. *Life* (June 2): 91.

Silber, Irwin. 2003. *Press Box Red: The Story of Lester Rodney, the Communist Who Helped Break the Color Line in American Sports*. Philadelphia: Temple University Press.

Smith, Wendell. 1943. "Publishers Place Case of Negro Players before Big League Owners." *Pittsburgh Courier* (December 11): 1.

Smith, Wendell. 1945a. "Players Get Try-Outs." *Pittsburgh Courier* (April 21): 1.

Smith, Wendell. 1945b. "The Sports Beat." *Pittsburgh Courier* (October 27): 16.

"Smitty's Sport Spurts." 1918. *Pittsburgh Courier* (May 14): 17.

Washington, Chester. 1938. "Pirates' Owner Would Favor Sepia Players in Organized Baseball; Lauds Gibson, Satchel." *Pittsburgh Courier* (February 12): 17.

"What's the Matter with Baseball? Prejudice!" 1933. *Chicago Defender* (September 16): 14.

"Willard Brown." 2010. Baseball in Wartime (May 6), http://www.baseballinwartime.com/player_biographies/brown_willard.htm.

5

Breaking the Color Barrier

THE YEARS OF MONARCHS AND
GRAYS AND THEN-BUCKEYES

As black sportswriters, led by men such as Wendell Smith and Sam Lacy, continued pressing Happy Chandler and major league baseball owners on the issue of integration, the Negro Leagues in the late 1930s and early 1940s became the domain of two dominant teams: the Homestead Grays and the Kansas City Monarchs.

As the drive toward integration became more intense—with the furor over the Jake Powell incident in 1938, the continued off-season success of black players against major leaguers, and the installation of a new major league commissioner who was less wedded to segregation of professional baseball— the competition on the field focused on the Grays and Monarchs, both loaded with extraordinary talent.

From the time owner J. L. Wilkinson of the Monarchs spearheaded the formation of the Negro American League (NAL), his team dominated that circuit. From the late 1930s into the early 1940s, the team rolled from one NAL championship to another, anchored by pitchers Satchel Paige and Hilton Smith and an all-star quality lineup featuring slugging outfielder Willard "Home Run" Brown, second baseman Newt Allen, and first baseman Buck O'Neil.

The Homestead Grays boasted perhaps the best middle-of-the-lineup slugging duo in the history of black baseball: Josh Gibson and Buck Leonard. Cum Posey's team dominated the Negro National League even more than the

Monarchs dominated the NAL. The Grays won consecutive pennants from 1937 through 1945.

In September 1942, baseball executives arranged for a showdown, a world championship, between the two clubs that had dominated each of their leagues in dynastic fashion. The series became a showcase for great talent, but especially for Satchel Paige. Beginning with an 8–0 win in the opening game in which he teamed with Jack Matchett in allowing the Grays only two hits to a remarkable relief appearance in the last contest, the Monarchs swept the Grays, four games to none.

In the last game, on September 29, under the lights at Philadelphia's Shibe Park, 15,000 fans watched the Grays pound out seven hits and five runs against starting pitcher Matchett, who was not supposed to be on the mound this day. The announced starting pitcher was Paige, but he was not in the ballpark. Suspicion and worry gripped the Monarchs; confusion reigned among the crowd. Where was the great one?

Satch later explained: "I was driving to that last game, must have been goin' pretty fast because a traffic cop stopped me" (Metcalf 2000, 114).

In Lancaster, Pennsylvania, Paige, because of his swift motoring, was fined $20. Shortly thereafter, he proved once again his mastery on the mound and shut down the Grays.

Other Negro Leagues teams were formidable. Abe and Effa Manley's Newark Eagles team, led by Mules Suttles, Willie Wells, Leon Day, and youngster Monte Irvin, were stiff competitors through these years. The Baltimore Elite Giants, who featured star catcher Roy Campanella, and the Birmingham Black Barons, who faced the Homestead Grays in both the 1943 and 1944 Colored World Series, were also highly competitive.

But the stage was set in the mid-1940s for the ascendancy of a team from a city that had known no black baseball championships of any kind—Cleveland, Ohio.

In the fall of 1941, an entrepreneur named Ernie Wright, who had turned a lucrative numbers racket in Erie, Pennsylvania, into a number of thriving black businesses such as the Hotel Pope, restaurants such as the Ramblers Club, pool halls, and barber shops, founded the Cleveland Buckeyes.

By 1942, playing in League Park, the Buckeyes had a team blossoming with new talent, including center fielder Sam Jethroe, one of the three Negro Leaguers who had worked out in the infamous Boston Red Sox tryout; pitcher and outfielder Willie Grace; third baseman Parnell Woods; and right fielder Lloyd "Ducky" Davenport. In 1945, the team acquired veteran catcher Quincy Trouppe, who became player-manager, and a slick-fielding shortstop named Avelino Canizares from Cuba. Suddenly, Cleveland, Ohio, a city that had a number of short-lived, unsuccessful black baseball teams, fielded a team loaded with talent and ready to challenge the likes of the Homestead Grays.

Ernie Wright had opened his bank account to assemble the team; its payroll was second only to that of the Homestead Grays. The investment paid dividends.

In 1945, the Buckeyes won the NAL. Bob Williams, editor of the Cleveland *Call and Post,* wrote of the Buckeyes that their performance was a relief compared to the team's first few years "when the Buckeyes looked like a team of scrub sandlotters, ready for the ash can," and fans left games convinced the team was "too mediocre even for the most tolerant or race-conscious individual." Williams went on to dare the Cleveland Indians, who shared League Park with the Buckeyes, to "play the championship Buckeyes at any time, any place" (O'Karma 2006).

Clinching the 1945 NAL pennant was not enough for the rejuvenated Buckeyes. They now readied themselves to take on the Homestead Grays and the likes of Cool Papa Bell, Josh Gibson, and Buck Leonard.

On September 13, 1945, Cleveland Stadium hosted game one of the Negro Leagues World Series. Willie Jefferson, the ace of the Buckeyes who had only lost one game during the entire season, was intent on not losing the second. For six innings Jefferson, along with the Grays' starter, Leroy Welmaker, shut down their opposing lineups as the scoreless game became increasingly tense.

In the bottom of the seventh, Quincy Trouppe of the Buckeyes drove a triple into the deepest part of the park. He scored on a sacrifice fly. In the eighth inning, the Buckeyes scored again as Willie Grace drove in a run with a single.

But in the ninth, the favored Grays, world champions of black baseball six years in a row, struck back. A Josh Gibson single drove in a run. With the game in the balance and the stadium now misty with light rain, Grays shortstop Sammy Bankhead headed to the plate with a man at first and one out. Jefferson, nearly unhittable the entire game, was now struggling, and Bankhead made solid contact, hitting a hard ground ball. The Buckeyes, however, turned a double play and ended the game dramatically as soaked fans roared approval.

For the ebullient Buckeyes team, this was only the beginning. For this series, at least, it was not the Grays that had the energy and momentum. Cleveland took game two by the score of 4–2, coming from behind in the ninth inning. In Washington for game three, the Buckeyes again silenced the usually hard-hitting Grays, winning 4–0.

The fourth game of the series was scheduled for Philadelphia. Could the Grays snap out of their listless hitting slump? The Buckeyes' Frank Carswell removed any doubt, as the big right-hander baffled the Grays inning after inning. Once again, the Buckeyes held the Grays scoreless, 5–0. The Cleveland Buckeyes had dispatched the Homestead Grays in a four-game sweep.

The black press in Cleveland hailed the championship. The city, after all, had experienced so few championships in any sports. The national black press also hailed the champions. Wendell Smith of the *Pittsburgh Courier* called the series sweep one of the biggest upsets in the history of baseball. But in the mainline city paper of Cleveland, in the sports section of the *Plain Dealer,* the victory and the championship of the hometown Buckeyes was allotted four paragraphs in the back pages.

On Sunday, September 23, 1945, the Buckeyes and Grays met once again, this time in a doubleheader, and this time only as an exhibition. They were invited to play in Yankee Stadium. Jonah J. Goldstein, judge of the New York County Court of General Sessions, who was asked to be a guest of honor and to throw out the ceremonial first ball, addressed the crowd. "Negro and white Americans," he said, "were good enough to fight together as one winning all-American team on the same far-flung battlefields. Negroes and whites, Americans all, are then surely good enough to play together on the same baseball fields. Baseball is an American game, played in the American spirit of fairness and democracy. Baseball is not a Nazi game based on the hateful rules of so-called racial superiority. Every American, every true lover of clean and wholesome sports, loves baseball because it symbolizes our democratic national spirit." Judge Goldstein was issuing a call to action. One of the major league baseball owners was about to act ("Goldstein to Seek Help" 1945, 11).

THE STEALTH CAMPAIGN OF BRANCH RICKEY

The Mahatma

In December 1881, on a small farm in Stockdale, Ohio, Branch Rickey became the second son of devout Methodists Jacob and Emily Rickey. He never attended high school but was such a voracious reader that he became a country school teacher. He learned enough Latin and higher mathematics on his own to enter Ohio Wesleyan University in Delaware, Ohio. To pay for living expenses, he took a part-time job at the local YMCA. Often, the YMCA in Delaware brought in speakers, some of them famous. One was the great educator Booker T. Washington. He was the first black individual Rickey had ever heard delivering a speech. Later, Rickey earned a law degree from the University of Michigan.

It was at Ohio Wesleyan that Rickey experienced an incident that touched him fiercely, one that he would relate on countless occasions through the years. In 1904, as student coach of the college baseball team, he and his teammates were on the road at the University of Notre Dame in South Bend, Indiana. The team's catcher was a kid named Charlie Thomas, the first black player ever to don the uniform of the Methodist school. At the Oliver Hotel in South Bend, where the team was to stay on the trip, Thomas was denied a room. A furious Rickey, unable to convince the hotel manager to back down, instead negotiated an agreement. Thomas would lodge with Rickey. Later, when the two were in the room together, Thomas began to weep. Rubbing his hands over each other he said, "Black skin, black skin. If I could rub it off and make it white" (Breslin 2011, 28).

Rickey's passion, in addition to his religious and moral convictions, was baseball. He became a catcher, good enough to make his way to the major leagues. In 1905–1906, he played for the St. Louis Browns and in 1907 for the New York Highlanders. Playing the game, however, was not to be his greatest contribution to baseball. He was a mediocre hitter and a catcher with a weak throwing arm. Besides, he refused to play on the Sabbath because of a promise he had made to his mother. The majors had little use for such religious scruples.

He tried to set up a law practice in Idaho for a time, but his heart was not in it. He wanted back in baseball. In 1912 the St. Louis Browns offered him an administrative position, and Rickey eagerly accepted. He served as an officer in the U.S. Army in France during World War I, mostly in the Chemical Warfare Service. When he returned to St. Louis, he moved across town and signed on as manager of the St. Louis Cardinals until 1925, when he took over as general manager. It was from this position as a baseball executive that Rickey would make an enormous contribution to the game.

With the Cardinals, Rickey developed the first farm system, in which a major league club controls a chain of minor league franchises through which it develops young players. Under Rickey's executive leadership, the Cardinals won six National League pennants and four World Series.

In 1942, following a disagreement with Cardinals ownership, Rickey became the general manager of the Brooklyn Dodgers. It was on this team and in this position that he would make his greatest mark on the game.

If cigar smoking was a vice, it was about the only one that Rickey apparently enjoyed. He did not drink or use profanity, beyond his oft-uttered "Judas Priest." He gave long answers to short questions and told folksy stories on the slightest whim, a number of which he had learned from his mother. He sometimes spoke at religious meetings as a lay preacher.

The portly Rickey, his bushy eyebrows rising to make a point, enjoyed lecturing players as well as audiences. Wielding biblical references and parables like swords, he could turn the game of baseball into life metaphors. Responsibility, duty, sacrifice—all of it was both the secret of living and the key to success on the diamond. He reminded sportswriters of India's nationalist leader Mahatma Gandhi, and newspapermen began to refer to him in print as "the Mahatma."

The Athlete

In his teenage years, Jackie Robinson had not been a baseball fanatic. He played the game and played it well, but he played all games well. Born to a sharecropper in Georgia, Robinson spent his early years across the country, in California, where his mother moved the family when he was an infant. After attending a technical high school and then Pasadena Community College, Robinson entered the University of California, Los Angeles (UCLA) in 1939.

It was there that sports aficionados began to take notice. This was a rare athlete. He lettered in four sports: football, basketball, baseball, and track. He was a superb swimmer and even had a mean tennis game. He was an honorable mention all-American in basketball. In track he set a national record for the long jump previously set by his brother, Mack, who also finished second to Jesse Owens in the 200-meter run in the 1936 Olympics in Berlin. The Robinson family nurtured more than one athlete.

Robinson left UCLA in 1941 because of financial hardship. For a time he earned money in Honolulu, Hawaii, playing semipro football. With the onset of U.S. involvement in World War II, he applied for officer candidate school and became a second lieutenant in the army and was sent to Fort Hood, Texas. He frequently played in camp ball games and was spied by Kansas City Monarchs pitcher Hilton Smith. The Negro Leagues hurler saw in the young kid speed, daring, and raw athleticism. He would later tell the Monarchs management of what he saw at Ford Hood.

Robinson had fierce pride. In June 1944, he took a blow of race prejudice and came back fighting. He refused a bus driver's order to move to the back of the bus, and the affair put him up against a court-martial for insubordination. The case went to trial. He was acquitted and given an honorable discharge.

In April 1945, Hilton Smith's advice to Monarchs' management paid off. Robinson joined the Kansas City club. He made $400 per month. In his first game for the Monarchs on May 6, Robinson, hitting third in the lineup, had an RBI double and a stolen base in a 6–2 win over the Chicago American Giants.

Although no one, including Robinson, knew it at the time, Jackie's career in the Negro Leagues would last only four months and fewer than 50 games. The rookie was a sensation, hitting almost .390. But he would later reflect on those days with the Monarchs with a better understanding of what black ball players had endured for decades. He said, "When I look back at what I had to go through in black baseball, I can only marvel at the many black players who stuck it out in Jim Crow leagues because they had nowhere to else to go. Finding satisfactory or even passable eating places was almost a daily problem. There were no hotels in many of the places we played. Sometimes there was a hotel for blacks with no eating facilities" (Robinson 1948, 17).

During those few months Robinson spent with the Royals, the Mahatma of Brooklyn had been looking for a player to break the color line with his Dodgers. By late summer 1945, he had chosen his athlete.

The Decision

Branch Rickey decided early in 1945 that he would attempt to break the entrenched policy of segregation of black players in the major leagues. Inside Rickey's ever-active mind were several forces driving his decision. Commissioner Landis was no longer alive and an impediment. The Dodgers team was in need of a powerful injection of youth and excitement to lead it back to the top and to draw new fans through the turnstiles. He could see, in his fertile business mind, rejuvenation not only of the Dodgers but of baseball itself with an influx of skilled black players. Despite the reluctance and outright opposition of other owners, he would tiptoe through the tall grass of opposition and pull off a business coup for the ages.

And always in the back of his mind was that day in his hotel room many years ago and that young black player sobbing, lamenting that he could not wipe off his color. This was Rickey's moral voice, his religious upbringing, engraved from his childhood that still demanded attention. Breaking baseball segregation was not only for Rickey a business windfall but also a moral crusade. For the Mahatma, it was perfect.

He went at his scheme with the utmost secrecy and deception. Rickey would not only blow smoke from his cigars, he would blow smoke in the eyes of the baseball world. Always a wheeler-dealer, a card player at heart despite his moral scruples, he conducted a campaign of deception worthy of a wily general planning an attack. In April 1945, he conducted a press conference announcing plans to create a Negro team that would compete in a newly formed league. Actually, Rickey was giving himself cover to search for the best black player to integrate the majors.

He needed scouts for his operation, people who could give informed judgments about Negro Leagues stars who might be able to handle the daunting pressures of being the first player to integrate. His trusted scout, Clyde Sukeforth, a former major leaguer, who became his lead agent. But Rickey also wisely turned to sportswriters Wendell Smith of the *Pittsburgh Courier* and Sam Lacy of the *Baltimore Afro-American*. The two had covered the Negro Leagues for most of their careers. The two consulted with Rickey with determined discretion.

In April 1945, Rickey asked Smith whether he knew of any blacks talented enough to play in the majors. Although the question, as framed, struck Smith as ludicrous, as the names of many Negro Leaguers swirled in his head, he told Rickey that Robinson would certainly make it in the majors.

Smith had already consulted with Lacy. "Wendell and I had a friendly exchange," Lacy remembered. "He thought Jackie Robinson would be the best choice. We agreed Jackie wasn't the best player at the time, but was the most

suitable player. He had played against white competition, was a college guy."
Lacy and Smith also considered the fact that Robinson was a family man, one
who had been in the service and might be better able to withstand racial taunts
(Mayo 2002).

As Rickey began to send agents to check out Robinson's background and
playing abilities, Rickey and Smith maintained a close correspondence. Smith
said later that he was almost certain at this stage that Rickey was seriously
considering signing Robinson to a contract but was reluctant to write anything
suggestive in the *Courier* lest the news compromise the possibility. Smith said
later, "I was tempted to write it, that the Dodgers were talking to him, but it
would have killed it. I was sworn to secrecy. When Rickey and I talked on the
phone, we never used Jackie Robinson's name. It was always 'the young man
from the West'" (Burroughs 1997, 7).

In August 1945, Rickey dispatched Sukeforth to Comiskey Park, where
Robinson was playing a series with the Monarchs to ask that he come to
Brooklyn to meet with Rickey in the offices of the Dodgers. When asked by
writers whether this was the beginning of integration in professional baseball,
whether he and the Dodgers were interested in signing Robinson, Rickey de-
murred. No, he said, "That would bring in a lot of problems which I am unable
to solve." Instead, Rickey claimed, he was exploring the idea of creating a "good
Negro league." This was more of Rickey's camouflage, his fiction, to disguise,
at least for now, his real intent ("Rickey Admits Calling in Jackie Robinson"
1945, 16).

On August 28, 1945, Sukeforth escorted Robinson into Rickey's office on
Montague Street in Brooklyn. Robinson later recalled his first meeting with
Rickey:

> He was taking off his coat, rolling up his sleeves. His mobile face had
> suddenly taken on a droll, cunning look. "Let's say I'm a hotel clerk. You
> come in with the rest of your team. I look up from the register and snarl,
> 'We don't let niggers sleep here.' What do you do then?" Again, before
> I could answer, the smudgy cigar shot toward my chin, and he was an
> umpire waving his huge fist too close under my nose, banishing me
> from the game. As a race-baiting fan he hurled pop bottles and insults.
> When the performance was over his shirt was soggy with sweat, his hair
> matted. His curtain line explained everything. It was the most dramatic
> [thing] I have ever heard, before or since: "Jackie, this talk of organizing
> a Negro team in Brooklyn was only a cover-up for my real plans. I want
> you to be the first Negro player in the major leagues. I've been trying to
> give you some idea of the kind of punishment you'll have to absorb. Can
> you take it?" " ("On This Day" 1965)

Robinson remembered Rickey concluding the interview by saying, "We can't fight our way through this, Robinson. We've got no army. There's virtually nobody on our side. No owners, no umpires, very few newspapermen. And I'm afraid that many fans will be hostile. We'll be in a tough position. We can win only if we can we can convince the world that I'm doing this because you're a great ballplayer and a fine gentleman." Rickey stressed that Robinson must endure not only the pressure of playing the game well but also the racial pressures—the bean balls that would be aimed at his head, the epithets, even possible physical attacks that could lead to increased racial violence and hatred. All of that would infuriate any man, would assault his dignity, but, in this case, assaults had to be endured, not with retaliation but with steadfast determination to see it through. Rickey quoted scripture about turning the other cheek. Robinson agreed. "I didn't know how I would do it," he said, "Yet I knew that I must" (Robinson 1995, 32–34).

On October 23, 1945, the color line in professional baseball officially broke, at least on paper. Rickey signed Robinson to a contract to play with the Dodgers' Triple A farm team in Montreal. It was Sam Lacy's 42nd birthday.

Wendell Smith broke the news to readers of the *Pittsburgh Courier:* "Baseball's long-established color line came smashing down with a resounding crash in Montreal, Canada, Tuesday afternoon when fleet-footed Jackie Robinson, ex-UCLA all-around star and Kansas City Monarch's shortstop became the first Negro to sign a contract in organized baseball. When the brilliant, broad-shouldered Pasadena (Calif.) athlete affixed his signature to the Montreal club contract, a farm team of the Brooklyn Dodgers, he established a precedent that blasted the sturdy, immovable barrier against Negroes since baseball's great empire was established" (Smith 1945a, 1).

Asked about his signing by the *New York Times,* Robinson declared, "I hope to make good and open the way for other in my race to do likewise. I sincerely hope that I am able and lucky enough to make the grade" ("Rickey Cites Wire to Refute Critics" 1945, 14).

Baseball writers and pundits eagerly sought out opinions throughout the baseball world on the signing. Although the black press hailed the occasion, there was some apprehension that if Robinson made the major leagues and if other stars would follow, the Negro Leagues themselves would be in grave jeopardy. Asked about the signing, Satchel Paige said, "They didn't make a mistake by signing Robinson. They couldn't have picked a better man" ("Rickey Cites Wire to Refute Critics" 1945, 14).

Civil rights leader Roy Wilkins, who was then assistant secretary of the NAACP and the editor of the organization's newspaper, the *Crisis,* said of the breaking of baseball's color line that "in a new and dramatic fashion the fact that the Negro is a citizen with talents and rights is being heralded to the nation." Adam Clayton Powell, black congressman from New York, declared that the signing was "a definite step toward winning the peace" in the battle for racial justice (Hogan 2006, 339, 342).

Many white players and owners were dismissive of the event. Clark Griffith, owner of the Washington Senators, fumed at Rickey's action, saying that the Dodgers were acting like outlaws in raiding the Negro Leagues. Like other owners, Griffith was almost certainly not concerned about the rights of the Negro Leagues; he was concerned about the pressure that the Senators and other teams would face if Robinson would succeed. He was also enjoying the profits from renting the Washington stadium to the Homestead Grays. He could see a financially comfortable arrangement being compromised down the road.

Over the next several months, owners in both National and American Leagues voiced nearly universal condemnation over the signing. Commissioner Chandler, however, stood firm against the entreaties.

Wendell Smith wrote on November 3, 1945, that Rickey had stood up against great odds and opposition for the right reason—he believed it was a moral thing to do. "He was motivated by a firm conviction," Smith said. "And although it may be hard to conceive that of a man who makes his living in such a 'blood and thunder' vocation as big league baseball, where gleaming spikes and menacing 'bean' balls are every-day ammunition, it is the truth" (Smith 1945b, 1).

Rickey himself told reporters that the Dodgers had scouted the Negro Leagues quite vigorously during the previous year, with special focus on Robinson. He did not mention that black newspapermen had aided his scouts in his search. And Rickey more than hinted that the Robinson signing was likely only the beginning. "In fact," he said, "we have several other Negroes in mind who will be signed to minor league contracts before the next season starts. I cannot tell you who they are or how many, but I do expect other clubs to follow suit." Rickey was not only defending his move but issuing a warning to all of baseball that other teams that did not follow his example could be left in the dust (Hand 1945, 12).

Rickey later talked about the civil rights implications: "The utter injustice of it always was in my mind—in St. Louis a negro was not permitted to buy his way into the Grandstand—you know that—and it has only been in recent years that he has been permitted to go into the Grandstand and of course there was no negro player in baseball. I felt very deeply about that thing all my life" (Rickey ca 1955).

Robinson prepared to go to Montreal to spend time in the minor leagues to prepare for the ultimate moment when he would first step on the field as a major league player. The great experiment would now begin.

But if the signing of Jackie Robinson marked a turning point in the nation's drive toward racial integration, no one would have guessed it at the annual

New York dinner for baseball writers. The event, as always, featured entertainment that often bordered on cruel and unusual punishment as performers roasted famous personalities. In early 1946, the entertainment took on a charged racial tone that infuriated much of the black press. With a bevy of sportswriters, major league team owners, and other sports notables in the audience, a comedy routine, with a stage setting of a Southern mansion, drew much laughter and hoots (after all, it was all in good fun), with actors playing Commissioner Chandler as a Southern plantation figure and Jackie Robinson as a butler:

> **Chandler**—Shall we all partake of some refreshments? (Colonels nod assent). No reason why we all shouldn't enjoy a little Southern hospitality. Southern, that is. (Claps hands and calls) Robbie-ee. Robbie-ee (Butler enters)
>
> **Butler**—Yassuh, Massa. Here Ah is.
>
> **Chandler**—Ah, there you are, Jackie. Jackie, you ole woolly headed Rascal. How long yo' been in the family?
>
> **Butler**—Long, time, Kuni, marty long time. Ebber since Massa Rickey done Bote me from da Kansas City Monarchs.
>
> **Chandler**—To be sure, Jackie, to be sure. How could Ah forget that Colonel Rickey brought you to our house. (Aside) Rickey—that no good carpetbagger! What could he be thinking of? (Daley 1946, 32)

If Jackie Robinson needed any more evidence that a monumental challenge to overcome racial stereotypes and prejudice loomed ahead, all he needed was the script of the baseball writers' dinner. Editors at the *New York Times* found the comedy so witty, they decided to publish it.

THE BARNSTORMING TOURS OF FELLER AND SATCH

In Des Moines, Iowa, in 1935, a 16-year-old pitching sensation took the mound for a group of semipro players to face the Kansas City Monarchs on a barnstorming tour. Satchel Paige pitched for the Monarchs; the 16-year-old was Bob Feller, a high school student from Van Meter, Iowa.

The Cleveland Indians were so enamored of the lightning-like fastballs of the youngster that they signed him to a contract. Although the shady action in signing someone so young was a violation of major league rules, baseball commissioner Landis allowed the signing to stand, fining the Indians $7,500. For the Indians, it was a small price to pay.

In July 1936, at age 17, Feller pitched in an exhibition game with the Indians against the St. Louis Cardinals. Sportswriter Harry Grayson watched stunned as the kid struck out eight batters in three innings. "You never saw anything like this kid!" said Grayson. "He practically steps toward third base when he throws, and the ball just explodes." "The kid has a chance to be the greatest of them all," said veteran umpire Bill Klein after seeing Feller for the first time. Klein would have known; he had called balls and strikes on such Hall of Famers as Grover Cleveland Alexander and Walter Johnson (Vass 2003, 46).

On August 23, 1936, Feller started his first official major league game against the St. Louis Browns. Because of his age and inexperience, Indians manager Steve O'Neil had a pitcher warming up in the bullpen in case of early trouble. Feller struck out the side in the first inning. The relief pitcher in the bullpen sat down. Feller struck out 15 that day. Two weeks later, he broke the American League single-game strikeout mark, fanning 17 against the Philadelphia Athletics. When the season ended, the boy returned for his senior year in high school in Van Meter.

Bob Feller went on to win 266 games in a remarkable career. He would almost certainly have won more than 300 games if it had not been for the onset of World War II. After the Japanese strike at Pearl Harbor, Feller was the first major league player to enlist. He served in combat on a battleship.

Soon after the beginning of his major league career, Feller barnstormed every winter, often facing Negro Leagues hitters. Although he stood by a remark he once made about Jackie Robinson having a slim chance of making a success in the majors and although he made other slighting remarks about the abilities of black players, Feller was an entrepreneur in his soul. He reflected on those barnstorming contests in the late 1930s. He knew that the competitive nature of the games between teams of which he had been a part and those of black players were exciting for fans. If black players were not going to be on major league teams, Feller reasoned, why not use competition between whites and blacks to draw big crowds.

"Why not capitalize on the separation?" he said later. "The racial rivalry tour came to me when I was aboard the battleship *Alabama* during World War II: the best blacks against the best whites across the country. When the war ended, in the summer of 1945, there was no time to organize anything. But there was plenty of time to figure something out for the winter of 1946" (Fussman 2007, 41).

The enterprising Feller leased two DC-3s from the Flying Tiger Line, set up a schedule, arranged rentals of the ballparks, and began the barnstorming series in Pittsburgh. His team played against Satch's squads in places as diverse as Yankee Stadium and the New Haven, Connecticut, race track.

In a game in Kansas City, Monarch hurler Hilton Smith, playing in front of his hometown fans of the Negro Leaguers, pitched his heart out but was behind in the ninth inning, 2–0. In the bottom of the ninth, Newark Eagles outfielder Johnny Davis belted a game-winning, three-run homer. As the hefty Davis gleefully romped around the bases, he picked up New York Yankee shortstop Phil Rizzuto and carried him around third base. "We both slid in at home plate together," Davis later recalled (Gay 2010, 237).

The barnstormers flew to the West Coast and played in stadiums from San Diego to Vancouver, 35 games in 30 days. "After it was over," Feller said, "I remember the black players coming over to shake my hand. Later on, some people said it really opened a door" (Fussman 2007, 42).

THE UNUSUAL FIGHT OF EDDIE KLEP

Eddie Klep was, in his own way, an integration pioneer. He was the first white man to play baseball in the Negro Leagues. Pitching in a benefit game for a local semipro team in Erie, Pennsylvania, against the Cleveland Buckeyes, Klep was impressive—so impressive that the owner of the Buckeyes, Ernest Wright, came up with a novel idea. There were no restrictions against white players joining Negro Leagues teams, at least to anyone's knowledge. Maybe the white kid would like to join the Buckeyes.

Wright asked Klep if he would be interested in leaving Erie for the road and a chance to play professional baseball. Klep saw nothing better in his future and jumped at the chance. He joined the Buckeyes.

On March 24, 1946, police in Birmingham, Alabama, arrived at Rickwood Field to enforce local ordinances designed to prohibit race mixing. Eddie Klep, a white man, met Jim Crow. The police forced Klep to take off his Buckeyes uniform, to dress in civilian clothes, and to sit in the stands specifically reserved for white patrons.

Fay Young, sportswriter of the *Chicago Defender*, mocked the ludicrous scene: "Sunday, one was pulled for the books down in Birmingham . . . the white man couldn't play with the Cleveland Buckeyes against the Birmingham Black Barons. Then the police decided he couldn't sit on the bench with the other players on the Cleveland Club. First, he had to take off his uniform. Next, he couldn't sit there as a spectator. That would be called social equality" (Young 1946, 15).

Although Klep pitched well in the first two games in which he was allowed to play, he lasted with the Buckeyes only until June, after an unfortunate performance that lost a game in the ninth inning. After his release by the Buckeyes, a bitter Klep returned to Erie and played for a time with a semipro team, but his life burrowed downward into petty crime. He later wore the uniform of the Rockview State Prison in Pennsylvania.

The odyssey of Eddie Klep's battle with racial integration inspired a folk song written by Chuck Brodsky called "The Ballad of Eddie Klep." But perhaps the best tribute was penned by Cleveland Jackson, a writer with the Cleveland *Call and Post*, who said: "Braving the taunts, insults and threats of an outraged southern public, Klep showed true blue. If Buckeye officials' reports are true, then Eddie Klep isn't ready for big league baseball. But in the hearts of every true American sportsman, there is an indelible feeling that little Eddie Klep is ready for the highest award in sportsmanship. He is a great little guy" (Tilove 2005).

INTO THE FIRE: SPRING TRAINING, 1946

Jackie Robinson joined the Montreal Royals in Florida for the 1946 spring training season. For Robinson, this spring training would be unlike any he would ever experience. Players normally think of spring in Florida and the first crack of the bats as the long-awaited break from winter, a time when all players harbor personal dreams of the season ahead. They get into shape and hone their skills. But for Robinson, Florida in 1946 was hellish—hardships and humiliations, challenges to his manhood and spirit, a test of survival.

As Jackie and his wife, Rachel, arrived in the back of a bus at the training site at Daytona Beach, degrading incidents soon mounted. They found few places to eat. Across the state, along with other blacks, they faced segregated health care systems, restaurants, beaches, swimming pools, recreational facilities, bathrooms, and the ever-present signs at separate drinking fountains marked "Whites Only" and "Colored." They had to rely on an informal network of black citizens to show them the limits of Jim Crow laws.

In addition to the major announcement of the signing of Robinson, Branch Rickey also quietly signed Johnny Wright, a quality pitcher with the Homestead Grays, to try out with the Royals in spring training. Robinson would not be alone to face his racial tormentors.

On the morning of March 4, 1946, Robinson and Wright walked onto the field for practice at Daytona Beach. During the coming six weeks in 1946, in a number of towns and cities, Robinson and Wright faced a wave of racist opposition, not only from players and fans. Some city officials made it clear that the Royals were not welcome to play on their fields with black players.

Look magazine interviewed Rickey at the beginning of spring training. The issue brought much national attention as a civil rights struggle. Rickey declared, "I cannot face my God much longer knowing that His black creatures are held separate and distinct from His white creatures in the game that has given me all that I can call my own" (Cohane 1946, 70).

On Sunday, March 17, 1946, in City Island Ballpark in Daytona Beach, Florida, Robinson took the field against the Royals' parent team, the Brooklyn Dodgers. On this day, the segregated section of Daytona's park quickly filled, as hundreds of black men, women, and children, many of whom had prayed for Robinson in their early morning church services, excitedly took their seats. This, of all days, was the one for them to be at the ballpark.

A nervous Robinson did not get a hit that day, but he made history and set a precedent. The Associated Press reported: "It was the first time a Negro player ever participated with whites in an exhibition game for which admission was charged in the state of Florida" (Lamb 2006, 107).

On March 24, 1946, in Jacksonville, Florida, a game between the New Jersey Giants and Montreal Royals was canceled by city authorities. They refused to allow Jacksonville's baseball field to be used by the Royals because of a city law that prohibited the two races from playing against each other or with each other. Shortly thereafter, Deland, Florida, canceled a game scheduled between the Royals and the Indianapolis Indians on the pretense that the field was undergoing repairs. Rickey and his Royals had been given an ultimatum: leave the two black players behind or face cancellation.

After some communication with Jacksonville city officials, the Royals, with Robinson and Wright on the team, showed up on March 28 in Jacksonville to play a game against Jersey City. The Royals thought that Jacksonville officials had changed their minds. They had not. When the Royals arrived at the ball field expecting to play, they instead got another taste of Jim Crow from the city's Bureau of Recreation. Outside the stadium, a man announced that "The game has been cancelled. There will be no niggers playing here" (Lamb 2006, 142).

By early April, Robinson and Wright had now been denied playing fields for three games. Rickey decided to contact stadiums remaining on the spring training schedule. A number of cities and towns insisted that Robinson and Wright not accompany the Royals to the games. Rickey was furious. "Without Robinson and Wright, there'll be no games," he declared. Thus, Rickey announced the cancellation of six additional games—in Sanford, Deland, and Jacksonville, Florida; Richmond, Virginia; and two games in Savannah, Georgia. Wendell Smith declared, "The stirring declaration pierced the usually impregnable armor of public office holders . . . and it left a scar that will become more prominent and discernable each day the world looks down with startled curiosity at the part of its anatomy that is being gnawed by the parasite of racial discrimination" (Smith 1946, 26).

NORTH TO MONTREAL

After the Royals wrapped up spring training in Daytona Beach, the team traveled north to begin play in its regular season International League schedule. On April 18, 1946, the Royals were in Roosevelt Stadium in Jersey City. Twenty-five thousand spectators filled the park as well as numerous members of the press. How would Robinson react? Would there be any friction between Robinson and his teammates or with the opposing players? How would he stand up to the escalating pressure now that the regular season was about to open?

This minor league game was not merely one that filled newspaper columns in the *Pittsburgh Courier, Chicago Defender,* and other black papers; this one earned 11 paragraphs in the *New York Times.* Readers across the country and around the world shared in this burgeoning civil rights story about a 26-year-old black man on a mission to succeed in a sport that had for so long banned his race from its professional ranks.

Robinson was spectacular that day. Displaying both power and flair, he led his team to a whopping 14–1 victory. He had four hits, scored four runs, and stole two bases. One of his hits was a three-run homer in the third inning. As he rounded third base and reached home plate, a white hand was extended there to greet him. It was the hand of teammate George Shuba. The *New York Times* captioned the photo of that handshake with the words, "The Highlight of a Brilliant Debut."

The photo circulated in newspapers across the country. "I just shook his hand. I didn't think too much about it," Shuba, then 21 years old, said later. "If the truth be told, he was the best ballplayer on the club. I was just focused on beating the other team. I didn't care if he was Technicolor, Jackie was my teammate" ("Gripping Memories" 2007).

The Jersey City game was both a personal triumph for Robinson and a signal that something extraordinary in the nation's culture was on the move. Nevertheless, Robinson and Rickey and others involved with the Dodgers knew that the world was not filled with George Shubas and that this bold experiment was going to get rough and possibly violent.

Indeed, the next stop for the Royals was Baltimore, a city that had Southern sympathies on the race question going back to the Civil War. Not surprisingly, the crowd in Baltimore greeted the new black player for the Royals with a startling display of profanity, hisses, boos, and threats. So hostile was the intense shower of verbal abuse that rained down from most of the areas of the stadium that Rachel Robinson was deeply frightened. The Robinsons survived Baltimore as they would survive other humiliating displays of mindless bigotry.

Along with trials, however, the coming season would also be full of memorable and warm times, friendships that lasted a lifetime, and a measure of respect that transcended the racial animosity. Much of it had to do with the city of Montreal, the home team for Robinson in 1946, the city that would witness half of his games during the year.

A cosmopolitan city, Montreal was the best possible minor league venue for Robinson. Rachel wrote later, "In the end, Montreal was the perfect place for Jack to get his start. We never had a threatening or unpleasant experience there, the people were so welcoming and saw Jack as a player and more importantly as a man" ("Plaque Placed" 2007).

They rented a house near Delorimier Stadium. They formed lasting bonds with a number of people, especially with famed Montreal sportswriter Sam

Maltin and his wife, Belle, with whom they shared dinners and occasional concerts on Mount Royal.

Montreal rocked with baseball pandemonium that summer, with fans cheering on Robinson and his teammates. He hit .349 batting and stole 40 bases. He was now, most baseball observers assumed, likely ready for Brooklyn and the majors.

On May 14, 1946, Johnny Wright was demoted to the Class-C Dodgers farm team in Quebec, the Three Rivers Royals of the Canadian-American League. At the end of the season, Wright barnstormed with Robinson's all-star team. He then decided to return to the Negro Leagues, joining once again the Homestead Grays for the 1947 season. He retired a year later.

Robinson wrote, "Johnny was a good pitcher, but I feel he didn't have the right kind of temperament to make it with the International League in those days. He couldn't withstand the pressure of taking insult after insult without being able to retaliate. It affected his pitching that he had to keep his temper under control all the time. Later I was very sad because he didn't make the Montreal team" (Robinson 1995, 44).

After the last game of the season, in which the Royals defeated the Kentucky Colonels for the "Little World Series" title, Robinson was swamped with joyous fans who chased him down the street after he left the stadium. Sam Maltin summed it up: "It was probably the only day in history that a black man ran from a white mob with love instead of lynching on his mind" ("Jackie Robinson's Montreal Home" 2011).

JACKIE ROBINSON IN EBBETS FIELD

In the spring of 1947, the Brooklyn Dodgers team did not choose Florida for its spring training schedule. The racial nightmares of a year before were still too painful. Instead, the team wisely traveled to Havana, Cuba, where black stars had both played and managed for decades. Negro Leagues stars were not novelties for Havana fans, who had seen over the years the likes of Oscar Charleston, Josh Gibson, Satchel Paige, and Cool Papa Bell.

Robinson was joined in camp by other black players who Rickey had recently signed, including Roy Campanella and Don Newcombe. Campanella, a stocky catcher, had begun his Negro Leagues career at the age of 16 with the Washington Elites, a team that moved to Baltimore the following season. He also played for a time in the Mexican League. In 1946, while Robinson played for Montreal, Rickey assigned Campanella to the Dodgers' minor league squad in Nashua, New Hampshire, whose young general manager, Buzzi Bavasi, and manager, Walter Alston, warmly welcomed him along with Newcombe, a strapping, hard-throwing right-handed pitcher from the Newark Eagles.

It was not as if Havana was some kind of racial nirvana. Just as in Florida, blacks faced certain segregation barriers, especially in housing. White Dodgers players stayed at the grand Hotel Nacional with its imposing Moorish architecture facing the gulf and its elegant swimming pool, bars, and other amenities.

For black players, it was the Hotel Boston in old Havana, nothing like the Hotel Nacional. Elegant pools were nowhere to be found at the Boston, but it was where black players had traditionally stayed in Havana. Although visibly annoyed, Robinson and the other blacks went along with the arrangement.

Most knowledgeable baseball observers now assumed that Robinson would head back to the states to play for the Brooklyn Dodgers. Campanella and Newcombe and others would have to wait. The official word came on April 10, a few days before the Dodgers' scheduled opening game of the 1947 season against the Boston Braves. Rickey signed Robinson to a contract with the Dodgers. He would not be playing second base, a position that would still be handled by veteran Eddie Stankey. Instead, Robinson would play first base and he would be in the starting lineup.

New York Times sports columnist Arthur Daley wrote: "Robinson has to be another DiMaggio in making good from the opening whistle. It's not fair to him, but no one can do anything about it but himself. Pioneers never had it easy and Robinson, perforce, is a pioneer. . . . It is his burden to carry from now on and he must carry it alone" (Daley 1947, 31).

On April 15, 1947, the Dodgers took the field. The first baseman, wearing number 42, was a 28-year-old rookie. He was a black man.

REFERENCES

Breslin, Jimmy. 2011. *Branch Rickey.* New York: Viking Penguin Group.

Burroughs, Todd. 1997. "Black Press Led Way for Robinson's Entry into Major Leagues." *New Pittsburgh Courier* (April 5): 7.

Cohane, Tim. 1946. "A Branch Grows in Brooklyn." *Look* (March 19): 70.

Daley, Arthur. 1946. "Sports of the Times: At the Baseball Writers Show." *New York Times* (February 4): 32.

Daley, Arthur. 1947. "Play Ball." *New York Times* (April 15): 31.

Fussman, Cal. 2007. *After Jackie: Pride, Prejudice, and Baseball's Forgotten Heroes: An Oral History.* New York: ESPN Books.

Gay, Timothy. 2010. *Satch, Dizzy, and Rapid Robert.* New York: Simon & Schuster.

"Goldstein to Seek Help for Negroes." 1945. *New York Times* (September 24): 11.

"Gripping Memories." 2007. Connect2OWU, Ohio Wesleyan University (March 21), http://connect2.owu.edu/ourtown/304.php.

Hand, Jack. 1945. "Dodger Boss Confident Negro Star Will Click." *Washington Post* (October 25): 12.

Hogan. Lawrence. 2006. *Shades of Glory: The Negro Leagues and the Story of Afro-American Baseball.* Washington, DC: National Geographic.

"Jackie Robinson's Montreal Home Commemorated." 2011. *New York Post* (February 27), http://www.nypost.com/p/sports/more_sports/jackie_robinson_montreal_apartment_bjKeByfXnv2kNAmx9jYdoK/1.

Lamb, Chris. 2006. *Blackout: The Untold Story of Jackie Robinson's First Spring Training.* Lincoln: University of Nebraska Press.

Mayo, Jonathan. 2002. "Ink-tegration: Writers Lacy, Smith Played big Role in Baseball Integration" (February), http://mlb.mlb.com/mlb/history/mlb_negro_leagues_story.jsp?story=lacysmith.

Metcalf, Henry. 2000. *A Game for All Races.* New York: MetroBooks.

O'Karma, Dave. 2006. "The Forgotten Championship." *Cleveland Magazine* (May), http://clevelandmagazine.blogspot.com/2009/07/read-about-cleveland-buckeyes-whose.html.

"On This Day", 1965. "Branch Rickey, 83, Dies in Missouri, *New York Times* (December 10): http://www.nytimes.com/learning/general/onthisday/bday/1220.html.

"Plaque Placed at Jackie Robinson's Montreal Home." 2011. CTV News (April 14), http://www.ctv.ca/CTVNews/Canada/20110228/jackie-robinson-montreal-baseball-110228/.

Rickey, Branch. Transcript of interview by Davis J. Walsh. Circa 1955. Library of Congress, Manuscript Division, Branch Rickey Papers.

"Rickey Admits Calling in Jackie Robinson." 1945. *Pittsburgh Courier* (September 1): 16.

"Rickey Cites Wire to Refute Critics." 1945. *New York Times* (October 26): 14.

Robinson, Jackie. 1948. "What's Wrong with Negro Baseball." *Ebony* (June 1): 17.

Robinson, Jackie. 1995. *I Never Had It Made.* New York: Harper Perennial.

Smith, Wendell. 1945a. "Baseball 'Color-Line' Smashed!" *Pittsburgh Courier* (October 27): 1.

Smith, Wendell. 1945b. "Why He Signed Jackie Robinson." *Pittsburgh Courier* (November 3): 1.

Smith, Wendell. 1946. "'Robinson Plays or No Game,' Rickey's Answer to Dixie." *Pittsburgh Courier* (April 13): 26.

Tilove, Jonathan. 2005. "Jackie Robinson in Reverse: Eddie Klep Integrated Negro Leagues." Newhouse News Service (March 2), http://jonathantilove.com/eddie-kepp/.

Vass, George. 2003. "The Naturals: Teenage Players Whose Innate Baseball Talents Made Them Special; Ty Cobb, Babe Ruth, Mel Ott, Bob Feller and Robin Yount Are Some Hall of Famers Whose Careers Started at an Early Age." *Baseball Digest* (August): 46.

Young, Fay. 1946. "Buck's White Pitcher Can't Play with Team in B'ham." *Chicago Defender* (April 6): 15.

6

Honors Due: Celebrating Black Players before Integration

COURAGE

As Jackie Robinson ran onto Ebbets Field as the Brooklyn Dodgers' opening day first baseman, the stands were packed, and a huge part of the crowd was made up of black patrons.

By the Fourth of July, the halfway mark of the 1947 season, Robinson had already surprised most baseball observers. Despite the searing pressure to succeed, to prove wrong those naysayers who doubted not only his abilities but his fortitude, he was hitting over .300, had a 20-game hitting streak, and led the league in stolen bases. And towering over these statistical measures was his demeanor. Shirley Povich, writing for the *Washington Post*, said, "Robinson doesn't scare easily, either. He's been hit by pitched balls seven times this year, more than any other player in the league, but you'd never know it the way he persists in his crowding-the-plate batting stance. He used to sit on the corner of the Dodgers' bench by himself, but now his teammates cotton to him and he's one of the boys" (Povich 1947, 8).

Nevertheless, the beginning of baseball's so-called great experiment, as reporters began to call it, was for Robinson a unique, personal ordeal. Here was a man with the hopes and fears of his race on his back, in the glare of a national stage, with a large percentage of the population hoping he would fail and be humiliated, and with the demand that he refrain from retaliation against insults and threats—all of it was, indeed, an experiment, and he was its subject.

So ingrained were the recesses of racism that even some of his new team-mates, mostly from the South, had quietly circulated a petition at the beginning of spring training in 1947 saying they would not play with a black teammate. The captain of the Dodgers was shortstop Harold "Pee Wee" Reese, a man with roots in rural Kentucky who had never shaken the hand of the black man and had never played ball with blacks because they were not allowed in the local parks. The schools were segregated. But near Reese's childhood home was a tree on which a number of black men, according to his father, had been lynched. Reese had never forgotten the feeling of injustice and evil that swept over him when he was told about the stories of what had happened on one of the large limbs of that tree. Now, faced with the petition, the Dodger captain refused to sign. The petitioners fell back.

From the first days of his major league career, Robinson felt daily the wrath of haters. He opened letters from people threatening to kill him. He constantly ducked pitches thrown at his head; he heard almost unrelenting heckling, taunts, and filthy name-calling from the stands.

On the field, the tormentors were many, but the most vicious was Phila-delphia Phillies manager Ben Chapman. A native Alabaman, Chapman was a notorious bench jockey who delighted in issuing a constant stream of epithets at opponents. He had especially expressed open disdain for Jews; but now Robinson came to the majors as something of a gift, the best target that a bigot could possibly attack, especially given the fact that Robinson was obviously under strict orders to rein in all impulses to retaliate.

Harold Parrott, traveling secretary for the Dodgers, said later that he had never heard in his lifetime such racial animosity and invective that Chapman incessantly hurled at Robinson—every insult imaginable, every disgusting, repulsive stereotype.

In later years, Jackie revealed how close he had come to cracking in those painful days. "For one rage-crazed moment," he wrote, "I thought to hell with everything. . . . I was going to go over there [to the Philadelphia bench], grab one of those white sons of bitches and smash his teeth with my despised black fist" (Robinson 1994, 9).

On May 9, 1947, a plot against Robinson was about to be executed by the St. Louis Cardinals. It was on that day that the Cardinal players, hosting Brooklyn for the first time since Robinson had joined the league, were going to demand that he be kept off the field. If not, the Cardinals would not play the game. Stanley Woodward, respected sports editor of the New York *Herald Tribune* re-ceived information about the planned strike by St. Louis players and exposed it. In a scathing editorial, Woodward wrote, "It is not generally known that other less serious difficulties have attended the elevation of Robinson to the major leagues. Through it all, the Brooklyn first baseman, whose intelligence and degree of education are far beyond that of the average ball player, has behaved himself in an exemplary manner" (Smith 1947, 14).

When revelation of the plot was revealed by Woodward, President Ford Frick of the National League denounced the planned revolt and declared that any players refusing to take the field against Robinson would be suspended from the league. "You will find," Frick angrily declared, "that the friends you think you have in the press box will not support you, that you will become outcasts. I do not care if half the league strikes. Those who do will encounter strict retribution . . . this is the United States of America, and one citizen has as much right to play as another" (Robinson 1963, 62).

Others quietly supported Robinson. In a game against the Pittsburgh Pirates in early May, Robinson collided at first base with Hank Greenberg, now in the last days of a Hall of Fame career, almost all of which he had played with the Detroit Tigers in the American League. The next time Robinson reached first base, Greenberg said, "I forgot to ask if you were hurt in that play?" After Robinson indicated that he was not injured, Greenberg said, "Stick in there. You're doing fine. Keep your chin up." Robinson always remembered that heartfelt gesture, especially because it had come from an all-star player who had himself been mocked and ridiculed because of his Jewish ancestry. Robinson said later, "Class tells. It sticks out all over Mr. Greenberg" ("Hank's Kind Word" 1947, M8).

But the venom toward Robinson kept coming. In one game on the road, the verbal assault from the bench and the stands reached such a crescendo that the game, for the moment, was not baseball but something else—racial hatred stirred to a boil. At that moment, Pee Wee Reese stared at the opposing bench, walked over to Robinson and stood by his side, a show of camaraderie that neither Robinson nor his wife Rachel ever forgot. "I remember Jackie talking about Pee Wee's gesture the day it happened," Rachel Robinson said. "It came as such a relief to him, that a teammate and the captain of the team would go out of his way in such a public fashion to express friendship" (Berknow 2005).

Looking back on the abuse and unrelenting attention directed at Robinson, Reese later remarked, "To be able to hit with everybody yelling at him, he had to block out everything but this ball coming in at 100 mph. To do what he did has to be the most tremendous thing I've ever seen in sports" (Singer).

The seemingly overwhelming pressures did not overwhelm Robinson. He hit .297 for the season, drove in 48 runs, and led the National League in stolen bases. The *Sporting News*, the long-standing newspaper devoted to organized baseball, had for decades played down the notion that integration would be a benefit to the sport. Now, in 1947, it gave Robinson its first rookie of the year award.

DOBY BREAKS AMERICAN LEAGUE COLOR BARRIER

In July 1947, three months after Jackie Robinson first stepped to the plate in Ebbets Field, Bill Veeck, owner of the Cleveland Indians, signed Larry Doby of the Newark Eagles. Unlike Robinson, who played an entire season in the minor leagues, Doby suddenly found himself in the Indians' starting lineup, the first black player to integrate the American League.

Born in South Carolina, Doby grew up in New Jersey. A natural athlete, he excelled in a number of sports at East Side High School in Paterson—especially in football, where he was an elusive and powerful running back and the only black player on the team. Doby attended Long Island University before signing a contract in 1942 offered by Effa Manley, owner of the Eagles, to play second base.

After serving in the navy for two years in 1944 and 1945, he rejoined the Eagles and hit well both in batting average and power. Lithe and graceful, Doby went on a tear with the Eagles in 1947, hitting well over .400. In mid-season Doby was approached by the Cleveland Indians. He became the first player to go directly from the Negro Leagues to the majors.

Jerry Isenberg, a columnist for the *Newark Star-Ledger,* talked about the constant humiliations Doby was forced to endure, especially in towns such as Washington. "It was so bad in Washington, which back then was essentially a Deep South town," said Isenberg, "that Larry wasn't allowed to use the visitor's clubhouse—he had to change in a black boardinghouse. No cab would pick him up, and there he was, walking down the street with his uniform on and his cleats over his shoulder, going to the tradesman's entrance at the ballpark so he could play against the Senators" (Fussman 2007, 32).

But Doby, just as Robinson, persevered. On October 9, 1948, at Cleveland's Municipal Stadium, the Indians defeated the Boston Red Sox 2–1 to give Cleveland a lead of three games to one in the World Series in which the Indians would prevail. The winning pitcher was Steve Gromek, who hurled a masterful complete game victory. The winning margin in the game was a home run hit by Doby.

Following the game, a photographer for the *Cleveland Plain Dealer* captured a joyous moment when Gromek and Doby hugged each other in the clubhouse, smiling broadly. In the history of black baseball, the photo, reproduced in newspapers around the country, would become an icon.

"That picture of Gromek and Doby has unmistakable flesh and blood cheeks pressed close together, brawny arms tightly clasped, equally wide grins," wrote Marjorie Mackenzie, a columnist for the *Pittsburgh Courier.* "The chief message of the Doby-Gromek picture is acceptance." The image, she said, "is capable of washing away with equal skill, long pent-up hatred in the hearts of men and the beginning of confusion in the minds of small boys" (Tygiel 1997, 239).

Doby later reflected on that World Series moment: "That was a feeling from within, the human side of two people, one black and one white," he said. "That made up for everything I went through. I would always relate back to that whenever I was insulted or rejected from hotels. I'd always think about that picture. It would take away all the negatives" (Goldstein 2002, A18).

During that 1948 run to the World Series championship, Doby was joined on the Indians by a long-familiar face to Negro Leagues fans—Satchel Paige. Doby was 24 years old; Paige was over 40.

Doby would make superlative marks in major league baseball: a seven-time all-star; the first black player to win a home run title in the major leagues; and the first black player to win an RBI title in the American League. After his player career ended after eight years in the majors, he became a coach and later the manager of the Chicago White Sox, the second black man (after Frank Robinson) to serve as a major league manager. He was inducted into the Hall of Fame in 1998.

AS THE MAJORS INTEGRATE, THE NEGRO LEAGUES DECLINE

Josh Gibson died in 1947 at the age of 35, three months before Jackie Robinson took the field for the Brooklyn Dodgers. Likely suffering from a brain tumor and wracked by alcoholism and drug addiction, Gibson's death on the eve of baseball's integration seemed especially tragic. The greatest slugger in the history of the Negro Leagues would never be able to demonstrate his skills to the entire baseball world.

For many other Negro Leagues players, the integration of the major leagues was a passionate dream never realized and, for some, it had been so tantalizingly close to their grasp. A hard-hitting, extraordinarily talented third baseman named Ray Dandridge, who had been signed by the New York Giants, quickly made his way through the Giants' farm system to the Triple-A Minneapolis Millers. There, he won the most valuable player award of the American Association in 1950. But Dandridge, who many believed was the best third baseman in the history of the Negro Leagues, was now nearing 40 years of age. He was never called up to the majors. For the rest of his life, he never forgave Giants owner Horace Stoneham for not giving him a shot at the majors. He told Stoneham, "The only thing I wanted to do was hit the major leagues. . . . You could have called me up for even one week! I could have said I hit the major leagues" (Tygiel 1997, 264).

Ironically, in Washington, DC, the two owners of the teams that played in Griffith Stadium—Clark Griffith of the Washington Senators and Cum Posey of the Homestead Grays—realized that they could make more money by keeping black and white baseball separate. Griffith was making a tidy sum renting Griffith Stadium to Posey's Grays, and Posey soon realized that with the advent of integration in the majors, the attendance at Negro Leagues games would inevitably suffer and would likely presage the end of Negro Leagues baseball itself. Especially for Posey, who had been at the center of Negro Leagues baseball for his entire life, Jackie Robinson's signing by the Dodgers seemed like the end of the road. Tragically, it marked the end for both him and his team. Posey died in 1946; the Grays played their final game in 1950.

Robinson's signing by the Dodgers did not immediately create a rush of activity by other team owners to walk through the long-closed door. The Cleveland Indians and St. Louis Browns integrated shortly after the Dodgers. By 1950, only two other teams had signed Negro Leagues players—the New York Giants and the Boston Braves.

Twelve days after Larry Doby appeared in the lineup of the Cleveland Indians, Kansas City Monarchs teammates Hank Thompson and Willard Brown were signed by the St. Louis Browns. Thompson started at second base for the Browns on July 17, and Brown joined him in the lineup in right field three days later. It marked the first time that two black players appeared in the same lineup in the majors. Thompson was later picked up by the New York Giants, and he, along with Monte Irvin and Giant rookie sensation Willie Mays, made up the first all-black outfield when they appeared in the 1951 World Series against the Yankees.

In April 1950, the Braves signed outfielder Sam Jethroe, one of the participants in the infamous Boston Red Sox sham tryout in 1945. Five years after that embarrassing day in Fenway Park, Jethroe returned to Boston—but not to the Red Sox. The Red Sox would be the last team in the major leagues to sign a black player—Pumpsie Green in 1959. Jethroe made the most of his chance at the big leagues. In his opening season with the Braves, he became the oldest player, at age 32, ever to win the rookie of the year award.

In May 1954, the Supreme Court issued the historic *Brown v. Board of Education* decision that essentially outlawed segregation in the nation's public schools. Argued by Thurgood Marshall, counsel for the National Association for the Advancement of Colored People (NAACP), the case became a momentous victory in a growing civil rights movement. By the fall of 1954, most major league teams had signed at least one Negro Leagues player. In October, when the New York Giants played the Cleveland Indians in the World Series, both teams, for the first time in the history of the series, were integrated.

On the one hand, integration of major league baseball was a pioneering step in the fight for equal rights; on the other hand, however, integration had a devastating effect on the Negro Leagues.

Star pitcher Hilton Smith of the Kansas City Monarchs said later of the black fans, "All the people started to go Brooklynites. Even if we were playing here in Kansas City, everybody wanted to go over to St. Louis to see Jackie. So our league began to go down, down, down" (Hogan 2006, 35). After Jackie joined the Dodgers, Buck Leonard quipped, the Negro Leagues couldn't draw flies.

In December 1947, the Negro Leagues applied for membership in the National Association of Professional Baseball Leagues. Their request: to become a minor league. It was denied. All-black teams would not be accepted into white baseball's fraternity.

Effa Manley, owner of the Newark Eagles with her husband, Abe, became the most vociferous defender of the Negro Leagues against what she regarded as outrageous treatment not only by major league owners but also by the black press and black fans. Known as a strong advocate for players, Effa Manley had fought for better travel and higher salaries. She and Abe were godparents to Larry Doby's first child. They loaned Monte Irvin money for a down payment on his first house. "After I quit playing, she started me out in business," said former player Lenny Pearson. "She interceded for me and spoke to people and helped me. She financed the first tavern I ever had. A beautiful, beautiful person in all ways" (Crawford).

Manley was also a social activist, serving as the head of a local chapter of the NAACP. She often used Eagles games to promote civic causes. In 1939, for example, she held an Anti-Lynching Day at Ruppert Stadium. She regarded the Eagles and the other Negro Leagues teams as black community pillars.

With the advent of integration, the Eagles entered into swift decline. Manley and the Giants lost Doby to Cleveland, Irvin to the New York Giants, and Don Newcombe to the Dodgers. All would have exemplary careers in the majors.

As the team lost players and attendance, Manley fumed about the black press and the fans now focusing on the major leagues rather than the Negro Leagues. A headline in the *Chicago Defender* on September 18, 1948, described her anger: "Effa Manley 'Hotter than Horse Radish.'"

Manley also responded with a withering attack against Jackie Robinson after a piece appeared in *Ebony* magazine in which Robinson listed a litany of problems with the Negro Leagues—questionable business practices of the owners, poor accommodations for the players, bad umpiring, and low salaries. After all, Robinson had played less than a season in the Negro Leagues. "No greater ingratitude was ever displayed," Manley said. "I wonder if he's speaking his own mind or if his statement was for a purpose even he does not understand." The problems Robinson cited, Manley went on, were mostly due to segregation and racism. It was not the fault of the Negro Leagues that blacks were denied hotel and eating accommodations. Black players made far more money per week than the average worker. Manley went on to appeal to black fans to continue to support the black teams. "Gullible Negro fans," she wrote, "who think the white owners take on colored players through any altruistic pangs of democracy had better quit kidding themselves. There's a potential of two million Negro fans to draw from" (Berlage 2005, 141).

But the Negro National League disbanded after the 1949 season. Interest in Negro Leagues games throughout the 1950s continued to plummet as radio and then television broadcasts drew crowds away from the stadiums. The 1952 East-West game drew only 14,122 fans, as opposed to three times that number in earlier years.

Also, through the 1950s, as more established and promising black players entered the majors, the talent level of the Negro Leagues continued to decline. At the same time, major league teams began to sign black players directly from high school and sandlot baseball.

The Negro American League limped along during the 1950s with an ever-changing roster of teams. By the late 1950s, however, all that remained of the Negro Leagues were a few traveling troupes owned by white promoters.

The Indianapolis Clowns, the prize possession of impresario Syd Pollock, was the last remaining black team that could attract big crowds. Although many of the players had outstanding talent, the Clowns, like the Harlem Globetrotters in basketball, put on a circus-like show. One of the players in the early 1950s was a young shortstop from Mobile, Alabama. In recalling his brief stint with the Clowns, he wrote: "They were the Globetrotters of baseball, and in fact, before I was with them, their big drawing card had been the famous Globetrotter, Goose Tatum. They say that Tatum was one of the fanciest first baseman you ever saw. The old Clowns also had a catcher named Pepper Bassett who would catch a couple of innings sitting in a rocking chair and a contortionist who coached first base standing on one hand." The youngster talked about the antics of King Tut and his sidekick Bebop. "They threw buckets of confetti into the crowd—all the same stunts the Globetrotters did. The fans ate it up." The young shortstop did not play long for the Clowns. His name was Henry Aaron (Aaron 1991, 31–32).

And so, both tragically and ironically, the price of integration by black stars came at a heavy price—the loss of a major black-owned and -operated enterprise and the careers of hundreds of players and other employees associated with various Negro Leagues teams.

CIVIL RIGHTS

In the struggle for black civil rights and equality, Jackie Robinson, Larry Doby, and others carried on the cause by courageously turning the other cheek. As the nonviolent civil rights movement—with its sit-ins, protest marches, and civil disobedience—was later to prove, this was a winning strategy. Baseball, however reluctantly, integrated even before President Harry Truman integrated the armed forces. In this sense, it led a way forward.

Martin Luther King Jr. later said of Robinson, "in the days when integration wasn't fashionable, he underwent the trauma and the humiliation and the loneliness which comes from being a pilgrim walking the lonesome byways toward the high road of Freedom. He was a sit-inner before sit-ins, a freedom-rider before freedom-rides" (Rampersad 1998, 7).

In looking back on Branch Rickey's actions in signing Robinson, Carl Erskine, great pitcher for the Dodgers in the 1950s, later said that a number of things were involved: improving the Dodger team, increasing attendance, all of the economic factors that made sense. But, above all, Erskine insisted, Rickey wanted "to break a tradition in America that Mr. Rickey thought was just plain wrong. He had to buck society to do that. He had to go up against a tradition that was solidly in place." And speaking of Rickey and Robinson, Erskine said, "it seems unreal to me now that one man's idea and one man's performance actually changed social behavior in America" (Fussman 2007, 76).

In 1949, soon after a few black players had entered the major leagues, John Henry "Pop" Lloyd, one the greatest shortstops in baseball history, was asked whether he regretted that his playing days at the turn of the century gave him no chance to play in the big leagues. He said: "I do not consider that I was born at the wrong time. I felt it was the right time, for I had the chance to prove the ability of our race in this sport, and because many of us did our very best to uphold the traditions of the game and of the world of sport, we have given the Negro a greater opportunity now to be accepted in the major leagues with other Americans" (Hogan 2006, 102).

Rickey, in a speech in Atlanta, Georgia, said in January 1956,

I know that America . . . is more interested in the grace of a man's swing, in the dexterity of his cutting a base, and his speed afoot, in his scientific body control, in his excellence as a competitor on the field,—America, wide and broad, and in Atlanta, and in Georgia, will become instantly more interested in those marvelous, beautiful qualities than they are in the pigmentation of a man's skin, or indeed in the last syllable of his name. Men are coming to be regarded of value based upon their merits, and God hasten the day when Governors of our States will become sufficiently educated that they will respond to those views. (Rickey 1956)

On December 1, 1955, in Montgomery, Alabama, a woman named Rosa Parks sparked a movement to challenge the segregated seating arrangements on the city bus system. She refused to sit at the back of a bus and was arrested. For 13 months, black leaders, led by Rev. Martin Luther King Jr., organized a nonviolent boycott challenging racial segregation that served as a model for other mass civil rights protests that would follow into the 1960s.

In September 1957, Governor Orval Faubus of Arkansas employed the National Guard to block the entry of nine black students who attempted to attend Little Rock's Central High School. The action so blatantly challenged the historic *Brown v. Board of Education* decision of 1954, declaring all laws establishing segregated schools unconstitutional, that President Dwight Eisenhower reluctantly sent federal troops to allow the students to enter the school. Although pleased that Eisenhower had acted, Jackie Robinson, now a company executive in New York, wrote to the president chastising the administration for its inaction in recent years to take leadership on civil rights issues. "I respectfully suggest," Robinson wrote to Eisenhower on May 13, 1958, "that you unwittingly crush the spirit of freedom in Negroes by constantly urging forbearance and give hope to those pro-segregation leaders like Governor Faubus who would take from us even those freedoms we now enjoy" (Robinson 1958).

For the rest of his life, Robinson became active in challenging the nation's leaders to advance the cause of equal rights.

Carl Rowan, esteemed journalist, diplomat, and one of the first black officers in the U.S. Navy, wrote a biography of Robinson in 1960. This was a time in the early stages of a civil rights movement that would lead to names of people and places forever ingrained in historical memory—the bravery of the freedom riders throughout the South in the summer of 1961 protesting segregation in bus and railway stations; the violence in October 1962 as James Meredith entered the University of Mississippi; the protests in Birmingham, Alabama, in the spring of 1963 that sparked police violence led by Commissioner Bull Connor, the arrest of Martin Luther King Jr., and his letter from Birmingham Jail; the June 1963 murder of civil rights leader Medgar Evers in Mississippi; the August 1963 March on Washington culminating in King's "I Have a Dream" speech at the Lincoln Memorial; the tragic bombing deaths of four young girls at the Sixteenth Street Baptist Church in Birmingham in September 1963; and the signing of the Civil Rights Act of 1964 by President Lyndon Johnson. Rowan concluded that "future generations will remember [Robinson] not as the baserunner who worried pitchers to their doom, but as the proud crusader against pompous bigots and timid sentinels of the status quo—another symbol of a new Negro American" (Rowan 1960, 339).

On election night 2008, Pulitzer Prize–winning author Jimmy Breslin was at Jackie Robinson Elementary School in Brooklyn, across the street from where Ebbets Field used to stand, current site of a housing project whose ground floor has a sign that reads "No Ball Playing." A New York City election official named Marie Lewis was at the Jackie Robinson school that momentous night in 2008 and, when asked if she had ever seen Robinson play, began swaying from left to right, mimicking the way Robinson used to taunt pitchers, dancing back and forth, unnerving them about whether he was about to dart toward second base. At the end of the evening, after the polls had closed, Breslin wrote, "a television showed Barack Obama and a whoop ran through the corridor of the Jackie Robinson elementary school and the election workers were kissing and Ms. Marie Lewis was swaying and swaggering, her feet remembering the start of the long march that got us here" (Breslin 2011, 146).

REMEMBERING

Griffith Stadium in Washington, DC, was near the famous Howard Theatre, the entertainment center in the nation's capital for the black community, a place whose stage featured such musicians as Duke Ellington, Louis Armstrong, Pearl Bailey, and Count Basie. When Frank Sullivan, who later worked on the staff of the Library of Congress, was a youngster, he would hear talk about the Homestead Grays from nearly everyone around the neighborhood. When he was able to attend games on his own, the adventures to the park were ones he cherished. "When the Grays came to town," Sullivan recalled, "the whole community would be excited. It was just like the Ringling Brothers Circus. After the game was over, the people would run out to the field and shake hands with the players, and they'd sign autographs. . . . The atmosphere inside Griffith Stadium . . . was like a rock concert" (Cattau 1990, SM22).

Bob Scott was a 16-year-old pitcher for a local team in Macon, Georgia, when he caught the eye of some of the players of the New York Black Yankees who were barnstorming after spring training in Florida. "I could throw harder than a mule could kick," he said. The Black Yankees signed him up, and he played for one season in 1950, when the Negro National League broke up. He also barnstormed with a Jackie Robinson all-star team. "Sometimes you'll be talking about it and it brings back tears, thinking about the good old days," said Scott, who later worked as a mason in Elizabeth, New Jersey. "Sometimes I think the good white players got cheated, too, because they never got a chance to play against the black players," Scott said. "If you never play against the best, you never know how good you are" (Coyne 2008, 10).

Herman Turner, a retired Cincinnati Public Schools educator, remembered the feelings he had when attending Negro Leagues games. "It was," he said, "manna from heaven. To see black guys play some ball in the white ballpark—Crosley Field—when the Reds were out of town; to eat a hot dog and peanuts for three cents a bag; to see the array of seats and all that green grass!" Turner recalled. "That was exhilarating" (Radel 2011).

Bob Motley began umpiring Negro Leagues games in the mid-1940s. He later wrote about the many star players he saw from his unique perspective as part of the games—about the crackling sound of Satchel Paige's best fastball ripping into the catcher's mitt; about Willie Wells wearing an old coal miner's hat to the plate, before the days of batting helmets; about the difference over the years in the expectations for starting pitchers. "Some Negro League pitchers," he wrote, "were such workhorses that they'd even pitch both games of a doubleheader. Larry Kimbrough of the Philadelphia Stars was ambidextrous; he'd pitch the first nine-inning game of a doubleheader right-handed and then the second seven-inning game left-handed (or vice versa)." Pitchers in those days had no idea whatsoever of such a thing as a "pitch count," Motley wrote. If manager Buck O'Neil of the Kansas City Monarchs would have tried to take star pitcher Hilton Smith out of a game because he had thrown a hundred pitches, "Hilton would have popped Buck in the mouth for saying something so insulting" (Motley 2007, 110).

In 1969, Roy Campanella, the Hall of Fame catcher for the Brooklyn Dodgers, whose career was ended by an automobile accident that cost him the use of his legs, remembered his early, hectic days on the road with the Baltimore Elite Giants: "We played all over the country, from Nevada to the East Coast. We'd go all over the country in a bus. We'd be in Detroit one night, Ohio the next, and Virginia the next. We averaged about 200 games a season. It was nothing to play three games in one day." Campanella especially remembered a day when he played two double-headers in one day, one set of games in Crosley Field in Cincinnati during the day and another set in Middleton, Ohio, that night. "I caught all four games," he said. "I think I am the only player to ever catch four games in one day. I loved to play" (Chass 1969, S4).

On August 28, 1967, Negro Leagues stars gathered for what would be the last East-West All-Star Game. It was played this time at Yankee Stadium rather than Comiskey Park. Governor Nelson Rockefeller of New York threw out the first pitch. The East All Stars took the field with 22-year-old Raleigh Tiger ace Pete Gilliam on the mound, a six-foot, five-inch power pitcher. The age of the pitcher who started the game for the West was somewhat in question; some fans claimed that he was 60 years old, nearly three times the age of the East starter. In three innings of work, the old man faced only 10 hitters, striking out 2. An enormous cheer filled the stadium when he baffled one hitter with a looping hesitation pitch. Satchel Paige, once again playing for a black team after his stint in the major leagues, was named the most valuable player of the game.

Veteran sportswriter Joe Posnanski spent a year on the road with 94-year-old former Negro Leagues player and manager Buck O'Neil, who shared memories and stories of his long life and career. A solid player and the first black man to coach in the majors, O'Neil became a tireless spokesman for the Negro Leagues Baseball Museum in Kansas City, which opened in the early 1990s. In remembering the many players he encountered, O'Neil said to Posnanski, "but before Jackie Robinson there were men who played baseball. And we were good. We could play, man. Double Duty Radcliffe could play. People who saw us, man, we could play. We made a difference in this world" (Posnanski 2008, 235).

They did, indeed!

REFERENCES

Aaron, Hank, with Lonnie Wheeler. 1991. *I Had a Hammer: The Hank Aaron Story.* New York: HarperCollins.

Berknow, Ira. 2005. "Two Men Who Did the Right Thing." *New York Times* (November 2).

Berlage, Gai. 2005. "Effa Manley: A Major Force in Negro Baseball in the 1930's and 1940's." In *Out of the Shadows,* ed. Bill Kirwin. Lincoln: University of Nebraska Press.

Breslin, Jimmy. 2011. *Branch Rickey.* New York: Viking Penguin Group.

Cattau, Daniel. 1990. "Forgotten." *Washington Post* (June 3): SM22.

Chass, Murray. 1969. "Campanella Recalls Negro League Days." *New York Times* (August 3): S4.

Coyne, Kevin. 2008. "Black Baseball's Rich Legacy." *New York Times* (April 27): 10.

Crawford, Aimee. "The First Lady of Black Baseball: Manley Was an Innovator in the Negro Leagues." *Negro Leagues Legacy,* http://mlb.mlb.com/mlb/history/mlb_negro_leagues_story.jsp?story=effa_manley.

Fussman, Cal. 2007. *After Jackie: Pride, Prejudice, and Baseball's Forgotten Heroes: An Oral History.* New York: ESPN Books.

Goldstein, Richard. 2002. "Steve Gromek, 82, a Pitcher Who Is Best Known for a Picture." *New York Times* (March 23): A18.

"Hank's Kind Word Makes Strong Fan of Jack Robinson." 1947. *New York Times* (May 18): M8.

Hogan. Lawrence. 2006. *Shades of Glory.* Washington, DC: National Geographic.

Motley, Bob. 2007. *Ruling over Monarchs, Giants, and Stars: Umpiring in the Negro League and Beyond.* Champaign, IL: Sports Publishing.

Posnanski, Joe. 2008. *The Soul of Baseball: A Road Trip through Buck O'Neil's America.* New York: HarperCollins.

Povich, Shirley. 1947. "This Morning." *Washington Post* (July 5): 8.

Radel, Cliff. 2011. "Negro Games Stir Memories." *Cincinnati: Our History* (February 28), http://cincinnati.com/blogs/ourhistory/2011/02/28/negro-league-games-stir-memories/.

Rampersad, Arnold. 1998. *Jackie Robinson: A Biography.* New York: Ballantine Books.

Rickey, Branch. 1956. Extract of Speech by Branch Rickey, Atlanta, Georgia, January 20. Branch Rickey Papers, Library of Congress, Washington, DC.

Robinson, Jackie. 1963. *I Never Had It Made.* New York: HarperCollins.

Robinson, Jackie to President Dwight D. Eisenhower. 1958, May 13. Dwight D. Eisenhower Library, Abilene, Kansas, White House Central Files, OF-142-A-3.

Robinson, Ray. 1994. "The Life and Death of an Enemy Within." *Sporting News* (October 31): 9.

Rowan, Carl, with Jackie Robinson. 1960. *Wait Till Next Year: The Life Story of Jackie Robinson*. New York: Random House.

Singer, Tom. "The Pioneer: Robinson's Entrance into the Big Leagues Spelled the Beginning of the End for the Negro Leagues." Negro Leagues Legacy, http://mlb.mlb.com/mlb/history/mlb_negro_leagues_profile.jsp?player=robinson_jackie.

Smith, Wendell. 1947. "Bigwigs of Baseball Support Jackie Robinson." *Pittsburgh Courier* (May 17): 14.

Tygiel, Jules. 1997. *Baseball's Great Experiment: Jackie Robinson and His Legacy*. New York: Oxford University Press.

Short Biographies of Key Figures

JAMES "COOL PAPA" BELL (MAY 17, 1903–MARCH 7, 1991)

The quip is ageless—"He's so quick he could flip a light switch and be under the covers before the room went dark." That was Satchel Paige's description of Cool Papa Bell. On the base paths, he was a terror to opposing pitchers and catchers, stealing bases at a rate never before matched in Negro Leagues play and turning normal singles into doubles. In center field, he played so shallow that many balls that otherwise would have fallen for base hits were, instead, turned into outs. At the crack of the bat, he could turn and tear toward a ball hit deep in the outfield and usually run it down.

His sleek 5-foot, 11-inch frame carried only 150 pounds. Yet he started his career as a pitcher with the St. Louis Stars in 1922. It was then that James Bell acquired his nickname. As a 19-year-old rookie, he faced the famed Oscar Charleston in a clutch situation and struck him out. His manager excitedly declared the youngster to be "Cool Papa."

In 1924, Bell became a switch-hitting outfielder with the Stars, leading them to two league titles. After other short stints in Detroit and Kansas City, he joined the Pittsburgh Crawfords in 1933 to play alongside Oscar Charleston, Josh Gibson, and Satchel Paige.

Like Paige and others, he traveled on various barnstorming exhibitions and played for a time in Santo Domingo, Mexico, and Cuba. He ended his active playing career with the Homestead Grays. Like many other black superstars of the Negro Leagues, the end of his career came as blacks were moving into the major leagues. Bell helped tutor such future major leaguers as Ernie Banks and Elston Howard.

OSCAR CHARLESTON
(OCTOBER 14, 1896–OCTOBER 6, 1954)

He had a barrel chest like Babe Ruth, the playing ferocity of Ty Cobb, and baseball skills that rank him as one of the greatest players in the first half of the 20th century. Oscar Charleston, known in the black press as the Hoosier Comet, served in the military as a teenager in the Philippines after lying about his age. At 21, he played in the outfield for the Indianapolis ABCs, displaying speed, power at the plate, and a fierce desire to win.

When the first Negro League was formed in 1920, the ABCs were part of the league, and Charleston soon became its marquee player. One of the leading hitters in all of the Negro Leagues, he also boasted a strong arm and unusual agility.

In the 1930s, Charleston teamed with Josh Gibson to make the Pittsburgh Crawfords one of the elite teams in the Negro Leagues. Later, Charleston became a manager and then helped Branch Rickey scout the Negro Leagues for a player to break the color barrier. Dizzy Dean, who faced Charleston a number of times in barnstorming games, said that Charleston had no weaknesses at the plate. You threw your best pitch, Dizzy said, and just hoped that Charleston would not drill it.

MARTIN DIHIGO (MAY 25, 1905–MAY 22, 1971)

There is a bust of a baseball player at Latin American Stadium in Havana that reads simply "The Immortal." It is that of Martin Dihigo, the only player to have his name enshrined in the baseball Halls of Fame in Cuba, Mexico, Venezuela, and the United States. Buck Leonard, one of the greatest Negro Leagues players, once said that Dihigo was the best all-around player he had ever seen.

It is a well-known story that Babe Ruth began his major league career as a successful pitcher and then, when his hitting prowess became the stuff of legend, switched to the outfield to become an everyday player. Martin Dihigo's story is even more dramatic. He began his career as an everyday player and then, in addition, became a star pitcher. By the end of his career, he had played almost every position on a baseball team and was exceptional at all of them. Blessed with a strong arm, extraordinary speed, quick reflexes, and a natural affinity for the game, Dihigo's versatility was itself the stuff of legend.

Cuban-born, he began his career in 1923 as an 18-year-old second baseman for the Cuban Stars. He played for such powerful teams as the Homestead

Grays, the Philadelphia Hilldales, and the New York Cubans and finished his career in 1944 in the Mexican League.

ANDREW "RUBE" FOSTER (SEPTEMBER 17, 1879–DECEMBER 9, 1930)

In the early years of black baseball, Rube Foster was a towering figure, not only in influence but in physical stature. At six feet, four inches, Foster was an intimidating right-handed pitcher who led the Cuban X Giants to a seven-game world championship against the Philadelphia Giants in 1903. In following years, he made his mark in every important leadership area of black baseball—as a manager, owner, and, eventually, as the organizer of the first Negro League. He got his nickname after besting the great major leaguer Rube Waddell in an exhibition game.

As both star pitcher and manager, he guided the Leland Chicago Giants to a 110–10 record in 1907. A strategist with guile and cunning, he used the bunt and hit and run well before many other teams. After gaining ownership of the Giants in 1910, he joined with businessman John Schorling the following year to form the Chicago American Giants. It was this team, at its South Side Park, that became one of the greatest in the early years of black baseball.

In 1920, Foster organized the Negro National League, the first of its kind. Serving as president, he brought keen insight and determined control to the enterprise, guaranteeing a decent wage for the athletes and giving black baseball a degree of order it had so long needed. For all of these contributions, Rube Foster has often been called the father of the Negro Leagues.

JOSH GIBSON (AUGUST 11, 1930–JANUARY 20, 1947)

He was often called the black Babe Ruth. Indeed, long-time Negro Leaguer Buck O'Neil once recalled the first time he heard the sound of Josh Gibson's bat connecting with a long home run. It was a sound, he said, he heard only a few times in all of his life around baseball. The sound was the same sound that he heard from Ruth's bat.

There is a tragic air surrounding the story of Gibson. So talented, so strong, so respected by fellow players—yet his career came at a time when there would be for him no major leagues. And death came to him at the young age of 35 in 1947, just at the time Jackie Robinson was about to make history.

Like many black players in the 1930s and 1940s, Gibson played in ballparks across the country as well as in Santo Domingo and Mexico. In Yankee Stadium, as well as other parks, he hit home runs that are still the stuff of baseball lore. Some baseball historians claim that he hit nearly 1,000 homers in 17 years of baseball, much of it on barnstorming tours.

When he was the star catcher for the Homestead Grays and Pittsburgh Crawfords, those teams were always among the best. Along with Satchel Paige, Gibson was the man who always drew the crowds and the admiring fans and about whom stories of greatness persisted through the years.

MONTE IRVIN (FEBRUARY 25, 1919–)

When enthusiasts play the game of "what if" regarding the history of baseball, one question that elicits vigorous debate is, "If not Jackie Robinson, then who?" One player who always ranks high in such an exchange of views is Monte Irvin. Like Robinson, he was a player with exceptional athletic skills, not only in baseball but in other sports. Irvin, for example, set a high school record in New Jersey throwing the javelin. Like Robinson, he had attended college. Like Robinson, he was entering his playing prime in the mid-1940s. Before the United States entered World War II, Irvin, indeed, had been very much on the minds of sportswriters and league owners as one of the men capable of withstanding the pressures and competing on a high level in the majors while breaking the color barrier.

Irvin joined the Newark Eagles in 1937 at the age of 18. He quickly dominated Negro Leagues pitching, hitting over .400 in 1940. By the following year, he was named to the East-West All-Star Game. In 1942, he moved to the Mexican League to earn a greater salary, and, a year later, he was called for duty by the U.S. Army. He served for three years.

In 1946, Irvin returned to the Newark Eagles, led the league in hitting and the team to a Negro Leagues World Series win. In 1950, he signed with the New York Giants and teamed with Willie Mays and Hank Thompson to form the first all-black outfield in the major leagues.

WALTER "BUCK" LEONARD
(SEPTEMBER 8, 1907–NOVEMBER 27, 1997)

In their heyday, the Homestead Grays, who won nine consecutive Negro National League championships between 1937 and 1945, had a lineup that intimidated even the most elite pitchers. In the middle of that lineup was Josh Gibson, a menacing home run threat each time he stepped in the box, and Buck Leonard, a powerful, smooth-swinging line-drive hitter who rocketed balls with a seeming ease. If Josh Gibson was the Babe Ruth of the Negro Leagues, then Buck Leonard, many said, was the Lou Gehrig. Leonard was also a sterling performer at first base. The press and the fans began to call them the Thunder Twins.

After beginning his baseball career as a semipro star in his hometown of Rocky Mount, North Carolina, Leonard played for the Portsmouth Black Revels, the Baltimore Stars, and the Brooklyn Royal Giants. By 1934, Leonard had joined the Grays and became a mainstay for the organization for 16 years, an unusually long playing career for the same team, either in the major leagues or the Negro Leagues. In the off-seasons, he, like many of the other top Negro Leaguers, traveled to Cuba, Puerto Rico, Venezuela, and Mexico. When he retired, it was noted that he had been the third highest paid player in Negro Leagues history behind Satchel Paige and Gibson.

In 1952, Bill Veeck, owner of the St. Louis Browns, offered Leonard the opportunity to play in the majors. Leonard, however, knew that he was far beyond his prime and politely declined. He joined his great teammate Josh Gibson in the Baseball Hall of Fame in 1972.

JOHN HENRY "POP" LLOYD (APRIL 25, 1884–MARCH 19, 1965)

In 1910, while playing with a Cuban team on a barnstorming exhibition, Pop Lloyd played shortstop against Ty Cobb of the Detroit Tigers. An open racist, Cobb refused to shake Lloyd's hand when introduced. Cobb once said that blacks should be clubhouse help or in the stands, not on the field. Noted for rough play and especially for high spiking, Cobb attempted to steal second against Lloyd. He was surprised and angered when his spikes slashed into Lloyd's leg and glanced off. Lloyd had put on a metal leg protector under his uniform and tagged Cobb out.

Lloyd was considered by most observers to be the greatest shortstop in the history of the Negro Leagues. In Cuba they called him El Cuchara (the shovel) for his ability to scoop up any grounder in the vicinity. When Babe Ruth was once asked who was the best all-around player he ever saw, he reportedly named Pop Lloyd.

Beginning his career with the Cuban X Giants, Lloyd later joined the New York Lincoln Giants as a player-manager, a position he held on most of the later teams on which he appeared. From 1905 through the early 1930s, Lloyd played on more than 10 teams. At the age of 44, with the New York Lincoln Giants, he was able to win a batting title.

Some sportswriters compared Lloyd to Honus Wagner, the great Major League Hall of Fame shortstop. Wagner later said it was he who was honored by the comparison.

EFFA MANLEY (MARCH 27, 1900–APRIL 16, 1981)

How many women have been inducted into the National Baseball Hall of Fame in Cooperstown, New York? The answer is one. Her name is Effa Manley, one of the most influential owners in the history of the Negro Leagues.

Manley grew up in a black family in Philadelphia headed by a black step-father and white mother. Although it is likely that Manley was fathered by a white man out of wedlock, Effa lived her life as a black woman. In New York, she met Abe Manley, successful in both real estate and the numbers racket, and they married in 1935. Together they organized a Negro Leagues team in Brooklyn called the Eagles and arranged for their games to be played in Ebbets Field, home of the Brooklyn Dodgers. Soon, they decided to merge the new team with the Newark Dodgers, a black semipro team, and moved the entire operation to Newark. It was in Newark that Effa Manley would make her mark in the history of black baseball.

An astute businesswoman, she not only took over the day-to-day opera-tions of the team but also the financial dealings of the Negro National League. Outspoken and loyal to the team players, she was also keenly aware that the Eagles must maintain a positive image, upholding the highest standards of the black community. Active in numerous civil rights causes, she often used Eagles games to promote such causes as antilynching.

Numerous Eagles players such as Larry Doby and Monte Irvin, who went on to stellar careers in the major leagues, often mentioned Manley as an in-spiration, helping them deal not only with on-the-field matters but also with personal problems. By the end of World War II, the Negro Leagues, thanks in part to the business acumen of Manley, were one of the largest black-owned enterprises in the United States.

ROBERT LEROY (SATCHEL) PAIGE (JULY 7, 1906–JUNE 8, 1982)

He was black baseball's greatest showman and raconteur and, many feel, the greatest pitcher in the history of the game of baseball—black or white. Long and lean, with a variety of pitches, many of which he gave special names such as the bee ball and jump ball, Paige also possessed a spectacular fastball that could frustrate most hitters, even if they knew it was coming.

Over a breathtakingly long career that began in 1923 with the Mobile Tigers, a team from his hometown, to a period in the major leagues that began in 1948 with the Cleveland Indians, Paige became something of a legend. He was most certainly the oldest rookie ever to play major league baseball, although his age, like many things in his life, carried an air of mystery. Dizzy Dean, a Hall of Fame pitcher who barnstormed with Paige, said Paige was the greatest pitcher he had ever seen. New York Yankee great Joe DiMaggio, who hit against Paige in winter league ball on the West Coast, said the same thing.

In the early 1930s, Paige was the ace of the Pittsburgh Crawfords, one of the top Negro Leagues teams, but the wanderlust and lure of the spotlight drew Paige to all quarters of the country and beyond to pitch. He played for teams in Chattanooga, North Dakota, Nashville, Pittsburgh, Kansas City, California, the Dominican Republic, Mexico, and Puerto Rico—anywhere he could show off his enormous talent; anywhere he could take on the best who would challenge him; anywhere he could tell jokes, quip, and banter with all who were privileged to watch and listen.

TED "DOUBLE DUTY" RADCLIFFE
(JULY 7, 1902–AUGUST 11, 2005)

Since the advent of baseball, nicknames have been a colorful ingredient of the sport. Ted Radcliffe's nickname resulted from his extremely unusual combination of skills and the fact that a famous sportswriter saw him in action. In the 1932 Negro World Series, playing for the Pittsburgh Crawfords before more than 40,000 fans in Yankee Stadium, he caught Satchel Paige in the first game of a doubleheader and then took the mound himself in the second game, pitching a shutout. In the stands that day was heralded sportswriter Damon Runyon. In his column the next morning, Runyon said that watching "Double Duty" Radcliffe was worth the price of two admissions. The nickname became permanent.

Radcliffe and Satchel Paige were lifelong friends; they grew up in Mobile, Alabama, in the same poor neighborhood and began tossing balls to each other when they were young children. In their long careers in baseball, Radcliffe likely caught Paige more than any other catcher in the Negro Leagues and on many barnstorming tours.

Most Negro Leagues players did not play for any one team for long. Radcliffe, one of the best Negro Leagues players in the game, was also one of the most traveled. From a white semipro team in Bismarck, North Dakota, to some of the most historic Negro Leagues teams such as the Homestead Grays, Pittsburgh Crawfords, Kansas City Monarchs, Birmingham Black Barons, and St. Louis Stars, Radcliffe was an extraordinarily talented and colorful performer and one of baseball's most versatile players.

JOSEPH "SMOKEY JOE" WILLIAMS
(APRIL 6, 1885–MARCH 12, 1946)

When Rube Foster's Leland Giants played an exhibition game in 1909 against a team in San Antonio called the Broncos, Foster was surprised by the sight of the opposing pitcher. The young hurler seemed, in many ways, much like an image of Foster himself. Tall, imposing, with a fastball that punished hitters, the young pitcher was named Joe Williams, and, like Foster, he was from Texas. Soon, Foster persuaded Williams, who was half black and half American Indian, to join the Giants. It did not take long for the flamethrower to earn nicknames. At first, it was Cyclone. The one that stuck was Smokey Joe.

As Williams moved from one Negro Leagues team to another, finally land-ing with the Homestead Grays in 1925, he had become so dominant that even Ty Cobb, who did not like playing against black opponents, admitted that Williams could have probably won 30 games a year in the major leagues. In barnstorming contests, Williams bettered such major league pitchers as Walter Johnson, Grover Cleveland Alexander, Rube Marquard, and Waite Hoyt.

Williams was to the early period of years of black baseball what Satchel Paige was to the later—the best pitcher in the game. On August 7, 1930, at age 44, Williams performed one of the most amazing feats in the history of Negro Leagues baseball. He struck out 27 Kansas City Monarchs in a 1–0, 12-inning victory.

Primary Documents

EXCERPT FROM MOSES FLEETWOOD WALKER'S *OUR HOME
COLONY: A TREATISE ON THE PAST, PRESENT, AND FUTURE OF
THE NEGRO RACE IN AMERICA*, 1908

The odyssey of Moses "Fleetwood" or "Fleet" Walker says much about postbellum race relations in the United States and much about the reasons that it took over a half century from the end of his own aborted baseball career to that day in 1947 when Jackie Robinson took the field for the Brooklyn Dodgers for blacks to be accepted into the major leagues.

While attending Oberlin College, where he studied Greek, Latin, and math, Ohio native Walker joined Oberlin's varsity team as a catcher. His brother Welday ("Weldy") was also on the team. Later, Walker attended the University of Michigan law school. In 1883, he signed with the Toledo Blue Stockings of the Northwestern League. A year later, when the Blue Stockings joined the American Association (which was officially considered a major league), Walker became the first regular black starting player in the majors. He played in 42 games in 1884 and hit .263; Weldy also joined the team and played in six games.

But Walker's major league career was short-lived. Through intimidation and even threats of mob violence, both of the Walkers lost their jobs with the Blue Stockings. Too many powerful owners and players refused take the field with African Americans. Walker continued to play baseball for a time, drifting between several minor league teams, before eventually giving up the game.

By the end of the 19th century, segregation of the races in baseball had become entrenched. Walker returned to Ohio, opened a hotel, managed several movie theaters, and even patented a few inventions related to the motion picture business. But, along with his brother, he also, for a time, published a small newspaper and wrote a short book called Our Home Colony, *which capsulated his thinking about race relations after the years of frustration and anger in his baseball career. Blacks, he had finally concluded, must not continue in their subservient position to whites in the United States. He argued for the separation of the races and for blacks to emigrate to Africa to start a new nation.*

The Negro Problem is the paramount question with over ten million black people in the United States. The relations of the two races, economic social and industrial, are being discussed from every Negro pulpit in the country. Negro teachers and politicians are disseminating their views in every community of black people . . . The leading Negro teachers and writers ask to be let alone with an equality before the law, and a chance to educate their youth, work and save money. The views advanced in the following pagesare not all new and will be found to be opposed to all of those mentioned above. We have endeavored to place facts side by side, and prove that absolute separation of the races is the only true solution of this troublesome question. Our own personal experience, in no way, has been allowed to bias our judgment. No one could entertain higher regard for the American white man and his magnificent civilization than the writer; and it is the appreciation of this fact, along with the infancy of Negro freedom, that forces the conclusion upon our mind that it is contrary to everything in the nature of man, and almost criminal to attempt to harmonize these two diverse peoples while living under the same government. If we have by this Treatise attracted the attention, or discussion of more able men to this phase of the Negro Problem, the result will be our reward.—Preface to *Our Home Colony* by Moses Fleetwood Walker, 1908.

Source: Walker, Moses Fleetwood. *Our Home Colony: A Treatise on the Past, Present, and Future of the Negro Race in America.* Steubenville, OH, 1908.

CLEVELAND GAZETTE REPORT ON 1886 REJECTION OF GEORGE STOVEY TO PLAY IN MAJORS, FEBRUARY 13, 1892

In 1886, George Stovey, a skilled, curve-balling left-handed pitcher, left the Cuban Giants in the middle of the night to pitch for Jersey City, a white team in the Eastern League. The theft of Stovey by the Jersey City team was the work of manager Pat Powers. Stovey pitched so well for Powers and the minor league

New Jersey team that Walter Appleton, a business manager of the major league New York Giants, expressed an interest in signing the young, light-skinned African American to pitch against the Giants' archrival Chicago White Stockings, a team owned and managed by Cap Anson, an outspoken racist. Appleton's deal for Stovey fell through at the insistence of Anson, who refused to play his team against a squad with a black player.

In 1892, the Cleveland Gazette, *owned by Harry Smith, a crusading journalist for black rights, managed to interview Pat Powers about the crucial events of 1886–1887 that further solidified the segregation of black players.*

Manager Powers of the New York League club submitted to an interview recently, of which the following is a part: "During the season of 1886 Jersey City was fighting it out with the then very strong Newark team, and I struck a day that looked dark. Mike Tiernan's arm gave out, and I didn't have any one to put in the box.

"The next day we were to play Newark, and the championship depended on the game. So I had to do some tall thinking to decide upon a play to let the Jersey people down easy.

"By luck I happened to think of a colored pitcher named Stovey in Trenton, a fellow with a very light skin, who was playing on the Trenton team. It was my aim to get him to Jersey City the next day in time for a game.

"I telegraphed a friend to meet me in Trenton at midnight, and went down to Stovey's house, roused him up, and got his consent to sign with Jersey City.

"Meanwhile some Trenton people got onto the scheme and notified the police to prevent Stovey from leaving town. I became desperate. I worked a member of 'Trenton's finest' all right, and finally hired a carriage, and, amid a shower of missiles, drove Stovey to a station below, where we boarded a train for Jersey City.

"I gave Stovey $20 to keep up his courage, and dressed him in a new suit of clothes as soon as the stores opened in the morning. I then put him to bed and waited for the game.

"When I marched my men on the field the public was surprised, and Tom Day, Tom Burns, Tucker, Greenwood, and 'Phenomenal' Smith, of the Newark team, gave me the laugh. Smith was then pitching his best game, and he went into the box. Stovey was put in to pitch for the home team, and dropped the Newarks out in one, two, three order.

"The game ended with the score 1 to 0 in Jersey City's favor, and Stovey owned the town.

"The same season, the New York League team had a fighting chance to win from Chicago, and Walter Appleton of the New York club, was very much in favor of having Stovey sent to Chicago to pitch the last four decisive games. In fact, a deal was fixed between Appleton, the Jersey club, and Stovey to this end. Stovey had his grip packed and awaited the word, but he was not called owing to the fact that Anson had refused to play in a game with colored Catcher Walker at Toledo and the same result was fear."

Source: *Cleveland Gazette*, February 13, 1892, Microfilm Copy, Volume 9.

EXCERPTS OF INTERVIEW WITH
BILL "PLUNK" DRAKE, 1971

Born in Sedalia, Missouri, in 1895, William "Plunk" Drake pitched for several top Negro Leagues teams in the early years of organized black baseball. Playing his first notable games for the Tennessee Rats, a touring team that integrated comedy routines into serious baseball, Drake gained his nickname for his propensity to pitch opposing hitters inside, often leaving many sprawling on the ground in self-defense.

While spending several seasons with the Kansas City Monarchs beginning in 1922, Drake pitched in two Negro Leagues World Series. Like many Negro Leagues players, he played baseball across the country, from North Dakota to California. While pitching for the Los Angeles White Sox, he played exhibition games against numerous white major league players, including Babe Ruth and the Meusel brothers Bob and Irish.

DRAKE: Well, I started in 1914 with a ball club called the Tennessee Rats. I played one season with them, and I joined a ball club called All Nations. We traveled in our own private car, about fifteen ball players of different nationalities—a Jap, an Indian, a Hawaiian, two Negroes, and some whites, and it was called All Nations. I played in 1915 with them, and in '16, I came here to play with the Giants. So I played with the Giants until 1922, and I was traded to Kansas City, and I played with the Kansas City Monarchs.

At that time, they was just about like the old Yankees. I played with them until '26, and after that I went to Memphis, Detroit, Indianapolis. That was about the biggest teams that I played with, and I played with other mid-west teams like Springfield, Illinois and Tennessee. In the winter months, why, I generally go to California and played with a team called the Los Angeles White Sox. We played eight big league ball players in the winter. So I was born in Sedalia, Missouri, June 8, 1895. I'm going on 77 years. So I spent practically about eighteen years, I would say, playing professional baseball for what you might call a "living". Some was good and some was bad, but that's my early days in baseball so if there's anything you'd like to know, why I might be able to tell you if you ask me.

Question: What memories do you most enjoy in your playing experiences?

DRAKE: That's hard to pinpoint, because I have some very fond memories, I recall we used to barn-storm with the Monarchs, and we'd go out in the small towns in Iowa, and we would take our tents and we would put them up and we would sleep in those tents. And we'd go to those restaurants and eat in the days, and in the evening we'd go fish, and we had just a dandy good time. I imagine you can have a better time in big cities like New York, Chicago.

Question: Did the Monarchs play most of their games in Kansas City, or did you barn storm?

DRAKE: No, we played—when I first went to the Monarchs in '22—they had an agreement with the Blues. The Blues were in the American Association at that time. And they devised a schedule, the Monarchs had an equal amount of games to play there as the Blues. So we played all our home games in Kansas City.

Question: What about the away games, was there actually a league schedule?

DRAKE: A league, yeah, we had a league. We formed a league in '20. We had members, the Chicago Americans, the Detroit Stars, Indianapolis ABC's, Birmingham Black Bears, and Memphis Red Sox. Then after that, in '23 they organized an eastern league, and they raided the West, the baseball players went East, some of them. I had offered to go on to Hilldale, but I wouldn't leave.

Question: I remember teams coming through the East like the Homestead Grays and the Indianapolis Clowns, were they in the league, too?

DRAKE: Well, the Homestead Grays were in the Eastern League. The Indianapolis Clowns just played what you might say, exhibition baseball. I knew the Clowns, in fact, a friend of mine, an old teammate of mine was a member, Oscar Charleston. Did you ever hear of Charleston?

Question: Yes.

DRAKE: One of the world's best. Charleston played with the Giants in '21. Our ball club was good enough to play the Cardinals. We played the Cardinals in some barn-storming games at the end of the season.

Question: This is the Monarchs?

DRAKE: No, the old St. Louis Giants.

Question: How did you do in so far as . . . ?

DRAKE: We played eight ballgames, and we won three out of them, wasn't too bad.

Question: Are those the Cardinal teams that Hornsby was on?

DRAKE: Hornsby didn't play, he just come out, frank like and say, "I won't play those Negroes here." Other than that, why, Jess Haynes and Clemens, and Thornare and Doc Levan, McHenry and all the other regulars played eight.

Question: So there wasn't too much of a problem with too many people who wouldn't play, just a few.

DRAKE: Hornsby.

Q1: Just Hornsby.

Q2: What about the Cardinal loners?

DRAKE: Well, you couldn't say they were bad because the schedule they played, they played us and we played them in Sportsman's Park. And you know at that time Negroes didn't go in the grandstand of Sportsman's Park. You know that.

Question: I remember when I first came to St. Louis looking about the pavilion and wondering what it was for.

DRAKE: Well, the pavilion, Negroes sat in the pavilion and in the bleachers.

Question: You could sit in the bleachers as well? I thought it was just the pavilion.

DRAKE: No, the bleachers. The only colored who sat in the grandstand was when I was a knothole gang and those was kids, they would sit back around the forty and . . .

Question: What about other ball players besides Hornsby, you must have barn stormed against some or . . . ?

DRAKE: Yeah, I barn-stormed against Ruth, the two Meusel brothers. And that's all we played on, of course, is ex-big-league ball players. We could play wonderful baseball out there. And Ruth was one of the finest men that ever I met. I know Ruth chewed tobacco. We were playing in Kansas City and Meusel, Bob Meusel, and Ruth came through there and they played with the local white club giving an exhibition of long distance hitting. Bob Meusel would give an exhibition of long distance throwing. And would throw it to the back field, and I said, "Ruth, give me a chew of tobacco." He chewed tobacco and I chewed tobacco, so he pulled his plug out, and I hit it and he hit it and he put it back in his pocket so I couldn't say anything about Ruth, really he was a pleasant fellow. But Hornsby wouldn't play against the Negroes—that's hearsay back in those days, but he didn't play.

Question: Some of the big league players that you played exhibitions against, was it a question of respecting you as a ball player?

DRAKE: They absolutely gave me all the Consideration in the world. I never had any trouble with any of them, big league ball players, so far as being nasty I never . . . and I played against one of the greatest old managers in baseball, Casey Stengal. I played ball against Stengal and he wasn't snotty. See, ball players are a little different people, they don't discriminate like some people do. . . .

Question: I guess whenever anybody asks questions about Negro baseball, they sooner or later get around to asking questions about Satchel Paige or Josh Gibson . . . ?

DRAKE: I met Satchel in 1926. I judged Satchel to be about 17 years of age he was with a ball club called the Chattanooga Look-Outs and I was with the Memphis Red Socks. Well, I didn't pay much attention to Satchel, he was just a big, ole tall boy: I know he could throw hard. And then a couple years later, he came to St. Louis with Birmingham, and I was told how hard he could throw, but he was pretty wild. So that's when I first met Satchel in '26, but I never played on a ball club with him other than All Nations, not the All Nations but I mean the Kansas City Monarchs. The Kansas City Monarchs used to send out a pitcher, like if they were going to play a real hard game, they'd send Rogan up one week, maybe they'd send me up the next week. But that's when I met Satchel, but I think Satchel, when he started to play with Cleve, I think that's when he made his fame. Although I'm pretty sure he played with the Grays, the Homestead Grays but he's a colorful fellow. He should have been a comedian instead of a ball player.

Question: Were there better pitchers, in your opinion, than Satchel Paige in the Negro leagues?

DRAKE: No, no, any time a man can throw I'd say 35, or 32 pitches out of 35 for a strike, no. I've seen the best, from Joe Williams to Slim Jones, all of those, and in my book, he's tops.

Question: Did you get to see much big league baseball after you quit playing yourself?

DRAKE: Yes.

Question: How would you compare Paige when he was in his prime with the top pitchers in organized baseball?

DRAKE: How would I compare them?

Question: Yes.

DRAKE: Right up there with them. I haven't seen no big league pitcher that could do any more than Paige could do. Remember Paige was around 35 years old when he went to the big leagues, an average ball player is through at 35, and he didn't do bad in the big leagues at 35. What do you think would happen if he went there at 25? . . .

Question: Do you remember any kind of press announcements, any kind of newspaper coverage that you would have ever gotten the way the white teams do?

DRAKE: Well, here's what would happen. They always give you a write-up in the late years we always had a score keeper, and they would send that box score to the press, and they would publish it in the morning paper. I've had some nice write-ups from white papers. I remember in Sioux Falls, South Dakota, I pitched a no-hit game there, an awful nice write-up. But so far as we having a press agent or something like that, no, we didn't have anything like that. The only news about us is what some man has voluntarily wrote about our ball team.

Question: In other words, the black athlete had to do something really exemplary even to get in the newspapers.

DRAKE: That's right.

Question: What about the really first class organizations like the Monarchs, did people think of you competing against the Blues? Did people follow you? Did you have the same kinds of fans that would come out to your games all the time and newspaper coverage as the Blues would have?

DRAKE: That was a wonderful reaction, for the Blues to play the Monarchs, it was just something exciting, and the crowds were wonderful. I can't recall now exactly what we did make out of that series, but when we played a team like the Blues, we were off salary. We played what we called "cold" playing, you get a certain percentage of the gate receipts, and they would run maybe a hundred or so dollars. But everybody was up in arms about us playing the Blues and we beat the Blues. But it never happened, we never played them any more. Of course we had a man who could make better contact: Wilkerson could make better contact than maybe Foster or some of those Negro managers or owners could. I don't know that a man could be any better than Wilkerson when they divided a season with him. If the Monarchs were playing 176 games, they divided it, half of them went to the Monarchs, and half of them went to the Blues. So he made wonderful contact.

Question: In Kansas City, did you have your own fans? For instance, were the big ball players of the Monarchs were they the kids heroes in the black neighborhood in the same way as the white ball player would be?

DRAKE: You sometimes couldn't hardly get to the ball park because of those kids all over you.

Question: They knew who you were?

DRAKE: Yes, they knew who you were, and that follows you everywhere. I used to go to a ball park in North. Dakota, and sometimes it would be five or ten minutes before I could get my paraphernalia, one kid would have my glove, one kid would have my shoes, you just couldn't carry your equipment. They'd take it away from you and bring it to the ball park. They just idolized those ball players, see.

Question: You mentioned before that you pitched a no-hit game one time. What other accomplishments in your career did you get most pleasure out of? Do you keep records for example, that you won twenty games in a year?

DRAKE: No, we didn't keep any, there's no record kept of the Negro ball players unless you kept it yourself. We used to kid each other, somebody would say, "Look at him, he's carrying his batting average on his cuff." No, we didn't keep no averages. No one else kept any. There's no where that you can write, there's no paper in the United States that you can write and find out what year I was born and when I started playing baseball. There's no record kept of that. . . .

Question: When the day came, when the Dodgers signed Jackie Robinson, were there any other Negro ball players, do you think, that were more qualified than Robinson to come up first?

DRAKE: Well. I'll tell you what I think. Just like you all are interviewing me. I think that's just what they did to Robinson. Robinson is due a lot of credit, because the boy went through, went through a whole lot. And they had to screen the right type of man for it because the whole future could have been killed by picking the wrong man. That's just my opinion. And Robinson went through quite a deal to make it, and he succeeded. Now there's some ball players, it's very easy for them to play, say for instance, if they wanted to send some white girl in on him or something like that, it would have killed his career. The boy carried himself like a gentleman. You can not take any man and do that with him. The boy didn't drink, he didn't smoke, and therefore he made a good leader. Say for instance, now, you take another man, a rough type that drank and didn't care, he'd 'a' killed the goose that laid the golden egg. So I really believe that they made the right choice when they picked him, and I think that's just what they considered when they picked Robinson, that he was the logical, at that time he was the onliest Negro that was logical for that thing. . . .

Question: Who were the people who got these black teams organized, I mean, how did you find out about a black team playing somewhere so you could go? Who did you have to go see to join?

DRAKE: Well, now, here's what happened. Managers, fellows that owned baseball teams, a lot of them was gamblers, saloon keepers, and he might have three, four hundred dollars, and he might buy a set of uniforms and go buy a team. They was just good sports that liked baseball. In the early days, as I say, the Negroes who owned ball clubs were saloon keepers or gamblers because the average workingman didn't have that kind of money, didn't have the time to buy a set of uniforms. I know, the fellow I worked for, when I come in, Charles Mills, he owned a saloon. He was a saloon keeper, but he had a white fellow in the background Ed Brock. Cause you recall, the Federal only played two years, '14, and '15, and it disbanded in '15. We played here in '16, we played at the old Finley Park which was located at that time at Grand and Laclede. Well, if Mills hadn't had a man like Brock, you ever heard of Johnny Brock? Used to play with the Cardinals? Well, his brother, he was an automobile salesman. Through Brock, we played at the Finley Park. And Rube Foster had a lot of money, C. I. Taylor, they all Negroes, they owned ball teams. It's just some men that just like sports and they'll buy some uniforms. I had a fellow that'd buy seven suits, baseball suits l. He was a bootlegger. He had the money, and I give him the idea. He bought the uniforms, bought an automobile, and I took those seven ball players and jumped in the car and lit out through the South. So that's the way those things in the early days originated. Some man with enough money to buy us some uniforms, now they weren't worried about salary, there was nothing about no salary, ball players would just go out there and play all day Sunday—hee-hee, and ha-ha, that's all they got.

Question: Did they pass the hat at all during the game?

DRAKE: Yeah, I've seen them pass the hat. Now, I think Foster was about the first Negro who had a salaried ball club, if not Foster then old man Leiand, otherwise Leiand handled the Leiand Jets in Chicago. Both ball players, they got paid for playing baseball. That was better than sixty years ago.

Question: What about Wilkinson? He seems so different.

DRAKE: Wilkinson, like I told you, doctor, was a white man, and he thought different. He was strictly business, it was strictly business with him, and the man knew baseball, made Tom Baird he had something the other fellows didn't have, he had a booking agent, see. He had a fellow that used to go out on the road and book games and look out for the team, find out about your accommodations, where you could eat or where you could sleep, and that made quite a difference. I know most of the booking back in those days was through mail, our games couldn't open til after they organized the league. After they organized the league, then they drawed up a schedule where you knowed where you were going.

Question: Did Wilkinson have money besides that or did he actually make money off the ball club?

DRAKE: He made money off the ball club. Where he first got his money, I don't know. He's always been connected with baseball. I know when I first went to him he had the All Nations ball club, and at that time he was interested in a team—Hopkins, Hopkins Sporting Goods in Des Moines, Iowa, and the year before that, he had this woman Carrie Nation, he had her on a ball club as an attraction. You remember Carrie Nation?

Question: Did she come with her hatchet?

CRAKE: I think she left her hatchet at home, but he had her on with All Nations one season.

Question: Nobody drank on that ball club when she was around?

DRAKE: No, no. He had a special car that he traveled around in, and a cook. He ate and slept right on the car.

Question: Do you think it was good business, that he got more out of the ball players by doing it first class? That they really wanted to play? That he could get better ball players?

DRAKE: A ball player is like a contented cow, a contented cow gives good milk, see? And you got to keep your ball players satisfied. A man can't give his best results when he's not satisfied, and to under-pay a man, he's not satisfied. He's not going to give his best. Wilkerson was pretty lucky. He was pretty lucky in selecting the right managers. He had managers that the ball players respected. See, Negro ball players respected a man if he was a good ball player. Now if he was just a mediocre ball player, they didn't pay much attention to him, but if he was a good ball player . . . that's why Charleston and those fellows made good managers, because they were outstanding good ball players. And when a man can tell you something, you agree with him. In your case, a man that never went to school, what can he tell you, you won't pay much attention to him, because there isn't much that he can tell you. You spent maybe fifteen years in school and he hasn't spent any. So to get respect from a manager, the Negro ball player, he had to be a good player himself.

Question: Does it surprise you that some of the best managers like Walther Alston and Earl Weaver were lousy ball players? I mean, one game in the major leagues and . . .

DRAKE: Yes, you do, you think about that. I was thinking about Joe McCarthy that managed the Cubs so long. He never played further class than triple A baseball, I think he played for a while with Louisville, but he turned out to be an outstanding manager. But I don't think a manager is any better than his players. In my opinion, a manager makes a team, and the team makes a manager regardless if you don't have the material to work with, you're not going to do much. But that's always been a mystery, too, why a man like Alston, I think he played one day in the big league.

Question: One time at bat.

DRAKE: And turned out to be one of your greatest—best managers. Look at Durocher, Durocher's one of those fiery managers. He's good and cocky.

Question: Then you get somebody like Ruth. I've heard a lot of ball players say that it's hard for a really good ball player to be a good manager, because everything came so easy to him that he can never tell anybody else how to play . . . just raid the Negro leagues, and Gibson, Page, Campanella, bring in a collection of all-stars and have them play for the Phils, and the league found out that that's what they were going to do, and they made sure the ball club was sold to somebody else.

DRAKE: Why I imagine that was their plan. Campanella, in my estimation, was a better catcher than Gibson as a receiver. Gibson was way farther the best hitter. He was a hitter more than Campanella was. When a man goes big league and accomplishes the things he did in the big league, he's got to be good. Course you know, in Negro baseball, back in those days you only had two newspapers. You only had the Pittsburgh Courier, and the Chicago Defender. Then they had, I think Ches Washington was the sports writer and Fay Young. Naturally, the Eastern ball players always got more publicity than the Western ball players. Now there's any number of good ball players that never was talked about. Nobody heard about them, because nobody wrote about them, and if you don't read about a ball player through the paper, how you going to find out about him? And back in those days, as always, they had to sell the ball players they was going to feature. Just like the Homestead Grays, Cyclone Joe Williams, they use to talk about him being fifty years old and pitching. He wasn't fifty, but we had to do something to attract attention. Everybody wanted to go out and see the man fifty years old play baseball. All the guys in the battery knew he wasn't fifty. He was an old man, and naturally, by writing about him, more people knew about Joe Williams. Just like the bally-hoo about Satchel and Josh Gibson, there's no bally-hoo about Campanella, because Campanella's made a name for himself in organized baseball.

Question: Does it bother you at times that the whole thing seems forgotten now? Whenever anybody talks about the Negro baseball league, whenever any white talks about it, all they can talk about is Gibson, Paige, maybe Williams, everything else seems forgotten? It seems a shame.

DRAKE: That's right. Well, it's just like when a man dies. When our President was assassinated, the country mourned, and mourned, and mourned, nobody now says anything about it. So Negro baseball's been dead ever since '47. When they organized baseball, when they started to put Negroes in baseball, that killed all your Negro baseball. Now there's no place for a Negro to play but in the big leagues, because you don't have no summer pool parks. There's no summer pool park in St. Louis. Where you going to play if you don't play in the little league out on Tandy, you don't have the chance to play any place.

Question: Were there a lot of Latinos in the Negro baseball league?

DRAKE: Latinos?

Question: Latinos and Cubans or Puerto Ricans.

DRAKE: Are there any?

Question: Were there when you played?

DRAKE: Yeah, there was white Cubans, but they were . . . Washington always had Cubans, Costa, Marsans, they were Cubans, but they were white Cubans. They had the same as we have here, the light and dark race. There's white Cubans and dark Cubans. Old man Griffith always did have several white Cubans on the Washington Senators.

Question: No, I meant in the Negro league.

DRAKE: We had one. Mendez, he was . . . the only Latin American ball players they had in Cuba, they had a Cuban ball club, the Cuban Stars. They come through here and played a series of games. They played every team in the league. But they weren't all Cubans, they weren't from Cuba. Molina owned them and they had a Cuban star out East, this little boy, Pompez on a ball club. In the East were Cubans, Rojo and all of them, they all were Cubans, but they was a Cuban ball team, but they played in the Negro league.

Question: Was that when you got friendly with some of the Cubans?

DRAKE: Yeah, that was when I cracked two, three of them.

Question: There's other stories that's part of the myth now, that the Negro baseball leagues were a lot rougher, there'd be a lot more head-hunting, and a lot sharper spikes, that people just took more chances. Is that really true? Was it a lot rougher game than the white baseball leagues were then?

DRAKE: Yeah, that's true, that's true. I played on a ball club where a boy used to file his spikes, he'd cut your throat if you got in his way then. I guess they just didn't know any better. They'd spike you, they'd hit you, they'd hurt you. You had to get out of their way, that's all there was to that. I know I was a rough ball player. I would hit a man, I would throw deliberately at a man. Deliberately I would throw at a man, other fellows, if you got in their way, they'd cut you. That's all there is to that. But them old ball players, they were pretty crass. You didn't hurt them too much, because they knew how to take care of themselves.

Question: You could've played for McGraw, too.

DRAKE: If that's the type of ball player he wanted, I fitted in his program, because I really believe in utilizing respect.

Question: Do you think part of that change because of baseball itself, when guys decided they could hit home runs, that it wasn't worth getting cut up? It was a lot easier to hit a home run instead of trying to steal a base.

DRAKE: I didn't quite get your question.

Question: I was wondering if the reason you think it changed, that people stopped trying to cut people up, do you think it was the baseball itself, that it was a lively ball?

DRAKE: No, I don't think that was important. Ball players got to be more human. Why would you hurt a man that's making $50,000 a year? And put him out for life? Ball players just used more judgment, they didn't do that.

I think they just stopped that themselves. I know just common instinct will tell you, I felt like throwing close to Ruth, but you couldn't do that. You see, you hit a man like Ruth it would be bad, because I've had that experience. I remember one time I was playing in Picher, Oklahoma and we stopped at Baxter Springs which was about thirty miles from there, there was no accommodations there. And Picher, Oklahoma is a mining town, and they had a big chet mine out in left field, and I'll never forget a big old boy named John. He was going up to Cubs, hit a ball off me into that chet mine, hit a home run, and when he sat down on the bench, it looked to me like he said, "I sure hit that off that shine." So when he come up to bat again, I would up and stuck this thumb up like I was going to throw him a curve ball, and I did throw him a curve ball on the outside, two of them, then I stuck the thumb up again and I threw a fast ball and hit him. And I didn't go back there the next day because the crowds didn't like it, they didn't like it at all. You got to be careful about who you hit, if it's a mediocre ball player, but you can't hit one of them stars. Suppose I hit a man like Ruth, what do you think the reaction would have been? You've got to use some common judgment and you'll get along real fine. You just can't hit everybody, I found that out early in life.

Question: Probably would be safer in Cuba.
DRAKE: That's right.

Question: On the way over here, we were talking about all forms of athletics, how there's a lot more organization, a lot more control, a lot more safety measures. So some of you older fellows think that some of these kids are coddled today? If they had to play the way you guys started out, they would have never made it?
DRAKE: When I first come here those old time ball players, we used to have what you call a uniform roll that you carried your uniform in. So I walked in the club house, and I unrolled my stuff. I had the best little shoes, and I heard one of them say, "He must have been doing something, he's got the tools to work with." And they gave me a uniform, and I went out. I throwed. So I impressed them, but those old ball players would watch you, and they wouldn't tell you nothing. They couldn't afford to tell you something, they'd only push themselves out of a job, cause when I came in, they only had twelve ball players on a ball club, twelve ball players. A young ball player come up like that and said, "I play first base" and the first baseman said, "I play first base on this team," and that meant he was going to do everything possible to keep him from playing first base. He wasn't thinking anything about your problems, he was thinking about his own job. It was pretty rough when I come on, awful rough. I fared rough: I seen some rough days, and I seen some good days. I recall, I had a boy, I was managing

a ball club in Tulsa, Oklahoma and the boy wrote me a letter and told me
that he was a left-fielder and would like to have a job. So I wrote and told
him, I said, "Well, if you happen to get up this way, why, I'd be glad to give
you a try-out." So one morning I walked into the hotel, and a boy walked up
and said, "My name is MacIntyre and I'm from so and so and so and so."
I said, "I remember, we're going to work out this morning so why don't you
come along?" So he come along out to the park and he had his glove and
his shoes. I gave him a uniform, and I said, "Trot on out there in left field,
I'm going to hit you some." And he said, "Where's left field? I've never been
in this park before." He didn't know where left field was, so he had a lot
of baseball in his background.

**Question: Did you find it tough as a manager to tell an older ball player that
that's it?**

DRAKE: That's hard, that's hard. You know, I'll tell you, doctor, ball players won't stick together. I had occasion to run into something in Memphis.
They used to have what they called a "Dixie Series" down there between
Birmingham and Memphis. So I went down, I been down there about six
weeks. I thought I'd go down there and cut in that Dixie Series. So they had a
meeting to discuss what percentages we were going to get, so the manager
was going to give the team 35%. So I spoke up, I said, "Thirty five per cent,
that's only 17 or 18%, for each team." So the next ball player to me said,
"You're lucky to be here at all." So I sat down. So we started the series and
they found out they were only getting 17% of the series and they wanted to
strike. I said, "This ain't no time to strike now." "Yes, it is," so they made me
their spokesman. I said, "You fellows aren't going to . . . " "Yes, we are, we
are." So it ended up, I told the manager, I said, "Mr. Lewis, the boys want
to see you in the clubhouse, they're not satisfied." So Lewis walked down to
the clubhouse, I told him just what's what. So he said, "What about you?"
I said, "I'm satisfied." He said, "Looks like everybody's dissatisfied but you,
Mr. Drake." So he made me go round again, right then I said, "The best I
can do is look out for my self cause they won't stick." They'll say anything
in the club house til the boss walks in and not a man has the guts, very few
of them have the guts to speak up for himself. But to tell an old man that's
all, that's a sad story. It's hard to tell a man that. I didn't wait for them to
tell me cause I knowed when I was over the hill. I just hung up my spikes.

**Question: Did you have any idea what you were going to do? While you
were playing, as you were getting older, did you give any thought as to what
you were going to do?**

DRAKE: None whatever. I didn't think about doing anything, and I didn't
do anything for a few years when I began to realize that after I went to the

war, I knew I would get a pension if I lived long enough to get old enough to get it. I got to thinking one day, "When the Social Security comes, I won't have to worry." I went and I worked for Famous and Barr for ten years, when I reached 62, I retired, that was in 1956 that I ever did anything. I haven't done anything since. I got along fairly well, nothing to brag about. I never made any plans, I didn't think about making any plans.

Question: Was that the case with most ball players, too? That "I'm the top man and . . . "

DRAKE: Some of them, some of the ball players are in pretty bad condition. I don't think any made enough money. None of them made enough money to retire playing baseball, that goes for a lot of your white ball players. That's why they established a Pension Fund for them, to take care of them when they get old. I was just more foxy than, cause I could do a lot more things than some of the other ball players could do. I had a way of taking care of myself.

Question: What about the owners? Were any of the owners any help as far as trying to come up with jobs for guys?

DRAKE: You mean back in those days?

Question: Yes.

DRAKE: Hardly any of them.

Question: You were just left on your own.

DRAKE: When the baseball season's over, because the owners never had enough for you to do, you had to get a job to work in the winter to make ends meet, course a lot of the ball players play winter baseball therefore they didn't need no job, that's why I used to play winter baseball, that's why I'd go to California. I always was loose cause I never did like to work, see, so I'd go out to California and play winter baseball.

Question: You didn't think of baseball as working? You enjoyed it.

DRAKE: No, I didn't think a ball player should work. I just didn't think a ball player should work, and I still think that today. I don't think a ball player should work. If you can't make enough money to live off, then give it up.

Question: You don't think of baseball as a job then? The way you would another job. Baseball was something you did because you were good at it, and you were getting paid for it.

DRAKE: But baseball is a profession, that's the way I look at it. It's a profession. If you can't make enough playing, let it alone. But we didn't make enough back in those days to . . . only to live off during baseball season.

Question: When you signed with somebody like the Monarchs or one of the league teams, did you sign a reserve contract, too? Did they have the right to trade you?

DRAKE: I played with the Monarchs five years, just a mutual agreement. I never signed no contract. That's why they laid off Robinson. If Robinson had signed a contract, they would have gotten something for Robinson. They couldn't have snatched him away. Their contract called for a reserve clause. In other words, you couldn't play with another team unless they wanted you. They could trade you, or they could release you, but other than that, you had to play with the Stars, the St. Louis Stars, or you didn't play at all. But Wilkerson, I don't know whether any ball players signed any contracts, I know I never did sign no contract with him. I don't think he had any contracts, cause I'm repeating, Robinson never signed any. Do you ever remember reading about anybody signing with the Monarchs? He didn't have no contracts signed. He didn't have no protection.

Question: Ernie Banks was stolen from one of the teams, too wasn't he?

DRAKE: From the Monarchs. The Cardinals could write him.

Question: The Cardinals were sort of late signing black ball players.

DRAKE: Yeah. You remember the Browns signed a colored boy out of Kansas City, Thompson and Brown, but they didn't do that in good faith. They just figured they might get a little more support from the Negro fans, and the fans are pretty hard to fool.

Question: I know what it did in Philadelphia. The Phillies waited a long time and I remember going out to Dodger games and half the ball park would be rooting for the Dodgers and there was only one reason, Robinson and Campanella, and Newcomb.

DRAKE: You know when Robinson and Campanella, I used to go out to the pavilion . . . there's people who come out to see ball games who didn't know who the umpire was, I've heard them holler about that little old man in the blue suit, "why don't he get out of the way?" They didn't know he was umpire. They used to bring baskets of chicken out there just like going on a picnic. They was just that crazy about Robinson, they was really crazy about Robinson when he was with the Dodgers.

Question: Somebody asked a question on radio a couple weeks ago about the Cardinals, they pointed out on the whole Cardinal roster there's one Negro ball player that they signed themselves and that's Bob Gibson. Every other one they got, they got in a trade. Either the scouts are stupid or they haven't been looking too hard, one of the two.

DRAKE: Well, you know, they claim there's a lot of conflict on the Big Red. They claim the Negro ball players, the football players don't get the consideration the white boys get. It's also been said that the Cardinals weren't particular about Negro ball players, because they could cut too many ball players. They could've got Banks and they could have got several ball players. It kind of shows that they got rid of some good ball players, and the ball players they got today like those Latin American ball players like one of them brothers. What's them brothers' name?

Question: Alou.

DRAKE: Alou brothers, see they're Cubans, or Puerto Ricans one, but I don't recall no other ball players that they signed for. I know they traded for Brock. In fact they haven't had too many, well, they got this boy Brooks Lawrence years ago. I don't know how they come about getting him. Do you remember they had this fellow Lawrence, a pitcher?

Question: Yeah.

DRAKE: They pitched him to death, though. But they seemed to think there's a little prejudice on the Cardinal ball club about employing Negro ball players.

Question: There's been a lot of talk about St. Louis, that the Cardinals were supposed to be the team that was going to go on strike, not play against Robinson. A couple of friends in the National Basketball Association claimed that the reason that the Hawks left here is that the last couple years they were starting five Negroes and nobody would come out to watch them.

DRAKE: Well, you understand, the Jewish population supported the Hawks, and after they lost that, why, they never went to the . . . but they won a lot of praises on up. Hawks basketball. And I don't think you could find a man any stronger racist than Enos Slaughter when he was with the Cardinals. He led all the fights against the Negro ball players. But that's just something in some men that you can't get out.

Question: There's Enos Slaughter and Dixie Walker who was the big leader on the Dodgers and ended up in Pittsburgh.

DRAKE: That's right. Well, the fellows would bring it on in and you can't expect to get it out of them.

Question: Then you get a guy like Pee Wee Reese who's had it bred and bored in him . . .

DRAKE: But he wasn't a racist.

Question: It must have taken an effort for him to realize that Robinson, that he's black, but he's a man.

DRAKE: Well, I don't know, you can take Walker and Slaughter, I don't know how limited their literary training was.

Question: Yeah, that could be. Slaughter never seemed to be the brightest guy in the world.

DRAKE: Well, then he's a hard man to deal with. Walker's from Alabama isn't he?

Question: Yeah.

DRAKE: Dixie Walker, isn't he from Alabama?

Question: Yeah.

DRAKE: It's just in them and it's going to die in them. But Harry Walker, his brother, he seemed to make a pretty good manager. He's dealing with Negroes. And Dixie dealt with them after a man told him he could go back and start picking cotton.

Question: But see here's the inequity of the whole thing—men like you did make that mark, or you made that mark and yet you didn't because it wasn't written down, or you weren't acknowledged as being as good as you really were, don't you sometimes feel a little bitter about it?

DRAKE: I don't feel bitter about it. I only say this, I said this when I received the letter, come along about sixty-five years, if I had come along in those days, I would have had the chance. But I didn't come along, so I don't feel bitter about it. It's just one of those things. It just didn't happen in my time. So I don't have anything to be bitter about.

Q1: That's a pretty wise way of looking at it.
Q2: That shows how important it is to talk to people like you so that kids now don't think that this is the way it always was.

DRAKE: That's right. Why should I feel that the Negro is getting the worst break on earth? Simply because I didn't get a good break, I didn't come along in time. I don't feel bitter. I didn't have the chance, I didn't come along in a day when that opportunity presented itself. Now if I had come along in those days, and I didn't get a chance, then I would have felt very bitter about it. But I think a man should be honest. I really think a man should be honest. But if I had told you that I did feel bitter, then I wouldn't be honest, I'd be lying. That's just the way I look at it.

Source: Oral History T-067, Interview with Bill Drake, Interviewed by Dr. Charles Knorr and Dr. Steven Hause, Negro Baseball League Project, 1971: Courtesy State Historical Society of Missouri-Research Center St. Louis.

EXCERPTS OF INTERVIEW WITH JAMES "COOL PAPA" BELL, 1970

Legendary pitcher Satchel Paige is credited with the quip that Cool Papa Bell was so fast that one time he hit a line drive past Satchel's head, and when Paige turned he saw Bell sliding into second base. Quips aside, the plaque honoring Bell in the National Baseball Hall of Fame in Cooperstown, New York says, "Contemporaries rated him fastest man on the base paths."

The switch-hitting center fielder played for the St. Louis Stars of the Negro National League from 1922 to 1932, leading them to league titles in 1928 and 1930. Joining the Pittsburgh Crawfords in 1933, he played alongside not only Paige but also other Negro Leagues stars who would be eventually honored in the Hall of Fame: Josh Gibson, Judy Johnson, and Oscar Charleston.

After playing in the Dominican Republic for several years, Bell returned to the United States in 1942 and finished his active playing career with the Homestead Grays. As his interview reveals, he actively helped Jackie Robinson prepare for his career in the major leagues.

BELL: See, now our league, the whole wasn't as strong as the Major Leagues because a lot of the ball players wouldn't play because they wasn't making enough money, a lot of them had jobs. But, you pick an All-Star team, and you could play, and have the same chance at beating any Major League team, and in our league, in later years, you could pick three teams out of each league, and put 'em in the Major Leagues, and they would hold their own there, if they had enough men. But you see, we didn't carry but about fourteen to eighteen men. In the Major Leagues they carry, you see, about twenty-five. Now, in a short series, we could beat 'em. You play from three to five games, we could beat 'em. But you play more than that, our pitchers, you know, wouldn't have enough rest. So we didn't have, we kept about five pitchers, sometimes we have three outstanding pitchers. And, it's not that we couldn't get the pitchers if they was making enough money, but so many good ballplayers wouldn't play ball 'cause they wasn't making it, it wasn't paying anything.

When I started, I didn't start playing ball just for money. My brother wanted me to play, if I could play professional ball. I was working at a packing house, and I was making more money at the packing house and playing on the lot. Now the team wanted me to play on Sunday, I pitched and played outfield, I was a pitcher when I played then, I pitched two years professional ball, and I was making something from, around thirty dollars a week working at the packing house. Our guarantee was twenty one, twenty cents, but we were working overtime. And he said I could play ball for him on Sunday, gave me twenty dollars a game on Sunday, then I would make my salary workin' . . . but, now they wanted me to play professional ball. And, I played for ninety dollars a month. But, if I hadn't awent I would have been making more money workin' than playing, you know, on Sunday. And my brother, because he could get along fine, and he said, "Well, just go ahead and play professional ball, professional ball." When I started and got in there I stayed in there for twenty nine years . . .

. . . it was during wartime, we was beating those Major Leaguers, they let 'em go. . . . they wouldn't play but about a month after we beat the Detroit Tigers. They wouldn't let 'em play the whole season, they used to play the whole season. They stopped that, and let 'em only play a month, after the World Series was over. But we was beating 'em so, out there, that word got back, here, to Atlanta, that's when the door was opened. They'd say, "these boys are beating these Major Leaguers out here". Now, they didn't have a full team, they had four or five Major Leaguers, and they had Minor Leaguers, you know, playing. Some of them had some ex-Major Leaguers. And said that, why can't you let these black ballplayers play. And Judge Landis went out there, to see about it. So, he stopped them from playing, but some of them still played, under assumed names. That's the way they did it out there. So they only let 'em play about a month after the World Series was over. . . .

Question: When you heard that Jackie Robinson had been signed, did you think that would be the beginning? Did you feel confident that . . . ?

BELL: Oh, I knew someone would follow. They was talking about it all the time, I didn't think it would happen that soon. In 1945 we played the Kansas City Monarchs, in Wilmington, Delaware, and the secretary of the team, he come to me, and he said that, "I want you to do a little favor." Well, I said, "Yea, what is it?" He said, "Well, I'm telling you, that after the season's over, maybe before the season's over, Jackie Robinson's gonna be signed into organized baseball." . . . And so, they told us, Jackie Robinson is a Major League ballplayer, but his best position is second base. So, either first base, third base, or outfield, he and a little flaw in going to his right in deep short, and they had told Jackie. We'll try and give him another chance, and let him play second base, but he won't play.

And, so he told me, he said, "Now, I want you to hit the ball to Jackie's right." And, I'm the type of hitter nine out of ten I could hit the ball to any field I want. Not that I would get a hit but I could hit it down the right. And, so he was trying to confuse him of that position. And, the first time up I hit the ball so he could had catch it, but he couldn't get in front of the ball. You're not supposed to backhand it. He was chasin' and made a couple of steps before he could pivot and throw it back. And, I beat the ball out. And, the first two times up I did that, and beat the ball out. And, I stole second base and trick slide. We had trick slide, puts his foot up touch that we just pushed other foot back like you see them running up and down slide by the base of a loose bag. He got that from us and I got it from old ballplayer. And, the next two times I walked and I stole two of my four bases. Never did get me out. And, but still when he was in the Major League that he wanted to play shortstop. . .

Question: Montreal?

BELL: Yea, he went down in, uh, he put him on second base when he brought him up, you see. He played, first base, Stanky was playing second base and finally, then Rodriguez said, "The best second baseman in the baseball was playing first base." He was talking about Jackie Robinson, but few people would believe it, because Stanky was a good second baseman. And, so he found a player he could put in there and he put him there. And he stayed there until he, until ten years, when he slowed up some . . .

Question: Perhaps, even if Rickey hadn't it, it was coming. It was going to happen. . . .

BELL: Oh, yea it was going to happen some time soon. But, after he found out that he, made this first step, that's what he wanted. The thing is that there's a lot of those owners wanted black. But, they didn't want to be the first one. Just like my old manager, he said, a black manager, he said, "Who want to make that first step?" That's the thing then. We had guys qualified for it and, but it just never happened. You don't know how the public is gonna react on this. And, you don't know how the ball players gonna react. See, most our black ball players, when they get through playing ball they have nothing to do, but baseball. Here lately they give 'em something to do. But you gotta star out there. Then when you come out, you're not qualified to coach, you're not qualified to scout, even if you made a big name as a ball player and he knows the game and everything, an outstanding ball player, and here he don't have no qualifications. . . .

**Question: How long were you playing, you said playing twenty nine years?
Would that be from 1924?**

BELL: It was 1922 through 1950. See you count it as a season. You don't
count it like you count a year. 1922–23 is just a year, but in baseball, it's two
years.

Question: A season then.

BELL: I was managing a farm team. The Monarchs went out to California during the winter in '48. Cleveland won the pennant. Satchel Paige was
with Cleveland at the time and they was playing some of our boys, but we
didn't have nobody much to play cause all of our best players was gone to the
majors and to the farms of the other majors. So we had to play what was left
and we didn't have too many experienced ball players. Satchel Paige asked
me if I wanted to come and play with them. But I said no, because I wasn't
in condition to play. And we had another experienced pitcher. But sometime
he needed a little relief. But these younger black ball players had the idea
that the major leagues was so much better. But the old players knew because
we had been playing against them—some of the major leaguers. So when
I went out there, I had been developing ball players, and I wasn't in good
condition to play. I was kind of a player-manager of the farm team. I couldn't
stay in condition like as if I was a young ball player. But if we played a tough
team, I'd get in there, after I let them star. But Satchel said, I want you to hit
while I pitch, see. He'd pitch from three to five innings. Then the last game
we played in 1950, we played in Garcia's home, he was with Cleveland too.
Mike Garcia, that was. And he pitched three innings. It was kind of raining,
and they wanted to see Bob Lemmon pitch too. He pitched two innings and
we had to call the game cause it was raining too hard and we won 1–0. I got
a run off Lemmon. But then I didn't play any more.

Question: Larry Doby. Did he play in the Negro Leagues too?

BELL: mmm-mmm.

Question: He did play there then.

BELL: He played on the same team that Monte Irwin played. The Eagles.
And Newcombe. We played against those guys.

Question: So the early players all came from the Negro Leagues?

BELL: Yea, they come from the Negro Leagues. But some of the other
guys. Now, Aaron he was playing with the Jacksonville Redcaps. He just
come on up, from when he was playing D.

Question: And Willie Mays? Did he ever play in the Negro Leagues?

BELL: Willie Mays played in Birmingham. You see, when they first came up, when they was young, most of them was on the bench and the older ones wanted to know why these guys got into the major leagues, but the majors wanted the younger players. There was a man on my team, but they wouldn't take him. I was looking to play myself. I stayed 13 years longer than I intended to play. But I was looking for a job, but I couldn't find one, a regular job that is. We had a boy down in Birmingham and our owner was told that there was a great ball player down there, he couldn't hit the ball, but he could run and throw, but he swings level. All you would have to do was just bring him up. He was supposed to be understudy for me (Bell) because I was going to quit as soon as I got a job. I had the intention of playing with a factory team in Pittsburgh, and working in the factory too, you know. We had a couple of boys already on the team. But they (the owners) wouldn't take the chance on Willie Mays, but look what a ball player he made.

Question: They kind of guessed wrong on him, didn't they? When you were talking earlier, did you talk much about all the different towns that you played? Not just the teams that you played for, but also the many places you played.

BELL: Well, no, we didn't much. But we played in most all the large towns here in the United States. We played in about every state in the New England states up there, big towns, small towns, especially out east. When I played in the West, we would travel a whole lot. Then when I had this farm team from '48 through '50, we played from Los Angeles back up to Canada, we were up in Edmonton, Canada.

Question: Now were these dates arranged singly, or were they pre-arranged like the baseball leagues?

BELL: Yea, they were prearranged. Before we would start, they would make these schedules up and we would follow those. Some times they would get rained out and you would have an open date or something.

Q1: But before the season it was all set up like it is now?
Q2: It was a regular league.
Q3: What was the name of that league?

BELL: We had three different leagues, four different leagues at one time. We had the Texas League, the Southern League, the Western League, that was in this area and then they had the Eastern League, back out there.

Question: Between all those leagues, did you have a World Series title?

BELL: Yes, we had a World Series. Now in this book, Only the Ball was White, I see in this book, they had the St. Louis Stars when they had reorganized again. That was the New St. Louis Stars. The old St. Louis Stars finished here in 1931. Almost all of the major league teams that came through here we beat all of them. The Warner brothers and Bill Terry and Heine Meine and Bill Walker, all those guys . . . we played them all down at Compton and Market.

Question: And you got big crowds for those games?

BELL: Yea, we got big crowds. On off season time, we drew pretty big crowds and we made pretty big money then.

Question: What was the charge of admission to the game?

BELL: I'm trying to think. Fifty-cent, seventy-five cents, maybe a dollar for some seats, or a dollar and a quarter.

Question: How did that compare to what the Cardinals were charging?

BELL: Well, I think at least that, or maybe they were charging a little bit more. The bleachers would be fifty cents, and the pavilion was seventy-five cents. I don't know much about it now, but I mean back in that time.

Question: Did you play much in the South?

BELL: Oh, yes, I played in the South, because we had teams in the South—in Memphis, Birmingham, and then we would play Montgomery and different towns around there. See our league was right here, but we would go down and play those people down there. And then when that was the farm team for the minors, then we played down there a whole lot. We played all around.

Question: But you didn't have any mixed audiences there, did you?

BELL: Oh, yes. Of course, it was white on the one side and black on the other.

Question: There was no major league baseball in the South.

BELL: No. There was no major league ball. And we played in the same parks that whites played in. Course they would have a rope to put across the stands, whites sit here and colored sit there.

Q1: That rope made them feel good though.

Q2: Mr. Bell pointed out earlier that the Cardinal games were segregated until around 1938 or so.

BELL: Until about 1938 or so you couldn't sit in the stands, just in the bleachers.

Question: I used to go to the girls' Knothole Gang and I don't remember any of that. You mean in Sportsman's Park, on Grand Avenue, don't you?

BELL: Yes. It was 1938 until they changed.

Question: Well, I was just a kid, I probably didn't even notice.

BELL: When we was playing here, they would come to all our ball games. We didn't charge them nothing either. But when we'd go there, sometime they's let you in, but sometimes they'd say, "the president's not here," or something. Or, "how many out there" and if there was about ten . . .

Question: You mean that whites could get in free?

BELL: Some of the ballplayers. Like I say though, I don't like to bring up those things to the public. Just like we're taping this. I don't want to be the one to say all that. But most other players or ball clubs would let us in.

Q1: Except in St. Louis you mean?

Q2: If you went to Cincinnati, let's say, you could then?

BELL: Yeah. But I guess it got different a little later on. But I didn't go to baseball games too much here, because I wasn't playing here. I was playing away after 1931.

Question: What teams were you with?

BELL: Pittsburgh Crawfords, Homestead Grays, out East. One year, in 1937 I played in Santo Domingo. We played about two months down there. That's Julian Javier's home. Now it's called Cuidad Trujillo. They changed it about six years ago to the name of the president down there. We went down there to play, but we didn't know that it was a political affair, but Trujillo wanted to get back into office and the people liked baseball down there. The people wanted a championship team to put him back into office. So they sent for a few of us, got people from all around. United States, Cuba, Puerto Rico, Panama. Orlando Cepeda's daddy was on the same team that I was on. He was a good ball player. We won the championship and they got back into office.

Q1: Trujillo, you mean?

Q2: You mean the election depended on who wins the championship? You were recruited for his team in other words?

BELL: Yeah. Satchel Paige was down there first. And he said that he needed some help. We have about five or six American boys on that team. Some Cubans and some from Santo Domingo. It was kind of tough down there.

Then when we come back, we toured the United States under the name of the Trujillo All-Stars. They gave me a whole set of uniforms, so I formed a team, although I didn't know nothing about managing, so we made another guy on the team manager and it seems like that satisfied them. Most people are kind of jealous, you know.

Q1: It was all kind of casual though, huh?

Q2: Of course baseball is enormously popular in the Caribbean. I guess that you drew big crowds, didn't you.

BELL: Oh yeah. We drew big crowds.

Question: Did you enjoy it down there?

BELL: Yeah, but it gets awful hot down there.

Question: Always a nice breeze though.

BELL: In the evening about four o'clock maybe.

Question: Did you play day games?

BELL: Yeah, day games. We'd go out about ten o'clock in the morning. You'd have to grease your face to keep from getting blistered.

Question: So you played all over the United States, Canada, Mexico, Cuba and the Dominican Republic.

BELL: And some of the ballplayers went to the Philippine Islands, but I never did go.

Question: When was that?

BELL: That was back in the twenties.

Q1: In the twenties.

Q2: Oh, yes, baseball was very popular there. In Japan too.

Q3: But I didn't know that early.

Q4: There was a great tour of Japan that the Yankees made in the 1920s. With Babe Ruth.

BELL: Babe Ruth went over there in 1931. He was out in California then. We had two colored teams out there then and we was supposed to play them. We played them, but Babe Ruth wasn't with the team, he was late and met them over there. They did play one team in California and they was supposed to play the other one on the way back from Japan, but they didn't.

Question: Who do you think were the greatest ballplayers you ever saw? I mean, ever played against.

BELL: I played against so many good ballplayers, that you cannot tell who was the best ballplayers. But they are in certain categories. You have number one, number two and number three. And then you have super-stars. The number one ballplayers are just above the number two and so on, and then the super ballplayer he is above the number one. So you have good ballplayers, stars and superstars. Just like picking these guys for the Hall of Fame. Some of them can do a little more than the others, but they are all super-stars. There's not that much difference. One can do two things, one can do three things, one can do all of them. So that's the way baseball will go. You have to have a combination. You have to do two things well. You have to throw and hit. Or if you are a catcher, receive well. If you are an outfielder, you have to be able to hit and run. See, some people can do every-thing. Field, steal bases, hit home runs. You have guys now hit thirty-five runs. But in the old days, you didn't have too many guys hit a lot of home runs. Fifteen or twenty was a lot of home runs.

Question: The ball was dead really.

BELL: Yeah, the ball was a little deader than the ball is today. Some of those balls we played with back in that time, if we were playing today with the different ball, there might be a lot more home runs. We had this boy. Josh Gibson playing catch he was the most powerful hitter I've seen, out of all the hitters I've seen—Babe Ruth and all of them. He hit the ball a dis-tance ball, but cut just right. Not that a lot of guys don't hit the ball as far as he did, but he hit 72 home runs.

Question: How many games was that?

BELL: We would play around 180 or 200 ball games. But now, some parks we use to play in wasn't fenced in. And if it was fenced in, couldn't tell how many home runs he would have hit, cause he hit the ball so far that the outfielders would stand 400 feet or more to catch the ball. We would play mostly two games every day at that time.

Question: Two games a day?

BELL: Sometimes three, some teams even played four. I played three games many a day. It was just my luck that the times we had four games scheduled, the other teams didn't show up.

Question: Did you charge separate admissions for each game? How did you do it?

BELL: Well, here's what we would do. For the three games, we would play a double-header and then a night game. But most times we would play a ten o'clock game, and then just sleep in the bus. We'd get up in the morning and put on our uniforms at eight o'clock and then just go and get something to eat, go to the ball park . . .

Question: Then peel it off at midnight, huh?

BELL: Sometime when we would get back home, it would be three, four o'clock the next morning.

Question: Did you travel mainly by bus?

BELL: Sometimes, by train, but they wasn't fast enough because they didn't make these small towns. So every team carried by their own bus. According to the times, they was doing all right, but it was just hard. You couldn't make enough money during the baseball season to hardly live out the winter, so you would have to find a job somewhere. That's why a lot of us played winter ball . . . Yeah, it's just a shame that the public doesn't know about these black ballplayers and, you know, it's just a shame.

Question: Who are some of these black ballplayers that you think that the public ought to know about and don't?

BELL: Well, they write about some of them. We had a kid when I first started named Samuel Bennett, we had George Meyers, Ted Trent and Davis and Wells, Willie Wells, one of the greatest of all the shortstops.

Question: This was in the 1920s?

BELL: Yeah, this was in the twenties. Right here, playing on Compton and Market. He started with us in 1924 and he played through 1931. But some of the old ball players now won't speak up like they should. They have favorites. But I don't care what color a ballplayer is, if he can play I give him credit for playing. I haven't seen no ballplayers who could beat Wells. They used to send scouts out to scout the colored ballplayers to pick the All-Stars and they had some scouts looking at Wells and one of the scouts wrote back that, "They got a shortstop out there that you could put six big-league shortstops out there and they couldn't catch the balls that he catch, if you put them all out there at one time." But we used to say little things like that, but he was the greatest fielder I've seen. We had a lot of good ballplayers, outfielders, catchers, infielders, first basemen. We had a great first baseman named Buck Leonard who played out East with me; and George Suttles, a big fellow we used to call Mule Suttles; and an outfielder named Turkey

Steams who hit the ball as far as anybody, as often as anybody; and Chino Smith; John Beckwith; and Oscar Charleston, supposed to be the greatest ballplayer back when McGraw saw him and said that he was the greatest ballplayer he had seen. Course there has been other ballplayers come up since then, you know. . . . Just like Satchel Paige said that I was so fast that I could turn off in the room; the light and get in bed before it got dark and that I was sliding through his legs at second base and the ball hit me in the back. Well, that's just something that Satchel says.

Q1: Well, Satchel has become famous for that.
Q2: He should have been a comedy writer.
   BELL: I broke the record from second base. The record in the major leagues is 13.3 and I did it in 12. A guy named Swanson had the record, with Cincinnati, I believe, and Archie Deacon, a St. Louis boy broke his record.

Question: Is that swinging the bat and then running?
   BELL: No, that's just starting from the plate.

Question: Were you right hander or left hander?
   BELL: I was a switch hitter.

Question: Were you ever clocked on how fast you could get down to first base?
   BELL: Here in St. Louis they say that I got on the base in 3 seconds.

Question: That's faster than Mickey Mantle.
   BELL: Between first and third base, I could go there in about four seconds and a half. Course, by the time you get there you begin to slow down.

Source: Oral History T-015. Interview with James "Cool Papa" Bell, Interviewed by Dr. Arthur Shaffer and Dr. Charles Korr, Black Community Leaders Project: Courtesy State Historical Society of Missouri–Research Center St. Louis.

EXCERPTS OF INTERVIEW WITH ERNEST BURKE, 1998

Born in Maryland on June 26, 1924, Ernest Burke lost both of his parents at an early age and was raised by a French Canadian family in Iberville, Canada. He returned to the United States to enlist in the U.S. Marines during World War II and fought in the Pacific. After leaving military service, he played for the Baltimore Elite Giants from 1946 to 1949.

After leaving the Elite Giants, Burke played for teams in the Western League and the Canadian Provincial League, appearing as a pitcher, third baseman, and outfielder.

Question: Okay, Mr. Burke, where were you born?

BURKE: I was born in Perryville, Maryland, 1924.

Question: As a child what recreational activities were available to you?

BURKE: When I was a child we had a stick. We rolled a rim or tire, and that was the only athletics that I have done, and all the rest of them in my neighborhood. I was the only black that lived in Perryville, Maryland, my family and that's the only recreation white or black had.

Question: Tell me about your first exposure to baseball, and when you first played.

BURKE: I entered into the Marine Corps in 1942—and I started playing baseball in Hawaii there and we won the, the Pacific Championship, and from that day forth I just kept playing, and I played such, against such men as Johnny Wrigley was in the CB's in the, in service, and he told me as good as I played I should be playing in the Negro League, which I didn't know anything about the Negro League, and so when I got out, ah I contacted the Baltimore Elite Giants in 42 ah 46, and uh, I continued on and played for them for two years, and what made, it so good, I didn't go on the farm team. When I joined them I came right up to the first, string, team, and I played with them for two years and then I played for the Canadian League.

And getting back ah, as far as the Negro League is concerned there was a lot of discrimination, a lot of times you couldn't go into restaurants to eat, ah you couldn't stay in the hotels, proper hotel not unless you were in a black neighborhood. We traveled by bus. A lot of times we had to change clothes in busses, an, and get out and play, an, and sometimes I remember even got behind a scoreboard or, or billboard and changed clothes, to play, baseball. And there's a lot of parks you went to that we wasn't allowed to use the locker rooms, and, showers and all that sort of thing.

It was bad, it was really bad, but overall we still had fun doing these things. We got in the bus, we had, we had jokers, and, guys that tell stories, and it was one big happy family. I can remember I, back there in those days they didn't slice bread they had a whole loaf of bread, and you'd go to the store and get a, we'd call it a chunk of bologna, but it was a, real thick piece of bologna and a onion and ate it and ah some bread. I can remember when I dug out the center of, of the bread and poured a can of baked beans in it, and take the inners, inners and, and sop the juice up, and ate that, and then got out and pitched nine innings.

I mean nine innings no reliever, no middle man, I don't know it's just, it was just, something else, but we survived. . . .

Question: How did your family, friends, and acquaintances react to you, as they became aware that you were a member of the Baltimore Elite Giants?

BURKE: Well I had family and friends they really was happy for me, that I was playing organized baseball. Even down, I had the team to come up an, and Havre de Grace, Maryland, and play, the little small teams there, a couple of times, and, you should seen the people turned out, white and black I mean, little stadium was full of people, lined up all down the lines, and, and everywhere that I came there and that the Elite Giants, that I played for, the Baltimore Elite Giants the team that I played for, was coming to Havre de Grace to play the little minor teams, and everybody said, "I never dreamed of a team like that coming here and playing." And I was responsible for it, and that made me feel good that the people responded.

Question: You mentioned travel conditions; tell me what, what travel conditions were like when you played outside of Baltimore?

BURKE: When we played outside of Baltimore, ah travel conditions, like I said before, it was bad, because if we stayed, went to a small town, especially a southern town, and pulled up to a gas station or something like that, they would come out and say what do you niggers want here, what can I what, what do you want, and we'd say we want gas. And they'd tell us to pull over to the side we'll get you in a minute. And I can remember one time we stayed at a service station almost two hours, before they came out and said, "You niggers back the bus up here and I'll give you some gas." And we had a bus, and it hold thirty or forty gallons of gas, and we asked him to fill the tank up, and he said, "well I'll give you five gallons of gas, and get your ass out of here, we don't want you niggers down here anyway." And that sort of things, you know, you had to hold your, hold your tongue, and ah, for people to come up and say things like that to you. I mean it's really something else. I could never believe that people would be so harsh, and so, so evil against another man because of the color of his skin.

Question: With travel where would you stay as a team?

BURKE: Well when we went to large towns, or large cities, they had the black neighborhood, an, and they had hotels, and a lot of people didn't have hotels, they had rooms that our owners used to rent for years, and years, and years every time we went there, so it was, you know, they knew that we were coming, so they had the rooms ready for each, for at different people's houses. And like when you're down south we stayed at houses, and there's one lady that owned a farm, her and her husband, and she used to feed, it makes no difference what ball team came there, she used to feed them, although we paid for it, but it was just like, I don't know, being in a camp or something like that, because they had the table set up with milk and, and just good food, and we'd go there to eat two times a day, or three times a day. And, you know, when we traveled we got two dollars a day for eating money . . .

Question: How did the pay as a baseball player compare to the pay non-baseball players earned for various jobs?

BURKE: Well, I can speak for myself. I got three hundred and fifty dollars a month, two dollars a day for eating money, and that's no comparison to what the white ballplayer was playing. And deep down in my heart, and it proved to be true that we were much able better ball players than the white, because we played, used to barnstorm against the, the white all-star teams, they used to pick up a all-star team, and we used to play. We used to beat them, sixty percent . . .

Question: Do you remember some of the players from the Major Leagues that would play in these all-star games?

BURKE: It's been so long ago, it, I know Al Kaline, I know Ted Williams um, oh Christ it's been so long ago I can't think of all of them, but those the ones that actually stuck in my mind.

Question: In what ways did the Negro League affect the black community?

BURKE: When we played in the Negro League before Jackie broke the color barrier, they supported us one hundred percent, one hundred percent. The stands was always full regardless of where you went. We had a east and west game that that we played in Chicago, Comiskey Stadium, and that stadium was packed. I mean it was standing room only, and it was packed, cause people come from all over the world, to see the all-star game there. And, as a, a phrase was made, when Jackie Robinson broke the, color barrier, says it was a damn shame for five hundred or, or eight hundred people to lose their job over one man, for to break the color barrier, because all the good ballplayers went into the Major Leagues, and that's when the, the Negro League folded.

Question: Did your playing season coincide with that of the Major League?

BURKE: Yes . . . The only difference, where the Major Leagues, they played, you know, one or two days, and, and traveled, and, and they had their day off here, and a day off there. Well we, when we wasn't playing in a league, we played every day, to in order to make money, so we'd get our pay. You know, and that's the way we, we played every day, and we traveled three, four hundred miles between games, different cities, and played. Sometimes I, I know that we left, got on the bus here in Baltimore, we went to Cleveland and maybe played a doubleheader, and we left Cleveland, and maybe went to Chicago and played a tripleheader where there's two team play, you know, four teams play, you know. And leave there and go to Texas, and make this, make this circle and end up back in Baltimore. And, I tell you, riding in the school bus, that was no picnic. We didn't have the seats that laid back or anything, but later on in the years that was something else, that was just like getting off the floor sleeping in a feather bed. It was just that much difference, with air conditioning . . .

Question: How did the Negro League players react in 1947 to the news that Jackie Robinson broke the color barrier?

BURKE: Well, they act great. They were happy, but as I always say, you know if you open up a crate of apples there always going to be one or two bad ones in there, and that's the same way with the Negro League players. There's always one or two saying, "I should have made it, I should have been picked." But ah, deep down in my heart I think Branch Rickey did the right thing by picking Jackie Robinson over all of the other Negro League players. Because, you must realize when Jackie went broke the color barrier, and he went to Montreal to play, all they wanted him to do was fight back, or call names or something, and they said well that's what you expect out of blacks. That's what you expect they can't handle the situation, and he didn't do that, and that's what broke, the color barrier. That's what went into the white society that he was there. See a white society said "The pastime of baseball was for whites, and whites only." And then when Jackie Robinson went up there, and broke the color barrier, they just opened their mouths and couldn't believe it. That's the reason why they wrote threatening letters, and death threats, and, called him all kinds of names . . .

Question: In what ways did your experiences as a Negro League player change your life and, and your future?

BURKE: Well it's just like I said when I first started playing baseball, in the Negro League, I signed a contract, and I was doing something that I like and I was getting paid for it, and it, it made me feel good to walk into Yankee Stadium or any of the Major League ballparks as far as that's concerned. It made me feel wonderful.

Source: Special Collections Department, Langsdale Library, University of Baltimore. Used with permission of the University of Baltimore

EXCERPTS FROM *CHICAGO DEFENDER* ARTICLE
ON THE FIRST NEGRO LEAGUES WORLD SERIES
CHAMPIONSHIP, OCTOBER 27, 1924

In 1924, executives of the two Negro major leagues—the Negro National League (NNL) and the Eastern Colored League (ECL)—decided to hold the first Negro Leagues World Series. To generate excitement across the country, the series would not only be held in the hometowns of the respective teams but also in parks in other major venues of black baseball. In all, the series would encompass a nine-game schedule pitting the Kansas City Monarchs, winners of the NNL, and the Hilldale Club, champions of the ECL.

The Monarchs, led by their pitching tandem of Wilbur "Bullet" Rogan and Cuban star Jose Mendez, both future members of the National Baseball Hall of Fame, faced the powerhouse Hilldale Club of Darby, Pennsylvania, a suburb of Philadelphia. First established as a boys team in 1910, Hilldale, led by manager and then owner Ed Bolden, assembled a squad that won the first ECL pennant in 1923. They featured a lineup that included such greats as catcher Raleigh "Biz" Mackey, third baseman William "Judy" Johnson, and left-handed pitcher Jesse "Nip" Winters, all three of whom were later enshrined in the Hall of Fame.

Philadelphia hosted the first two games of the series, followed by games three and four in Baltimore; games five, six, and seven in Kansas City; and the final games in Chicago. Game three in Baltimore ended because of darkness with the score tied 6–6 in the 13th inning. After Kansas City won the first World Series championship five games to four, the Hilldale Club took the second series between the same clubs a year later.

"KANSAS CITY WINS CHAMPIONSHIP: DECIDING GAME BEST OF SERIES: PITCHERS' DUEL TO MENDEZ, 5–0"

By Frank A. Young

The Kansas City Monarchs were crowned champions of the baseball world Monday afternoon when they won a pitchers' battle that had raged for seven innings between Jose Mendez, veteran Cuban twirler and manager of the Kansas City Monarchs and Lee, the underhand ball artist of the Hilldale club, Eastern champions. The final score was 5 to 0, the Monarchs staging an attack in the eighth that would not be denied. They hit Lee for five of the six hits he yielded in that frame. The game was far better than the score shows. In fact to say that the game was one of the best ever played in Chicago by any two teams would not be exaggerating and to say it was the best seen in recent years would be only telling the truth.

In fact the whole series has been hotly contested. Both teams have felt the pressure and have at times made misplays due to overanxiety or excitement.

Hilldale Good Club

To say the Monarchs won because they played better baseball than the Hilldale team would hardly be fair to either club. It would not be the truth, for after seeing the Easterners show the fight and play the game as they play it, it will be safe to say that Hilldale has a most wonderful ball club whose infield is just as good if not a trifle better. The outfield of the Hilldale club outclasses that of the Monarchs. In Thomas and George Johnson Hilldale has a group of fly chasers that any major league owner would buy if they were white.

I am not going into the merits of the given players at this time, but I am going to say that it seems as though it was not for Hilldale to win this series.

The attendance record shows that Chicago outdrew Baltimore and that Philadelphia outdrew Kansas City and Chicago with that Saturday crowd. Chicago, although the fans apparently wanted to see the two teams play, did not have the Sunday attendance that Kansas City had.

To the Philadelphia dailies and the Kansas City dailies credit must be given their sports departments, the Ledger and Bulletin in Philly and the Kansas City Star-Times and Journal-Post giving front page space and carrying the scores play by play. The Journal-Post went so far as to use the pictures of Winters and Rogan in the Sunday morning edition, the first time in history of the paper that a Colored man's picture, other than Harry Wills', found its way into print unless he had committed a crime.

The opening game of the series was won by the Negro National league champion with Rogan pitching 6 to 2. Winters came back the next day and the Monarchs were like babies before his baffling delivery. The clubs moved to Baltimore where the game was tied in the fifth. The Monarchs took the lead in the ninth only to have Hilldale tie up the county. The Western club took the lead again in the twelfth only to have it tied again. The umpires called the game at the end of the thirteenth. In the play-off the following day, Monday, Hilldale came from behind to tie the score in the last of the third and won a 4 to 3 in the last half of the ninth.

The series moved to Kansas City, opening there on Oct. 11, continuing there on Oct. 12 and 13. Rogan lost to Winters on the opening day in the Missouri city when the Hilldale club, going to bat in their half of the ninth with the score 2 to 1 against them, hammered out the tying run and three more, winning 5 to 2 giving them a lead of three games to one. On Sunday the Kansas City club backed William Bell up with some good fielding and won 6 to 5.

Again Hilldale came from behind to tie the score in the fourth. Kansas City took the lead in their half of the fourth and Hilldale, fighting as they always were, tied it up in their half of the sixth. It remained until the eighth when Sweatt's triple sent Moore in with the winning run.

After a day's rest, Winters lost a 12-inning game to the Monarchs, Mendes getting credit to a win when he relieved Drake in the tenth with the score tied, one on and one out. Sweatt tripled and Rogan then hit to Judy Johnson and the throw to Carr caused him to pull his foot off the bag and S. Bell, who ran for Sweatt, scored.

Then came the Chicago games. Currie lost a game that should have been his. Itube pitched splendid ball but could not win. The ninth was too much. Yet Currie surprised lots of Chicago fans.

Lee made the mistake Monday of changing his style of pitching. As long as he threw the underhand ball the Monarchs had made but one hit up to the eighth. When he changed his style away went the game on healthy swats by the Kansas City club.

The series is history now . . . All in all it was a great series, a forerunner of something that is to become an institution in our midst each year, and the best thing that ever happened for Colored baseball.

Source: Courtesy, *Chicago Defender*

EXCERPTS OF INTERVIEW WITH
LARRY DOBY, 1996

The story of Jackie Robinson breaking the color line in major league baseball with the National League's Brooklyn Dodgers on April 15, 1947, and his courageous stand against the racial slurs and hostility that it entailed became a central focus of sport legend and lore, both at the time of his momentous struggle and through the years. Largely shadowed by Robinson's epic battles is the story of Larry Doby. On July 5, 1947, less than three months after Robinson's first game with the Dodgers, Doby took the field as a member of the American League's Cleveland Indians.

A lithe athlete who starred in basketball, football, and baseball at Paterson, New Jersey's East Side High School, Doby joined the Newark Eagles in 1942, spent two years in the U.S. Navy, and then rejoined the Eagles, leading the team, along with his friend Monte Irvin, to the 1946 Negro Leagues championship over the Kansas City Monarchs.

When Cleveland Indians' owner Bill Veeck signed Doby to become the first black player in the American League, it placed on the young center fielder the same kinds of intense racial pressures faced by Robinson. As Robinson did, Doby battled the bigotry with uncommon grace and toughness, standing his

*ground against threats and insults to become a major league star and member
of the Baseball Hall of Fame. He was the first black player to jump directly from
the Negro Leagues into the majors, the first black player to hit a home run in
the World Series, and the first black home run champion.*

I didn't know any of the guys or idolize a ballplayer or look up to anybody
when I started my career. Actually, I hadn't seen too many baseball games because there weren't many Negro League teams coming through my hometown
of Paterson, N.J. In my senior year of high school, I saw some Negro league
players, but I didn't model myself after any of them. However, as I came out of
high school and started playing with the Negro leaguers, I desperately wanted
to be a part of it. I loved the way the players went about their business with
smiles and enthusiasm and energy. I ended up playing about two years in the
Negro leagues, and they were good years, years full of fun.

I have seen some of the guys over the years, and it's pretty amazing to think
that even though we're older and we've all gone through so many ups and
downs in all these years, we still talk about those days and get these great big
smiles. I was a very young man when I played Negro League baseball, but it
was the kind of baseball that I'll never forget. I played a couple of months after
high school, then I went to the service, came out and played for Newark in
1946. And then on July 5, 1947, I went to Cleveland—the major leagues. It all
seemed to go pretty fast.

The big thing I remember about the Negro leagues is getting paid to play
baseball. Honestly, I probably would have played just for the fun of it, without
getting paid. Another thing that was important to me was getting to play with
and against some great ballplayers in their own right—Josh Gibson, Satchel
Paige, Cool Papa Bell, Buck Leonard. They were all great guys who could really
play the game.

It's a shame more of them didn't get a chance to play in the majors.

Buck O'Neil is right when they ask him if he's upset that he didn't get the
chance to play against the best ballplayers in the world. Buck looks them in the
eye and says to this day that he played in the Negro leagues—and who is to say
that the Negro leagues didn't have the best ballplayers in the world? I agree
with him. I know that if the chance to play would've been there, there are many
African Americans who could've played back then. But that's the past. I loved
playing with those folks in the Negro leagues. It was much easier playing with
those guys. It was a lot easier just being one of the guys than being the first
African American to go in the American League. I came in only 11 weeks after
Jackie Robinson came into baseball with the Dodgers, so I faced the same type
of segregation and prejudice.

As far as I was concerned, I was just 18 years old and things in the Negro
leagues were incredible. I couldn't wait to get to the ballpark every day, riding

the bus and all that stuff—I never thought it was that tough. A lot of people say it was a tough thing, but I didn't think it was that tough because you got on the bus and did what you wanted to do. If you wanted to sleep, you went to sleep. If you wanted to stay awake, you stayed awake and partied with the other guys. Somebody wants to sing or play cards or whatever, you did that. Let me tell you, though—the guys who sang were usually the guys who thought they could sing.

Seriously, though, we had a lot of fun just being together and with everybody in the same boat, so to speak, we were close and had good times doing the simpler things. We'd go to Kansas City or Pittsburgh and we'd get the good crowds and we knew that we were doing well. We saw the faces of the people watching us in those stands and we knew they loved watching us play the game of baseball. We played together on the field and hung out as a club a lot off the field.

Associate and communicate, that's what we did back then, and we didn't need anyone to break it down for us. When you're having fun, you don't try or care to little out why.

It wasn't as much fun at the beginning of my major league career, though. A lot of guys kept to themselves, and I was very much alone in the beginning. I didn't feel like I could do anything on that bus the way I could in the Negro leagues. It's funny how you remember. I had a couple of Cleveland scouts looking at me at the time. In early June, I went to a ballgame with a scout—the Yankees were playing Cleveland—and then July 4, we were playing a doubleheader in Newark. I played in the first game, and then the second game, my teammates gave me a going-away present. There wasn't jealousy. No one was saying things like, "Why not me?" or "Why is this kid going?" And that wasn't because they were any less competitive. It was because they cared and some of them could see hope in a kid with some talent going to the big leagues. They were happy for me and wanted to show me they were proud, telling me to go for it.

I got on the train to Chicago and signed a contract on July 5. It was clear-cut. You knew what you had to do. If you played well, you stayed and you got your chance. If you didn't play well, you weren't going to be on the team. I'm happy the way things worked out because if you went through the minors, you'd be going through the same problems and the same segregation but without being at the very best level. Going from the Negro leagues to Cleveland was a good thing for me. I also preferred not going to the minors, going through more and more towns where I wouldn't be able to stay at the same hotels or drink at the same water fountains as the other guys. I went straight from the Newark Eagles to the Cleveland Indians. The rest as they say is history.

Source: Larry Doby and Mark Balk, "The Pioneer Leagues," *The Sporting News*, March 4, 1996, 47.

"AS 'SPEEDBALL' SATCHEL PAIGE AMBLED INTO THE EAST-WEST GAME AND SIMPLY STOLE THE SHOW," *PITTSBURGH COURIER,* SEPTEMBER 1, 1934

The East-West All-Star Game was the brainchild of two enterprising black newspaper reporters, Bill Nunn of the Pittsburgh Courier *and Roy Sparrow of the* Pittsburgh Sun-Telegraph. *The man they approached to make it happen was black entrepreneur Gus Greenlee—banker, nightclub owner, central figure in a numbers racket, boxing promoter, and the owner of the Pittsburgh Craw-fords. It was Greenlee who, in 1932, financed in Pittsburgh the construction of the first Negro Leagues park—Greenlee Field—that rivaled some of the parks of the major leagues. A year later, the innovative Greenlee, in the midst of the Great Depression—which was not only especially hurting the black popula-tions across the country but also attendance at Negro Leagues games—saw much wisdom and possible profit in the idea of the two sportswriters to high-light, as never before, the abilities of black baseball stars.*

After extensive negotiations headed by Greenlee, the first East-West All-Star Game was scheduled for Comiskey Park in September 1933. The players were chosen by ballots submitted by fans to black newspapers, most prominently the Chicago Defender *and the* Pittsburgh Courier. *So successful was the first game in 1933 that the All-Star game in Comiskey became an annual event, sometimes drawing as many as 50,000 spectators.*

The second East-West All-Star Game, called "epic" by Bill Nunn, featured the exploits of the great Satchel Paige.

By William G. Nunn
Comiskey Park, Aug. 26.
We saw a baseball epic unfold itself on this historic field this afternoon.

No diamond masterpiece was this game! No baseball classic! Those words are relegated into the limbo of forgotten things in describing the titanic strug-gle for supremacy which marked the second meeting of the baseball cream of the East and the West, in which the East won 1–0 and evened up the series at 1-all.

And Satchel Paige, sensation of the Pittsburgh Crawfords, "stole the show."

NO GREATER EPITAPH—

No greater epitaph can ever be written about the man who ambled to the pitching knoll in the sixth inning here this afternoon with 25,000 wild-eyed fans on the edge of their seats, with a man on second and none out—retired the side while that man fiddled nervously around the keystone station, and then went on to give one of the greatest mound exhibitions modern baseball has ever seen as he twirled three more scoreless innings to enable the East to chalk up their first victory.

Today's game was more than a masterpiece! It was more than a classic! It was really and truly a diamond epic! . . .

This article is a paean of praise to the "man who stole the show" and to the marvelous performances of those diamond stars of sun-tan hue, who once again demonstrated to the world at large that they are on a par with major-league performers. For those two teams reeled off a "once in a lifetime" performance.

Close your eyes if you can for a moment. Comiskey Park, situated on the Southside, is a natural amphitheater. The double-decked grandstand extends to the far reaches of right-center and left-center field. Only in deep center are bleacher seats.

Sunday was one of those perfect baseball days. Not a cloud in the sky to mar the perfect azure-blue of the heavens . . . And the lower tier, as far as the eye could reach in all directions, packed with thousands and thousands of people, who came to the game. The official attendance was 20,582. Figures from the gate, however, informed us that more than 25,000 fans were on hand to witness the game. Of that number, more than 4,000 were white. . . .

No greater pitcher ever performed at Comiskey Park than did the Satchel Paige of Sunday.

Old-time patrons of this park who have seen the burning speed of Walter Johnson, Ed Walsh, Smoky Joe Wood, Lefty Grove, Rube Waddell, Schoolboy Rowe, and other American League immortals and have witnessed the curves and brainy twirling of such unforgettable as Addie Joss, Russell Ford and Wild Bill Sullivan will concede the fact.

Paige today was unhittable . . .

Source: Pittsburgh Courier Archives

EXCERPT FROM "BASEBALL 'COLOR LINE' SMASHED! JACKIE ROBINSON SIGNED BY BROOKLYN FARM CLUB," *PITTSBURGH COURIER*, OCTOBER 27, 1945

When Pittsburgh Courier *sportswriter Wendell Smith sat down to write his news story for October 27, 1945, it was with a sense of triumph. For a number of years, several reporters for black newspapers had been on something of a crusade to persuade anyone who would listen, especially the owners of major league teams, that many black players not only were on a talent level equal to the best of white major leaguers but also that major league baseball would benefit financially by integrating black players into professional baseball. Not only Wendell Smith but also Ira Lewis, president of the* Pittsburgh Courier; *Sam Lacy, sportswriter for the Baltimore* Afro-American; *Joe Bostic of*

Harlem's the People's Voice; *Fay Young of the* Chicago Defender; *Art Carter of the Washington* Afro-American; *and others, in column after column, interview after interview, promoted the desegregation of baseball.*

And now it had happened, and appropriately it was the Pittsburgh Courier *that broke the story. Years later, Jackie Robinson himself acknowledged the enormous role of the black press in changing the face of baseball.*

By Wendell Smith

Baseball's long-established color line came smashing down with a resounding crash in Montreal, Canada, Tuesday afternoon when fleet-footed Jackie Robinson, ex-UCLA all-around star and Kansas City Monarch's shortstop became the first Negro to sign a contract in organized baseball. When the brilliant, broad-shouldered Pasadena (Calif.) athlete affixed his signature to the Montreal club contract, a farm team of the Brooklyn Dodgers, he established a precedent that blasted the sturdy, immovable barrier against Negroes since baseball's great empire was established . . .

Robinson's entrance into the ranks of organized baseball was acclaimed throughout the two countries Wednesday—the United States and Canada. Baseball's most rabid enthusiastic fans—Negroes—received the sensational news with joyous emotion and viewed it as an event of far-reaching racial progress. The special signing was of such tremendous significance that it was covered by every major news service in the United States and Canada. The Pittsburgh Courier had the sensational news "break" at noon Tuesday, approximately two hours before the story was officially released to the press.

It was Robinson, himself, who gave the story to The Courier. As late as last August, the new member of the famous Montreal Royals promised Herman Hill of the Courier's West Coast bureau that he would let him know first if and when he was signed by Brooklyn or any other team in organized baseball. He kept his word Tuesday noon when he put in a long distance call to Hill in Los Angeles from Montreal and said these historic words: "I am signing a contract with Montreal in an hour from now!" . . .

It has been common knowledge for a long time that Branch Rickey held more than just a passing interest in Negro ball players. Publicly, however, he has expressed interest in Negro baseball as an organization rather than in the individual players. But behind the scenes, he has been working tediously and carefully on the question of how to "break" a Negro player into the Brooklyn system. . . .

Dodger scouts were trailing Robinson all over the country watching his every move—while he performed with the Kansas City Monarchs. On two occasions he was called in by Rickey and it was probably during one of those "secret conferences" that the Dodger owner decided to elect Robinson as the first Negro player to join the ranks of organized baseball by placing him on a team in the Brooklyn farm system.

Source: Pittsburgh Courier Archives.

EXTRACT OF SPEECH BY BRANCH RICKEY, ATLANTA, GEORGIA, JANUARY 20, 1956

In the fall of 1955, the Brooklyn Dodgers for the first time in their history won the World Series. The team captured the National League pennant and the series with sterling play from, among others, Jackie Robinson, Roy Campanella, Don Newcombe, and Jim Gilliam—all black men—and Sandy Amoros, a Cuban, whose dramatic catch in left field of a line drive hit by Yogi Berra of the New York Yankees saved the seventh and deciding game for the Dodgers and pitcher Johnny Podres.

A few months later, Branch Rickey, although no longer part of the Dodger organization, was in Atlanta, speaking about his momentous involvement as the Dodger president in signing Jackie Robinson years earlier. As he looked back on the end of the color barrier in baseball, Rickey spoke of the social implications of baseball's integration and the drive for social justice that it represented. For sure, much of Rickey's motivation in signing Robinson had been business related; nevertheless, it had also been from a firm belief that black players should not be denied opportunities because of color.

This address in Atlanta was unlike any usual speech by a baseball business executive; indeed, it was something of a historical treatise. Invoking the work of historian and sociologist Frank Tannenbaum of Columbia University— who, in 1947, published Slave and Citizen, *a comparative study and point of departure for much later scholarship on slavery and race relations in the United States—Rickey hailed the day when individuals would not be judged by the "pigmentation of a man's skin, or indeed in the last syllable of his name." Instead, he said, they would be judged "of value based upon their merits, and God hasten the day when Governors of our States will become sufficiently educated that they will respond to those views."*

I felt that the time was ripe, that there wouldn't be any reaction on the part of a great public if a man had superior skill, if he had intelligence and character and had patience and forbearance, and "could take it" as it was said here. I didn't make a mistake there. I have made mistakes, lots of mistakes.

A man of exceptional courage, and exceptional intelligence, a man of basically fine character, and he can thank his forbearers for a lot of it. He comes from the right sort of home, and I knew all this, and when somebody, somewhere, thinks in terms of a local athletic club not playing some other club because of the presence on the squad of a man of color. I am thinking that if an exhibition game were to be played in these parts against a team on whose squad was Jackie Robinson,—even leaving out all of the principle of fair play, all the elements of equality and citizenship, all the economic necessities connected with it, all the violations of the whole form and conceptions of our Government from its beginning up to now,—leave it all out of the picture, he would be depriving some of the citizens of his own community, some wonderful boys, from seeing an exhibition of skill and technique, and the great, beautiful, graciousness of a slide, the like of which they could not see from any other man in this country. And that's not fair to a local constituency.

I am wondering, I am compelled to wonder, how it can be. And at the breakfast, recently, when a morning paper's story was being discussed and my flaxen hair daughter said to me, "He surely didn't say it." I thought, yes it is understandable. It is understandable. And when a great United States Senator said to me some few days after that, "Do you know that the headlines in Egypt are terribly embarrassing to our State Department?" And then he told me, in part, a story whose utter truthfulness I have no reason to doubt, about the tremendous humiliation—"The Land of the Free and the Home of the Brave,"— "where we are talking about extending to all civilizations, tremendous and beautiful freedoms, and the unavoidable, hypocritical position it puts us in internationally," "How could anybody do it," said my daughter.

That night we had a family discussion. It lasted a long time. My five daughters were there, mother was there, auntie was there, four sons-in-law were there,— it was Christmas time. And I said to them what I want to say to you tonight. It is understandable that an American with a certain background, certain exposures in the field of education, would represent a more or less a plausible inheritance in regard to the assimilation, the relationship, the acceptance in our current life of the negro.

The whole thing as a difference between the acceptance in Brazil, for instance, Spanish and Portuguese countries, and the British West Indies and America, a very remarkable thing, but understood by all historians and all writers on the subject. Portugal was the first one to import slaves from Africa,—took them into Portugal. It was the last one to give up the slave trade. 19,000,000 go into one country alone in South America,—imported slaves over a period of over four hundred years. Now, slavery antedated negro slavery,—oh many years, really thousands of years, before any negro was taken out of Africa. It was an accident, a misfortune, a thing that could be remedied. All slavery throughout the centuries preceded African importation of slaves. It was the result of war, it was a result of debt. There were several things that led to it, but always there was manumission in front of the man. Freedom obtainable. And the laws going back clear beyond Seneca, and Cicero refers to it,—all the way through all those centuries, manumission was a comparatively easy thing. The law of that time, all of it—Plato, the Roman jurisprudence is based upon it, that you can become free. You may be a slave today,—you can be a Moor, you can be a Greek, you can be a man of high intelligence. Slavery was a matter of accident or misfortune. And the Spanish Law,—the Latin nations inherited that law both in its enactment and in its interpretation were favorable to manumission,—making men free. It was not a matter of color at all and the law supported that and the importation of slaves into South America, and all of South America, into Mexico earlier, a few were there subsequently, and in all the Caribbean countries which are now predominant,—all of it came in the line of probable manumission, so that when, say, 90% of all the slaves who had been slaves came to be free in Brazil, for example. Then would come in the other importations and the other men who were slaves. There was a group of qualified free men to take care of the small number, 10%, who were slaves. That was Latin America.

They had no problems such as we had here in the south following the Civil War, where there was nobody to take care of a great number of free men and no previous free men in the colored race to adapt themselves to those conditions. And, of course, there was disgraceful governmental conduct. Now the difference, miracle that it is, mystery that it is, and yet greed at the bottom of it the slave trade was immensely profitable,—Liverpool was,—I was going to say, was built out of it, and America followed suit on it. And whereas the law that men are equal long before, I say, the negro came into the picture.

The church has always, and it has been a tendency of the Christian church too to undertake to establish the equality of all men in the sight of God. And to the extent which that prevailed to that extent it became inevitable that all men should ultimately become free. That was the greatest force in the world,—to give every man moral stature. Of course the Emancipation Proclamation by Lincoln made the southern negro slave free, but it never did make the white man morally free. He remained a slave to his inheritances. And some are even today . . .

Character is a great thing to have in an athlete, a team. It's a great thing. And when I wonder if there is any condemnation, any explanation, anything that can be done to make an extenuating circumstance out of something that violates the right of a part of our citizenship throughout the country when I know that the Man of 1900 years ago spent His life and died for the sake of freedom,—the right to come, to go, to see, to think, to believe, to act. It is to be understood, but it is too profoundly regretted.

Education is a slow process. It may solve it. It is inevitable that this thing comes to fruition. Too many forces are working fast. This so called little Robinson,—we call it the "Robinson Experiment,"—tremendous as it will be for Jackie to have so placed himself in relation not only to his own people in this country, but to his whole generation and to all America that he will leave the mark of fine sportsmanship and fine character. That is something that he must guard carefully. He has a responsibility there.

Frank Tannenbaum, in his book on *Slave and Citizen*,—he is a professor of Latin American history in Columbia University, points out,—I think it is the bible on the subject—it really is. I'm not sure, I'm not sure that legislators ought to drive against a prominent and very antagonistic minority. I'm not sure that they should drive F.E.C. too fast too far. I'm not sure that the 18th Amendment might repeat itself. That you would have an organization of glued antagonisms that would be able to delay the solution of a problem that is now in my judgment fast being solved, and when you once gain an eminence you do not have to recede from it. The educational process is something.

Four things, says Tannenbaum, is solving this question, with an unrealized rapidity. First,—proximity. Clay Hopper, Jackie's first manager. I've never told it in public. I've never allowed it to be printed if I could help it, took me by the lapels of my coat as he sat there sweating in his underclothes watching a game over on the inside park at Daytona Beach. And this boy had made a great play in the fourth inning and I had remarked about it and the two of us sitting there together, and this boy coming from—I shouldn't have given his name,—forget the name and I will tell you the story. I'll deny that he ever said it. He took me by the front of my coat when in the seventh inning Jackie made one of those tremendous remarkable plays that very few people can make,—went toward first base, made a slide, stabbed the ball, came with it in his left hand glove and as he turned with the body control that's almost inconceivable and cut off the runner at second base on a force play. I took Clay and I put my hand on his shoulder and I said, "Did you ever see a play to beat it?"

Now this fellow comes from Greenwood, Mississippi. And he would forgive me, I am sure, because of the magnificent way that he came through on it. He took me and shook me and his face that far from me and he said, "do you really think that a 'nigger' is a human being, Mr. Rickey?" That's what he said. That's what that fellow said. I have never answered him until this minute.

And six months later he came into my office after the year at Montreal when he was this boy's manager. He didn't want him to be sent to him. And he said to me, "I want to take back what I said to you last spring." He said, "I'm ashamed of it." "Now," he said, "you may have plans for him to be on your club,"—and he was, "but," he said, "if you don't have plans to have him on the Brooklyn club," he said, "I would like to have him back in Montreal." And then he told me that he was not only a great ball player good enough for Brooklyn, but he said that he was a fine gentleman. Proximity. Proximity, says Tannenbaum, will solve this thing if you can have enough of it. But that is a limited thing, you see.

And the second thing, says Tannenbaum, is the cultural inter-twining through the arts, through literature, through painting, through singing, through the professions, where you stabbed through the horizontal strata of social makeup, and you make vertical thrusts in that cultural inter-twining. That inevitably will help solve this problem,—and he believes with rapidity.

And third, the existence in our democracy here of a middle class, the middle class in Great Britain,—the middle class in probably every country, I think, that makes secure, if anything does, a democracy such as we know. This group here like this,—these groups throughout America of all colors. That existence in this country will bring it about surely and faster than people know.

And fourth, the recognition of the moral stature of all men, that all humans are equal. This thing of freedom has been bought at a great price. That all men are equal in the sight of God. That all law must recognize that men are equal,—all humans are equal by nature. The same pains, and the same joys, and in our country the same food, the same dress, the same religion, the same language, the same everything. And perhaps quite as questionable an ancestry civically in this country on the part of the black men as we can trace many of the forbearers in the white race of the other settlers of this country.

Gentlemen, it is inconceivable to me that in view of domestic tranquility and home understanding that anywhere, anytime, anybody, can question the right of citizens of this country for equal economic opportunity under the law. How can it be. And how can anyone in official authority, where more attention is given to remarks than would come from an ordinary civilian, be so unremindful of his country's relationship that he could bring us into [?] and disgrace. Internationally.

These four things I mention will work, I think, in due time with a sureness that will make possibly the very next generation wonder and look back, as I said that you quoted me in Cincinnati, I had forgotten that I had ever said it look back with incredulity upon everything that was a problem to us today in this country, and will wonder what the issue was all about. I am completely color-blind. I know that America is,—it's been proven Jackie,—is more interested in the grace of a man's swing, in the dexterity of his cutting a base, and his speed afoot, in his scientific body control, in his excellence as a competitor on the field,—America, wide and broad, and in Atlanta, and in Georgia, will become instantly more interested in those marvelous, beautiful qualities than they are in the pigmentation of a man's skin, or indeed in the last syllable of his name. Men are coming to be regarded of value based upon their merits, and God hasten the day when Governors of our States will become sufficiently educated that they will respond to those views."

Source: Branch Rickey Papers, Library of Congress, Washington, DC.

JACKIE ROBINSON TO PRESIDENT DWIGHT D. EISENHOWER, MAY 13, 1958

Jackie Robinson decided to retire from baseball after the 1956 season. He signed a two-year contract to become a vice president and director of personnel for Chock Full o' Nuts, a chain of New York–based lunch counters.

In the fall of 1957, in Little Rock, Arkansas, a group of nine black students enrolled in segregated Central High School. As they attempted to enter the school, angry mobs, backed by the Arkansas National Guard, blocked their entrance, supported by Arkansas governor Orval Faubus. It was only after the intervention by President Dwight Eisenhower, who ordered the 101st Airborne Division of the U.S. Army to Little Rock and federalized the Arkansas National Guard, that the students were allowed to enter the school. Their first year at Central High, where they faced down constant harassment and taunts, became another step in the nation's drive toward civil rights. The treatment of the students undoubtedly brought vivid memories to Jackie Robinson about his early years in the majors.

In May 1958, a few months after the showdown in Little Rock, Robinson heard President Eisenhower speak about the need for blacks to slow down in their efforts toward integration. Angered and hurt, he sent this passionate response to the president.

May 13, 1958

The President
The White House
Washington, D.C.

My dear Mr. President:

I was sitting in the audience at the Summit Meeting of Negro Leaders yesterday when you said we must have patience. On hearing you say this, I felt like standing up and saying, "Oh no! Not again!"

I respectfully remind you, sir, that we have been the most patient of all people. When you said we must have self-respect, I wondered how we could have self-respect and remain patient considering the treatment accorded us through the years.

17 million Negroes cannot do as you suggest and wait for the hearts of man to change. We want to enjoy now the rights that we feel we are entitled to as Americans. This we cannot do unless we pursue aggressively goals which all other Americans achieved over 150 years ago.

As the chief executive of our nation, I respectfully suggest that you unwittingly crush the spirit of freedom in Negroes by constantly urging forbearance and give hope to those pro-segregation leaders like Governor Faubus who would take from us even those freedoms we now enjoy. Your own experience with Governor Faubus is proof enough that forbearance and not eventual integration is the goal the pro-segregation leaders seek.

In my view, an unequivocal statement backed up by action such as you demonstrated you could take last fall in dealing with Governor Faubus if it became necessary, would let it be known that America is determined to provide—in the near future—for Negroes— the freedoms we are entitled to under the constitution.

Respectfully yours,
Jackie Robinson

Source: Jackie Robinson to President Dwight D. Eisenhower, May 13, 1958, National Archives and Records Administration, Dwight D. Eisenhower Library, White House Central Files, Box 731, OF-142-A-3.

Glossary

Barnstorming: In the late 1880s and the first half of the 20th century, many black teams would travel, usually by bus, across the country playing local mining, mill, or manufacturing teams; other touring teams; and even white major and minor leaguers playing in their off-season. Barnstorming made money for local towns that hosted the events and some cash for the ballplayers themselves.

Chicago Defender: Founded in 1905, the *Chicago Defender* became the nation's most influential black weekly newspaper by the beginning of World War I. More than two-thirds of its readership was outside the city of Chicago. Along with the *Pittsburgh Courier,* the *Defender,* led by sportswriters Frank and Fay Young, played a very active role in encouraging the integration of black baseball players into the major leagues.

Chitlin' circuit: Barnstormers roaming from one part of the country to the other to play exhibition games had to be careful where they sought food and a place to stay. "Hittin' the chitlin' circuit" was a phrase used by black players on the road looking for safe havens.

Clown team: Clown teams, usually sporting very talented players, performed comic routines that included exaggerations of racial stereotypes. The Indianapolis Clowns, featuring the antics of King Tut, billed as the "Crown Clown" of baseball, were the preeminent clown team. Tut dressed either as an Egyptian pharaoh or in a tuxedo and top hat and performed numerous skits during the games. Eventually the team was so talented that it became part of the black major leagues. The great major league home run king Henry Aaron began his baseball career with the Clowns.

Color line: The baseball color line was the unwritten policy excluding African American baseball players from organized white leagues before 1947. As a result, various Negro Leagues were formed, which featured those players not allowed to participate in the major or minor leagues. Well before the turn of the century, black players were no longer on the rosters of professional white teams.

Comiskey Park: A former ballplayer and owner of minor league teams, Charles Comiskey, at the turn of the century became owner of the Chicago White Sox. In 1910, in replacing old South Side Park, in which the White Sox had been playing, he built Comiskey Park. The baseball venue was one of those stadiums in which Negro League teams played when the white teams were on the road. In 1933, and for the next two decades, Comiskey Park hosted the East-West All-Star Game.

Eastern Colored League (ECL): In 1923, Ed Bolden, owner of both the Hilldale Daisies and the Philadelphia Stars, founded the Eastern Colored League, composed of such teams as Hilldale, the Cuban Stars, Brooklyn Royal Giants, Bacharach Giants, Lincoln Giants, and Baltimore Black Sox. Designed to compete with the established Negro National League, the ECL lasted for five years. The Hilldale team defeated the Kansas City Monarchs in the 1925 Negro League World Series.

East-West All-Star Game: The brainchild of Gus Greenlee, owner of the Pittsburgh Crawfords, the game was modeled after the major league All-Star Game. Because the league structures were constantly changing and because some of the better players in black baseball were on independent teams, the East-West All-Star game matched players geographically. Newspaper balloting from the public was conducted by the two major black newspapers, the *Chicago Defender* and the *Pittsburgh Courier*. Comiskey Park in Chicago was selected as the site of the game because of its central location in the country. More than the Negro League World Series, the East-West All-Star Game was the highlight of each Negro League year.

Great Black Migration: During World War I, the largest movement of blacks northward since the end of the Civil War began, as men, women, and families from various Southern states left to settle not only in Eastern cities such as Philadelphia and New York but also in cities in the Midwest, especially Chicago. Stirred both by the disfranchisement of black voters in the South as well as growing mob violence and overt racism, blacks began to take new factory jobs in Northern cities opened up by wartime industrial needs. The huge increase in black population across the North made it possible for the growth of black baseball teams and the Negro Leagues.

Hall of Fame: The National Baseball Hall of Fame and Museum in Cooperstown, New York, founded in the mid-1930s by Stephen Clark, owner of the Singer Sewing Machine Company, is the preeminent museum and research facility for the study of the history of baseball in the United States. By 2011, 35 Negro League players and executives had been elected to the Hall of Fame.

Independent club: Before 1920 and the creation of the first Negro League, hundreds of all-black teams played across the country without having an affiliation to a league. Such teams as the Cuban Giants, the Kansas City Monarchs, and Homestead Grays all began as teams that played other independent teams in exhibitions and barnstorming travels. By the end of World War I, black baseball had become a powerful form of entertainment for urban black populations, and their prominence made it financially possible for entrepreneurs to establish formal league organizations.

Jim Crow laws: The term *Jim Crow* originated in the minstrel shows of the early 19th century that depicted blacks in inferior and derogatory ways. In the post–Civil War era, Jim Crow laws came to mean legislation designed to restrict voting rights, public access to accommodations, and other actions that segregated black people, making them second-class citizens.

National Association of Base Ball Players (NABBP):   Founded in 1858 by 16 baseball clubs located in the New York metropolitan area, the NABBP was the first organization that set out to provide a basis for defining, organizing, and governing the sport. In 1867, the NABBP, at its annual convention, officially barred blacks from its teams.

Negro American League (NAL):   After the end of the Eastern Colored League in 1928, members of the league reorganized a year later as the NAL. The post-Depression NAL included such teams as the Kansas City Monarchs, Memphis Red Sox, Atlanta Black Crackers, Chicago American Giants, Indianapolis ABCs, and Birmingham Black Barons.

Negro League World Series: Modeled loosely after the Major League World Series, the Negro League World Series was a postseason competition to determine a champion of the Negro Leagues. Between 1924 and 1927, the Negro League World Series pitted the top club from the Negro National League against the top team from the Eastern Colored League. After a hiatus during the Great Depression and World War II and the realignment and demise of various teams and leagues, no World Series was held. Between 1942 and 1948, the World Series matched winners of the Negro American League and the Negro National League.

Negro National League: The first successful organized Negro League was established on February 13, 1920, at a YMCA in Kansas City, Missouri. Andrew "Rube" Foster was the driving force behind the organization of the league and served as its president. The league disbanded from 1931 to 1933, was rebuilt, and survived until 1948. The clubs included the Pittsburgh Crawfords, Homestead Grays, Baltimore Elite Giants, Newark Eagles, Philadelphia Stars, and New York Black Yankees.

Pittsburgh Courier: Founded in 1907, the *Pittsburgh Courier* was, by the 1930s, one of the most highly circulated black newspapers in the country and one in which readers could follow closely the results of Negro League competition. Its sports editor, Wendell Smith, vigorously denounced segregation in the major leagues and contributed directly to the signing of Jackie Robinson by the Brooklyn Dodgers.

Plessy v. Ferguson: A U.S. Supreme Court decision in 1896 that upheld a Louisiana law requiring separate but equal facilities for blacks, *Plessy v. Ferguson* firmly established segregation as legal doctrine.

Rickwood Field: In 1910, industrialist Rich Woodward, owner of the minor league Birmingham Barons, built Rickwood Field. In 1920, with the advent of the Birmingham Black Barons, a team included in the new Negro Southern League, Rickwood Field became the home for both the white and black teams. Rickwood has been preserved and is listed on the National Register of Historic Places.

Shadowball: Negro leaguers often performed this pantomime stunt before games. It involved frenetic action with players making astonishing leaping catches and other agile moves—all without the benefit of a ball. The term *shadowball* was later used as a metaphor for the Negro Leagues and the exclusion of African Americans from organized baseball.

Spiking: To injure another player with baseball shoe cleats while sliding. Black infielders were special targets of white base runners in games involving both races.

Sporting News: Almost from the beginning of professional baseball, the *Sporting News* established itself as the national magazine on baseball. Founded by St. Louis sportswriters Alfred and William Spink, the magazine at first focused not only on baseball but also on wrestling, horse racing, and other sports news. It later turned its attention almost entirely to baseball. Although its coverage of black baseball was sparse, it did address the issue of possible black participation in the major leagues. Its position on the issue varied over the years. At the time of Jackie Robinson's first game with the Brooklyn Dodgers, the magazine was skeptical of the move.

"Whites only": Especially in the Southern United States, restrictive signs were constant and humiliating reminders to blacks that they should "stay in their place." The signs were commonly outside restaurants and other public areas, but black baseball players on interracial teams would, on occasion, find such signs pinned to their lockers.

Annotated Bibliography

Cattrell, Robert. *The Best Pitcher in Baseball: The Life of Rube Foster, Negro League Giant.* New York: New York University Press, 2001.

One of the towering figures in the history of the Negros Leagues, Andrew "Rube" Foster was not only a star player but also a manager and founder of the Negro National League. This admirable biography places Foster in the forefront of the drive for equality in the early years of professional black baseball.

Clark, Dick, and Larry Lester. *The Negro Leagues Book.* Cleveland, OH: Society for American Baseball Research, 1994.

Founded in 1971, the Society for American Baseball Research (SABR) was organized by historians and other serious students of baseball history. Among the research areas promoted by SABR was the history of the Negro Leagues. The organization formed a committee to advance such scholarship. This book is the product of the work of members of that committee. From their exhaustive research came a wealth of information, including team rosters, league standings, and a register of players and their individual statistics. The book remains a principal reference tool.

Dixon, Phil. *Wilber "Bullet" Rogan and the Kansas City Monarchs.* Jefferson, NC: McFarland, 2010.

Exhaustively researched and including interviews with several ex-ballplayers, this study acts as both a biography of Wilber "Bullet" Rogan, one of the Negro Leagues' most versatile players, and as a history of the great Kansas City Monarchs, which, in the 1920s and 1930s, won two Negro League World Series and five pennants. Author Phil Dixon, a board member of the Negro Leagues Baseball Museum, has written several excellent books on baseball history.

Gay, Timothy. *Satch, Dizzy, and Rapid Robert: The Wild Saga of Interracial Baseball before Jackie Robinson*. New York: Simon & Schuster, 2010.

Through the lives of three of baseball's greatest pitchers—Satchel Paige, Dizzy Dean, and Bob Feller—author Gay traces the years of barnstorming when black and white players competed in postseason exhibitions across the country, much to the displeasure of major league baseball's executive leadership. Bolstered by many first-person interviews, the work is especially rich in describing the personal interactions when legends of the Negro Leagues met legends of the major leagues in head-to-head competition.

Hogan, Lawrence. *Shades of Glory: The Negro Leagues and the Story of African-American Baseball*. Washington, DC: National Geographic, 2006.

Commissioned by the National Baseball Hall of Fame with funding from Major League Baseball as part of the 2006 special induction ceremony of Negro Hall of Famers, this volume is a distillation of an 800-page manuscript entitled "Out of the Shadows," which was begun by a stellar research team of historians, one of whom was Lawrence Hogan. Filled with photos and profiles, this book is perhaps the best single volume covering the beginnings of black baseball after the Civil War through the end of the Negro Leagues.

Holway, John B. *Voices from the Great Black Baseball Leagues*, rev. ed. Mineola, NY: Dover, 2010.

A highly respected newspaper reporter and writer, John Holway began researching baseball in the mid-1940s. In 1976, after traveling across the country and interviewing veterans of the Negro Leagues such as Buck Leonard and Cool Papa Bell, he published *Voices from the Great Black Baseball Leagues*, a collection that brought to life the stories of players who had been virtually unknown to most Americans. This latest revised edition remains a principal source of first-person accounts.

Kilma, John. *Willie's Boys: The 1948 Birmingham Black Barons, The Last Negro League World Series, and the Making of a Baseball Legend*. Hoboken, NJ: Wiley, 2009.

This is the story of the first year of the fabulous Willie Mays in professional baseball. In 1948, the remarkably talented 16-year-old kid from Birmingham, Alabama, joined the local Negro Leagues Birmingham Black Barons to play at Rickwood Field. Rich in anecdotes and first-person accounts, the book offers an intimate look at the veterans who taught Mays the ways of the game and the lessons needed to cope with institutional racism. It also provides an account of the last of the Negro World Series—the Black Barons against the Kansas City Monarchs.

Kirwin, Bill, ed. *Out of the Shadows: African American Baseball from the Cuban Giants to Jackie Robinson*. Lincoln: University of Nebraska Press, 2005.

This book is compilation of essays from *NINE: A Journal of Baseball History and Culture* by leading scholars on the history of black baseball from the 19th century to the end of the Negro Leagues. It represents the best scholarship covering the historical and cultural aspects of the growth of the Negro Leagues, the ultimate desegregation of professional baseball, and the persistent issues of racism.

Lanctot, Neil. *The Negro Leagues: The Rise and Fall of a Black Institution*, paperback ed. Philadelphia: University of Pennsylvania Press, 2008.

Through careful research in black newspapers and first-person interviews, author Neil Lanctot not only presents a valuable general history of the Negro Leagues but gives careful attention to the way in which the teams were assembled and run. The book traces the teams in the context of black business enterprise and the ways in which they functioned in a separate economy geared toward the black community.

Leonard, Buck, and James A. Riley. *Buck Leonard: The Black Lou Gehrig: The Autobiography of Hall of Famer Buck Leonard.* New York: Carroll & Graf, 1995.
One of the few autobiographies authored by a former Negro Leagues player, this is the story of Buck Leonard, long-time first baseman of the powerful Homestead Grays. Hitting behind catcher Josh Gibson (who was called by sportswriters in the black press the black Babe Ruth), Leonard was known as the black Lou Gehrig. From the mid-1930s until his retirement in 1950, Leonard not only hit for high batting averages but often led the Negro National League in home runs. He was later voted into the Hall of Fame. Well-known baseball historian James Riley acted as coauthor.

Lester, Larry. *Black Baseball's National Showcase: The East-West All Star Game, 1933–1953.* Lincoln: University of Nebraska Press, 2001.
Even more than the Negro Leagues World Series, the East-West All-Star Game at Chicago's Comiskey Park, beginning in 1933, became a showcase for black athletes unlike any other. It attracted huge crowds, much press attention, and spurred the players to give their greatest effort. This book traces the games, year by year, and re-creates, as closely as possible, the box scores and inning-by-inning accounts.

Lomax, Michael E. *Black Baseball Entrepreneurs, 1860–1901.* Syracuse, NY: Syracuse University Press, 2003.
Before the creation of the Negro Leagues, a number of post–Civil War teams made up of black players emerged in several cities in the North. They included such teams as the Philadelphia Pythians, the New York City Gorhams, the Cuban Giants, and the Page Fence Giants, and they led the way to increasing professional organization of black teams and leagues. This book offers a solid background of 19th-century black baseball business enterprise.

Luke, Bob. *The Baltimore Elite Giants: Sport and Society in the Age of Negro League Baseball.* Baltimore: Johns Hopkins University Press, 2009.
The Elite Giants of Baltimore boasted some of the outstanding black players of the Negro Leagues in its later years—Roy Campanella, Joe Black, and Jim Gilliam—all of whom would become Brooklyn Dodgers. The book is especially valuable for its insights into a team and its players during the first years of integration of Negro Leagues stars into the major leagues and into the complex effects of the transition on the city of Baltimore.

O'Neil, Buck. *I Was Right on Time.* New York: Simon & Schuster, 1996.
When film maker Ken Burns produced his landmark, 18½-hour, Emmy Award–winning PBS series *Baseball* in 1994, the most prominent voice for the history of the Negro Leagues was John "Buck" O'Neil. A slick-fielding first baseman and teammate of such legendary stars as Satchel Paige and Josh Gibson, O'Neil became something of an ambassador for the history of the Negro Leagues, making appearances around the country telling the stories of the athletes he knew so well, and working hard to help publicize and grow the Negro Leagues Baseball Museum in Kansas City, Missouri.

Paige, Leroy "Satchel." *Maybe I'll Pitch Forever: A Great Baseball Player Tells the Hilarious Story Behind the Legend.* Lincoln: University of Nebraska Press, 1993.

The Negro Leagues' preeminent pitcher was also its greatest showman. This account of his life, spanning the years of the growth of the Negro Leagues through the breaking of the color barrier, is filled with humor, pathos, and the extraordinary drive of Paige to keep on performing as the years passed.

Peterson, Robert. *Only the Ball Was White: A History of Legendary Black Players and All-Black Professional Teams.* New York: Oxford University Press, 1992.

Robert Peterson's account of black baseball, first published by Prentice Hall in 1970, was a pioneering work. At the time of its publication, little was known of the Negro leagues. Peterson, who, as a boy in Warren, Pennsylvania, saw a number of barnstorming games and later played college baseball, began his project in the mid-1960s, interviewing star players and researching black newspapers. The work itself is a part of the history of the Negro Leagues, because it spurred ever-increasing research on a neglected subject.

Pollock, Alan. *Barnstorming to Heaven: Syd Pollock and His Great Black Teams.* Tuscaloosa: University of Alabama Press, 2006.

Alan Pollock's father, Syd Pollock, owned the Indianapolis Clowns, a black touring baseball team that featured an entertaining mix of athletic ability and comedy. From the late 1920s to the mid-1960s, the team crisscrossed the country, playing on every kind of field, from little league parks to Yankee Stadium, from the Canadian Rockies to the South. Alan Pollock grew up around his father's team and describes in vivid detail the routines of Richard "King Tut" King as well as the extraordinary successes of the team against all challengers, including barnstorming major leaguers.

Ribowsky, Mark. *Josh Gibson: The Power and the Darkness,* paperback ed. Champaign: University of Illinois Press, 2004.

There is both awe and tragedy in the story of Josh Gibson, perhaps the greatest baseball slugger of all time. He was one of the Negro Leagues' greatest stars, popular, and a fearsome hitter who, many insisted, rivaled any in the history of baseball. But there was also the sadly troubled personal life that led to an early demise. Gibson never had a chance to take his game to the major leagues. This biography is one of the best of any Negro Leagues star as well as a penetrating look at the world in which he moved.

Riley, James A. *The Biographical Encyclopedia of the Negro Baseball Leagues.* New York: Carroll & Graf, 1994.

This landmark reference work on the history of Negro Leagues includes over 4,000 entries, mostly short biographies of players. The book required a herculean research effort by prolific baseball writer James Riley and is an invaluable tool for anyone exploring the subject.

Robinson, Jackie, and Alfred Duckett. *I Never Had It Made: An Autobiography.* Hopewell, NJ: Ecco Press, 1995.

Originally published in 1972, the year Robinson died, this autobiography, written with freelance writer Alfred Duckett, is valuable not only for Robinson's own recollections of his life before baseball, his days at UCLA, his time in the military, and his baseball career but also for his impressions of race relations in the United States.

Snyder, Brad. *Beyond the Shadow of the Senators: The Untold Story of the Homestead Grays and the Integration of Baseball*. New York: McGraw-Hill, 2003.

A number of baseball owners made a healthy profitable enterprise of renting major league baseball stadiums at exorbitant prices to Negro Leagues owners for use when their major league teams were on the road. This book offers a close look at the machinations of Washington Senators owner Clark Griffith; his dealings with Cum Posey, owner of the Homestead Grays; and an enterprising newspaper editor, Sam Lacy, who carried on a vigorous campaign, along with other black newspaper owners and writers, to integrate the major leagues. It also captures the excitement for black Washingtonians as they begin to flock to see baseball at its highest level—not from the Washington Senators but from the Homestead Grays.

Tye, Larry. *Satchel: The Life and Times of an American Legend*. New York: Random House, 2009.

Much legend and lore surrounds the life of Satchel Paige, perhaps the best pitcher in the history of baseball. His incredible talent, his wanderings across the country and abroad playing for numerous teams, his memorable quotes, his brief career in the major leagues at an age when most baseball players would have long been in retirement—all are skillfully crafted into Larry Tye's biography.

Tygiel, Jules. *Baseball's Great Experiment: Jackie Robinson and His Legacy*, 25th anniversary ed. New York: Oxford University Press, 2008.

Historian Jules Tygiel's much-admired biography begins with Jackie Robinson's first game with the Montreal Royals, the Brooklyn Dodgers' farm team, on April 18, 1946. The game broke professional baseball's long-standing segregation. A year later, Robinson was in Brooklyn, breaking the color line in the major leagues. Gleaned from interviews from numerous players and executives and meticulous research in archives and newspapers, the book stands as a major contribution not only to the history of baseball but also to the tortured path of U.S. race relations.

White, Sol. *Sol White's History of Colored Baseball with Other Documents on the Early Black Game, 1886–1936*, rev. ed., with an introduction by Jerry Mallory. Lincoln: University of Nebraska Press, Bison Books edition, 1995.

Sol White was the first historian of black baseball. From his own experiences as a player and manager, White in 1907 wrote his reminiscences about organized teams both integrated and "colored" on the East Coast and in the Midwest in the 1880s and 1890s. Only four copies of the original publication exist; this revised paperback edition with an introduction by historian Jerry Mallory includes not only the original work authored by White but also a solid introduction to the history of black baseball and the groundwork it laid for the later Negro Leagues.

Index

About the Author

ROGER BRUNS is a historian and former deputy executive director of the National Historical Publications and Records Commission at the National Archives in Washington, DC. He is the author many books, including *Icons of Latino America: Latino Contributions to American Culture; Preacher: Billy Sunday and the Rise of American Evangelism;* and *Almost History.* He has written several biographies for young readers of such figures as Martin Luther King Jr., John Wesley Powell, and Thomas Jefferson.